# ELVIS PRESLEY

## A Study in Music

Robert Matthew-Walker

Midas Books

By the same author for Midas
*Muhammad Ali – his fights in the ring*
*Rachmaninoff – his life and times*

First published in 1979 by
Midas Books
12 Dene Way, Speldhurst
Tunbridge Wells, Kent TN3 0NX

Reprinted 1980, 1981, 1982



ISBN 0 85936 162 4



Book Production by Chambers Green Ltd., Tunbridge Wells, Kent.
Printed and bound in Great Britain by Billing and Sons Limited,
Guildford, London, Oxford, Worcester.

# Preface

I became interested in popular music as a form of relaxation and entertainment when a music student in the 1950s. I found its clarity, simplicity and directness attractive. But I was totally unprepared for the impact on me of Presley's 'Heartbreak Hotel'. It was unlike any music I had ever heard. I was astounded by it, and for a quarter of a century Elvis Presley's performances have moved, excited, exasperated or disappointed me—but the fascination has remained.

Presley's death in 1977 prompted a number of books on him. But I felt that his essential importance—his life's work as a singer—remained largely untouched. To some, Presley was always an outsider: faintly vulgar, possibly tasteless. I determined to try to explain his importance through a study of the hundreds of songs he recorded over almost 25 years.

This book is not, therefore, a standard biography, although I make no apology for tracing his life in Part I. For it is only when the background to a man's life is grasped that his life's work falls into place. The main body of this book, Part II, traces Presley's recording career in chronological order of recording session. Within each session, the titles are dealt with in alphabetical order. I refrained from using musical examples or technical language, for the general reader would be left in the dark. On the rare occasions when technical terms are used the meaning is clear. Part III is a final summing-up of Presley's importance, influence and achievement.

This book could not have been written without the help and encouragement of several people. Todd Slaughter, President of the Official Elvis Presley Fan Club of Great Britain, supplied much material. His own book—*Elvis Presley*—remains the best short biography. The full-hearted co-operation I have received from my old colleagues at RCA deserves special mention. In particular, Peter Bailey supplied many records, and Dave Machray helped greatly in the initial stages. Paul Rustad, whose complete collection of Elvis Presley recordings was placed unhesitatingly and selflessly at my disposal, also discussed various aspects of the book with me at several stages, and took part in stimulating conversations on Presley's performances.

My thanks are also due to Mrs Barbara Kettle-Williams, who typed much of the manuscript, and to Dr Tim Dowley, whose constructive advice I have unhesitatingly taken. Without my wife's loving forbearance and reassurance, this study would have remained unwritten.

RM-W
London SE12
May 1979

# Contents

**Part I The Man.**

| | | |
|---|---|---|
| 1 | 'A Nice Kid'. | 1 |
| 2 | The Young Singer. | 7 |
| 3 | Superstar. | 12 |
| 4 | The Last Decade | 22 |

**Part II The Music.**

| | | |
|---|---|---|
| 5 | The Sun Recordings, 1954-5. | 31 |
| 6 | The Early RCA Recordings, 1956-8. | 35 |
| 7 | From Nashville to Hollywood, 1960-66. | 48 |
| 8 | Change of Habit, 1966-8. | 68 |
| 9 | The Return of the Master, 1968-9. | 75 |
| 10 | On Stage, 1969-74. | 83 |
| 11 | The Final Years, 1975-7. | 102 |

**Part III The Musician.**

| | |
|---|---|
| Appendices' Conclusion | 109 |
| I Filmography | 119 |
| II Select Bibliography. | 135 |
| III Select Discography. | 136 |
| Index | 144 |

# PART I
# THE MAN

## 1 'A Nice Kid'

When Vernon Presley first met Gladys Smith in Tupelo, Mississippi, towards the end of 1932, their families, like most of working-class America, were suffering from the Depression. The Wall Street crash had occurred three years earlier. Of all the states in the Union, none was more severely affected than the singular state of Mississippi. In 1933, Tupelo—the small town where Vernon and Gladys grew up—had a population of around 7,000. Tupelo was a stop on the Chicago-New Orleans railroad, and the court house of Lee County was situated there.

Life in Mississippi was basic and hard. The state population numbered almost two million, half of which was black: Mississippi had the highest proportion of blacks of any state. It also led in other statistics: it was the state where the most lynchings had taken place—almost 600 in seventy years, less than fifty of the victims being white men. Integration was almost unknown, blacks and whites tended to keep to themselves.

The marriage rate in Mississippi in the early 1930s was more than double the national average, but the divorce rate was only fractionally higher. During times of economic stress, it is not unusual for family ties to become stronger, and the highest birth-rates are almost always found among the lowest-income families. Moreover, the white population was greatly influenced by fundamentalist religion, which preached a strict moral code. Vernon and Gladys were both regular churchgoers. Last, and most importantly, the age of consent for marriage was the lowest in the U.S.A. Boys could marry at fourteen, without their parents' consent, and girls at twelve.

It is not surprising then, to find that Vernon and Gladys married while they were still in their teens. In 1934, shortly after her marriage, Gladys discovered she was pregnant. She had to give up her job as a sewing-machine operator, Vernon attempted to find work on the land, and succeeded sporadically, but economic conditions made life extremely hard. Vernon's father, Luther Presley, a farm-worker, averaged $40 a month in pay as a young man, but in 1932 Luther was taking home less than $25. A farmer could sell a cow for $90 in 1930, but by 1935 it would fetch a mere $36. Wool cost 27½ cents a pound in 1930, but had fallen to less than 19 cents when Gladys left her job in the rag trade. Wages fell and the standard of living was desperately low.

Vernon was forced to change jobs; he became a milk delivery-man. He now received steady pay and his employers helped find a home for the young couple.

Towards the end of her pregnancy, Gladys was thought to be expecting twins. Two boys were born in the afternoon of 8 January 1935. But one, Jesse Garon, did not survive; he was buried the next day in an unmarked grave, in Priceville Cemetery, Tupelo. The surviving boy was christened Elvis Aron.

It is common for parents who lose a baby to idolise their surviving children. Vernon and Gladys were no exception. Elvis remained their only child, and Gladys doted on the boy to a degree which might have brought problems in later life. The family was sustained by the love showered on Elvis and by the qualities of small-town life in southern U.S.A.—honest, hard-working, God-fearing neighbourliness—not so admired as they once were. The regular church-going of Elvis's parents, members of the Pentecostal Church of the First Assembly of God—a small wooden building on Adams Street—not only taught Elvis standards of behaviour, which are apparent in early recorded interviews with him, but also led to his first musical awakening.

In later life Elvis recalled: 'We were a religious family, going round together to sing at camp meetings and revivals. Since I was two years old, all I knew was gospel music.' His mother told Elvis that when he was two years old, he would stand by her in church, wriggling from her lap on to the floor, to join the choir. He added 'I could carry the tune, even though I didn't know the words. That music became such a part of my life, it was as natural as dancing.'

For a musical boy, the attraction of the choir was considerable, and unwittingly Elvis's hymn-singing proved the best musical education he could have had. Singing is the most natural musical expression, and the harmonies of the choir must have entered his subconscious. The family sang together at camp meetings, during which Elvis's grandfather Luther and father Vernon would feature prominently. Luther was a noted local musician, and had arranged several well-known hymns. Much later, Elvis was to record one of his grandfather's arrangements. Luther made one or two recordings of his own, and his talent was inherited by Vernon, who had a fine voice.

Other musical influences at the camp meetings were remembered by Elvis: 'During the singing, the preachers would cut up all over the place, jumping on the piano, moving every which way . . . I guess I learned a lot from them.' This is a penetrating remark. When Elvis burst upon the world popular music scene in the mid-1950s, many people felt his stage movements were done for vulgar effect. Such a view is quite wrong. Elvis moved naturally, responding physically to the heart of the music—the beat—as did the preachers of his youth.

But the singing was the main attraction for him. Elvis recalled:

> When I was four or five all I looked forward to was Sundays, when we could all go to church. I loved the old church, filled with sunlight, and the security of my mother and father beside me. This was the only singing training I had—I never had lessons. I'd just try to sing as loud and in tune as I could. I was always singing. People living on the same housing project as me would stop and listen.

As a toddler the boy had few friends outside the family. But at the age of five, Elvis began school, and came into contact with children of his own age. Gladys, however, doting on him, would never let him out of her sight. 'I couldn't go down to the creek with the other kids,' he later recalled. He was not an outstanding pupil, and surprisingly few of his contemporaries remembered much about him; but his love of music was clear for all to see.

In September 1939 Germany invaded Poland; this marked the outbreak of World War II. At the end of 1941, Japan attacked Pearl Harbor; the United States became a fighting part of the Allied cause. Vernon and his brother Vester were liable for call-up, but both suffered from diabetes, and were exempted. They followed the war news in broadcast bulletins, and Vernon, Gladys and Elvis became avid radio listeners. This led to another formative musical influence on Elvis. 'I used to listen quite a lot, and I loved records by Sister Rosetta Thorpe and country singers like Roy Acuff, Ernest Tubbs, Ted Daffan, Jimmie Rodgers, Jimmy Davis and Bob Wills.'

Another singer he could have mentioned was Red Foley, who recorded the song 'Old Shep'. This became very popular, and must have made an impression on Elvis, for one day at school when he was in the fifth grade he sang the song for his teacher, Mrs Grimes. She was impressed, and arranged for Elvis to sing it again for the principal. He, too, was moved by the boy's singing, and entered Elvis for a local talent show, which was part of the annual Mississippi-Alabama State Fair. Although his voice had not yet broken, the years of singing had moulded it into an expressive instrument. 'Old Shep' is not an easy song, and Elvis sang it unaccompanied at the contest. He thought he came fifth, but in fact he was placed second, and won five dollars and free rides on all the amusements and side-shows at the fair. But when Elvis arrived home his mother was more concerned over some misdemeanour, and beat him. Much later in life, when Elvis was asked about his mother, his reply was revealing:

> I used to get mad at Mama once in a while. But I guess a growing boy always does. I was the only child and Mama was always right with me. Maybe she was too good. I could wake her up in the middle of the night if I was worried about

something. She'd get up, fix me a sandwich and a glass of milk, and talk to me; help me figure things out . . . I suppose because I was an only child I was a little closer. I mean, everyone loves their mother but I was an only child and my mother was always with me, all my life, and it wasn't like losing a mother, it was like losing a friend, a companion, someone to talk to. I would wake her up any hour of the night and if I was worried or troubled about something she'd get up and try to help me. I used to get very angry at her when I was gowing up, it's a natural thing, isn't it? A young person wants to go somewhere, do something and your mother won't let you and you think, well, what's wrong with you? But later on in years you find out that she was right, that she was only doing it to protect you and keep you from getting into trouble and getting hurt. And I'm very happy that she was kind of strict.

Mrs Faye Harris, a neighbour and friend of the Presleys in Tupelo, recalled:

Gladys thought Elvis was the greatest thing that ever happened. And she treated him that way. She worshipped that child from the day he was born until the day she died. She would always keep him at home, and when she let him go out to play, she was always out looking to see that he was alright. And wherever she went, whether it was out visiting or down to the grocery store—she always had her little boy along . . .

The end of the war brought no improvement in the rural townships of the deep South. It was impossible for Vernon to find continuous work in Tupelo, and in 1948 the family decided to move to Memphis, Tennessee. Vernon packed the family's belongings into their green 1939 Plymouth, and drove to the capital of the neighbouring state. They lived for several months in one room on Poplar Avenue in downtown Memphis, about a mile from the Mississippi River. Vernon managed to get regular employment, and Gladys worked part-time in sewing shops, a restaurant and a local hospital. Elvis was enrolled in L.C. Humes High School, a forbidding three-storey brown-brick building on Manasas Street. Only white children went there and although it had 1,700 pupils, it had only six classes.

The Presleys' living accommodation was primitive. They shared a bath with three other families. In these cramped conditions Elvis began to sleep-walk. Red West, a later friend and confidant, wrote:

Like most transplanted kids in a new town, Elvis withdrew into a shell of timidity and shyness. Whatever he lacked in friends on the street, Gladys Presley more than made up for with her attention and affection.

In the summer of 1949 the Presleys moved into a three-roomed ground-floor apartment in a concrete federal-funded housing project called Lauderdale Courts, on Winchester Street. This complex was constructed for families with an income of less than $200 a month. The rent was $35 a month.

Although they were poor, Vernon and Gladys did all they could to give their son what he wanted. By the time the family moved to Memphis, Elvis had his own guitar. This must have entailed a major sacrifice for his parents: he really wanted a bicycle but accepted the $12 musical instrument instead. His interest in the guitar quickly grew. As a keen singer, he could now learn to accompany himself. In the eleventh grade, he performed a song called 'Cold, Cold Icy Fingers' at a school concert. This was so successful that Miss Scrivener, a history teacher,urged him to sing an encore. He went on to give a public performance at the Memphis Veterans' Hospital in early 1950.

By November 1950 Elvis, then approaching his sixteenth birthday, obtained a job at Loew's State Theater, Memphis for $12:50 a week. He worked from 5 pm to 10 pm each night. He enjoyed his evening work, and gave all the money he earned to his mother. The drawback was that he kept very late hours and regularly fell asleep in class the following day. When his mother learned of this, she insisted that he quit the job. But the family finances were still rocky and early in 1951 Elvis was obliged to return to Loews. He left their employment a second time when the manager, Arthur Groom, fired him after a fight over a candy-seller.

Elvis's next job was with the Marl Metal Products Company—but this was a full night-shift. Inevitably, Elvis again fell asleep in class, and Gladys once more told him to give up evening work, exclaiming 'We're not *that* poor.' In spite of their low income, the family managed to get by.

Although Elvis was a quiet and reserved child, he matured early; his adult voice developed sooner than most other boys'. His passionate interest in music and singing gave him an outlet for self-expression. This was not the only way in which the adolescent asserted his individuality, as Red West recalled:

> . . . 17-year-old Presley was a nice kid, even if he looked a little out of place in the sea of kids with their crew cuts and pink scalps. Pasty-faced with . . . long brown hair, in duck-tail fashion, the handfuls of Vaseline he put on it made it look much darker than it was . . . He had a preference for leather jackets and would often tie a red bandana around his neck, in the fashion popular with inter-State truck drivers of the era . . . When he wasn't wearing a leather jacket and jeans, it was some outrageously-coloured pair of pegged pants. In the sea of 1,600 pink-scalped kids at school, Elvis stood out like a camel in the arctic. Intentionally or not, his appearance expressed a defiance which his demeanour did not match . . .

Elvis's individuality in clothes attracted unwelcome attention from his contemporaries. Red West continued:

. . . someone was always picking on him, don't know why. He was easy-going enough, well-mannered, was always respectful of his elders, and he never wised off anyone. In many ways, he was a very good kid, a lot nicer than some of the others around . . .

Red was able to help Elvis out of a few scrapes, and their long association began at this time. Red recalled another, more significant school variety concert at Christmas 1952:

. . . one of the big events of the year was the school variety concert. It consisted of about 30 acts . . . the person who ran the show was a history teacher (Miss Scrivener) . . . I put an act in the show. I played the trumpet and I got together a guitar and a bass. It was a heck of a big day and we were all very nervous . . .

Red had finished his act when he got the shock of his life, seeing Elvis come out on the stage with his guitar:

To be honest, I never thought he would have the guts to go out there in front of those people . . . Then it happened. Elvis put one foot up on a chair to act as a prop, and he started to plunk away at the tune 'Old Shep'. Then he whipped into a fast song, then a ballad . . . Hell, do you know while Elvis was singing the love songs, there was one old lady crying? . . . When he finished his show, the kids went crazy; they applauded and applauded. They just went mad . . . He seemed to be amazed that for the first time in his life someone other than his family really liked him. I'll never really know when Elvis got bitten by the bug of loving the applause of the audience, but my guess is that it happened right there in Humes High School. At last, it seemed, he had found a way to make outsiders love him . . . As shy as he was, he had a definite magic on stage . . .

This concert took place a few months before Elvis graduated; the success made his last months at school more pleasant. He was popular and much in demand, no longer the Outsider. Elvis graduated in the summer of 1953. He was now eighteen and got a job with the Precision Tool Company. He had no clear ambition, and whatever ideas he may have had about becoming a singer he kept to himself. He clearly realized that he had to have regular employment to help with the family's finances. He later became a truck-driver with the Crown Electric Company earning about $35 a week. Crown was situated on Poplar Avenue, where the Presleys lived when they first moved to Memphis. With Elvis working, the family could afford to move to a bigger and better apartment on Lamar Avenue. To better himself, Elvis studied in the evenings to become an electrician. But his day time delivery route as a truck-driver took him along Union Avenue, where a small building had caught his interest.

# 2 The Young Singer

At 706 Union Avenue, Memphis, was a small building which housed the Sun Recording Studio. It was owned by a former radio announcer, Sam Phillips, who opened the studio in 1950. Phillips had already recorded local singers such as Howlin' Wolf, Junior Parker and B.B. King, as well as Johnny Cash, Jerry Lee Lewis, Roy Orbison and Charlie Rich—all of whom went on to make important careers for larger and more famous record companies. Two years after starting out, Phillips launched his own Sun label (his previous recordings were licensed to other labels). A lucrative spin-off was the Memphis Recording Service, a facility for budding artists who wanted to make recordings. For four dollars anybody could go in and record two songs. Apart from being a profitable sideline, it was also an excellent free way of finding local talent. One Saturday afternoon in 1953, just before his mother's birthday, Elvis dropped by the Memphis Recording Service office. As he recalled:

I went to Sun, paid my four bucks to the lady, because I had a notion to find out what I really sounded like. I had been singing all my life, and I was kind of curious. But when I heard the recording it was terrible—I was terrible—I sounded like someone banging a trash-can lid.

Apart from natural curiosity—wanting to know what his voice sounded like—another reason for making the recording was that Elvis decided to give it to his mother for her birthday. Gladys was delighted with it. 'She played it over and over until it was plumb near worn out.' The recording was an acetate (a direct-cut on to disc), so its playing life was considerably shorter than that of a normal commercial record—probably not more than fifty or sixty times at most.

Gladys was not the only person to disagree with Elvis over the quality of his recording. The young woman who worked for Sam Phillips, Miss Marion Keisker, was attracted by the quality of Elvis's voice. When he was half-way through his first song, 'My Happiness', she managed to get a spare tape-machine switched on, and caught the second part, as well as the whole of his other number, 'That's When Your Heartaches Begin.' She decided to tape Elvis's voice because she remembered Sam Phillips' advice: 'If you can find a white singer with a black man's voice, we could make a fortune.' She clearly thought that Elvis was such a singer, and played the tape to Phillips. He was not impressed, but Marion Keisker kept badgering him to use Elvis.

After several months driving for Crown, and pursuing his electrical studies at night, Elvis returned to Sun on 4 January 1954 to invest another four dollars. This time the two songs were 'Casual Love' and 'I'll Never Stand in Your Way'. Miss Keisker was out of the office, but Sam Phillips himself was there. He heard Elvis, and again was not impressed with his voice. He felt Elvis had a great deal to do before he could record commercially, although he now admitted he had 'something'. He noted Elvis's name and address in case he should ever need him.

A month or two later (eight months after Elvis originally visited Sun) Phillips came across a demonstration disc of an unknown black singer's performance of 'Without You'. Phillips was unable to contact the singer. But when Miss Keisker heard the number she suggested Presley as the performer. Presley recalled: 'It was 12 o'clock on a Saturday, and they said "Can you be here by three?" I ran all the way. I was there by the time they hung up the phone.'

All afternoon Presley sang 'Without You', and another song, 'Rag Mop', but the results were, by all accounts, very disappointing. Phillips was on the point of sending Elvis home when he asked if Elvis would like to choose something to sing. Elvis needed no second bidding, and all the musical influences of his life poured out: gospel songs, country and western songs, blues, current hits, songs from films, urban songs, black artists' songs that dominated the old rhythm-and-blues charts but hardly ever broke into the national charts. It was an amazingly varied performance.

This made Phillips decide to stick with Presley. He called a local musician, the 21-year-old guitarist Scotty Moore, to see if he could work with Elvis for a later recording session. Elvis visited Moore's home that evening, and astonished Mrs Moore by his flamboyant dress, strangely at odds with his quiet and reserved personality. A neighbour, Bill Black, a bass player, heard the music at Moore's house and dropped by, but neither he nor Moore were impressed with Elvis. However the three agreed to record a session at Sun the following Monday evening.

The first song recorded was 'I Love You Because'. Four takes were made. The first version released was spliced from takes two and four. The first take, complete with talking, remained unissued for twenty years. After this song had been recorded, the boys took a break, during which Presley picked up his guitar and starting to play and sing 'That's All Right Mama'. Scotty and Bill joined in freely and, without anyone realizing what was happening, the music came together.

This time Phillips *was* impressed. He sent the boys back into the studio to repeat on tape what they had created in the engineering room.

This was it—what they had instinctively been striving towards for so long: a fusion of separate elements, joined by a steady, unvaried syncopated beat, but sung in an original manner by a singer whose voice had a naturally distinctive quality. It was totally unsophisticated and direct, like the best of country music. It was sincere, like the best gospel music. It seemed to be reaching for some unattainable goal, like the best of blues music. It was rhythmically solid and firm, like the best dance music. And above all there was the voice, and the extraordinary way Elvis used words. The way the elements blended was utterly original.

Sam Phillips was well pleased with the results of the session. He took an acetate of the intended single to Dewey Phillips, a white disc-jockey on station WHBQ, Memphis. Dewey was as impressed as Sam, and agreed to play 'That's All Right Mama' over the air on his show, *Red, Hot and Blue.* The result was extraordinary: following the broadcast of the acetate, WHBQ was besieged with calls enquiring about the singer.

Elvis's reticence got the better of him. He decided not to listen to the broadcast, but went to see a movie. 'I was too nervous to sit with Mom to hear the transmission . . . my parents came looking for me because the radio station received lots of calls.'

The radio listeners were even more astonished when they discovered Elvis was a white boy; many people, hearing the disc over the air, imagined he was black. Discrimination was still prevalent in the deep South in the mid-1950s. It was rare for local radio shows to mix white and black singers, and normally Dewey's programme was devoted to black artists. By the time the evening was over, Presley had been dragged from the cinema to be interviewed by Dewey over the air, and every listener knew he was white.

Sam Phillips now moved quickly. The record was already in production when Dewey Phillips played it. This was probably the evening of Wednesday 8 July 1954. By 18 July the record was on sale in the stores. By 31 July it stood at number three in the Memphis Country Music chart. At first some disc-jockeys objected to playing a black song by a white singer—a white singer who sounded as though he was black. But not for the first time the commercial success of the single swept away such reservations.

Elvis, his parents, Sam Phillips, Scotty, Bill and Marion Keisker were all thrilled at the success of 'That's All Right Mama'. The hit led to calls for Elvis and the boys to appear in public. They were booked for appearances at both Nashville's famous *Grand Old Opry* and Shreveport's *Louisiana Hayride* — both of which were broadcast — but Elvis's appearance at the *Opry* was disastrous. As he left the stage, the MC, Jim Denny, told Elvis he should quit singing and go back to driving a truck. Presley was deeply upset by this remark, and never forgot it, but the appearance at Shreveport was quite another matter. Elvis hit it off both with the audience and the show's director, Horace Logan A few weeks later, they played a return engagement and their success was so remarkable that Logan offered Elvis a year's contract.

It did not take Elvis long to pick up the essentials of microphone technique, but he never really lost his inherent shyness. Recordings of his last shows, although visually flamboyant, reveal that underneath the trappings he was still a nervous public speaker.

Engagements for the boys meant that they were now earning enough money for Elvis to leave his job with Crown, although Vernon had some misgivings. From this moment Elvis Presley became a full-time professional singer. Within the next few months, a local disc-jockey, Bob Neal, took over the affairs of the 'Hillbilly Cat', as Presley was called, as well as those of the band, which had been joined by the drummer D.J. Fontana. The success of the first single in the local charts, and the growing number of concerts in neighbouring states, led to more sessions with Sam Phillips. But Phillips did not keep a detailed log of Elvis's recording sessions. Consequently, much detailed information is lost—or, rather, was never recorded—and a great deal of conjecture is necessary. However, it is a fact that in August or September 1954 Elvis recorded at least three more titles, 'I Don't Care If The Sun Don't Shine', 'Good Rockin' Tonight' and 'Just Because'. It is also very likely that 'Harbour Lights' was recorded at this time, although it was not released until 1976, on the album *A Legendary Performer* Vol. 2. 'Good Rockin' Tonight' repeated the success of the first single, reaching number three in the Memphis charts. This was released in January 1955, by which time Presley had recorded (probably the previous December) four more titles 'Milkcow Blues Boogie', 'You're A Heartbreaker', 'I'm Left, You're Right, She's Gone'. and 'I'll Never Let You Go'—the last possibly in January 1955.

'Milkcow Blues Boogie' was Elvis's third single, but it did not quite repeat the success of the first two. However his public appearances were growing, both to build up a fan club and to provide him with valuable experience in performing before a live audience. Bob Neal was able to get Elvis on *The Hank Snow Jamboree*, a southern tour which began on 1 May. This was a major step forward, and in the event it was a fateful move. For promoting the tour was Colonel Tom Parker.

Colonel Parker was born in 1909. In 1953 he was granted the title of Honorary Colonel of Tennessee by Governor Clement. Tom Parker worked for his uncle, who ran the Great Parker Pony Circus, until the age of eighteen. He left to work on his own, becoming a free-lance press agent and promoter, and his success in these fields led him to work for the country singer Eddy Arnold. He became Arnold's personal manager, and was instrumental in getting Arnold signed with RCA in the 1940s. Arnold and Parker separated, most amicably by all accounts, in 1951, when Colonel Tom became Hank Snow's manager.

The Colonel saw that Presley had a tremendous impact on the youthful element in the audiences, but had apparently been aware of Elvis for some time. Now he saw for himself. In a move which left no ill feeling, the Colonel eventually took over Elvis's management. First he won the confidence of Vernon and Gladys, and, once he had become Elvis's manager, he attempted to get Elvis signed to a major record company.

It was clear that Sam Phillips did not possess the resources to capitalize on his 'find', nor could he give the financial support usual for the kind of tour Elvis had undertaken with Hank Snow. Atlantic Records, a new label run by a great record man, Ahmet Ertegun, offered $25,000 for the Presley contract. This was a tempting offer but Atlantic lacked the strength of the major companies. It was CBS (in the United States, Columbia) and RCA which possessed the resources that the Colonel was after. In the event, it was the Colonel's previous connexions with RCA, together with that company's growing country-and-western roster (in the early days, Presley was still regarded as a Southern country singer) which clinched the deal. CBS, then run by the legendary Goddard Lieberson, whose judgement was almost infallible if, in the last resort, a shade too elegant to embrace the rawness of Presley, might have posed problems for the Colonel.

And so Steve Sholes of RCA signed Elvis Presley to that company. The price for Elvis's services—together with all the Sun material, both released and unreleased tapes—was $35,000, plus a $5,000 non-recoverable advance to Elvis himself. The young man had never seen so much money before, and started a fashion in spending which many young pop stars later copied. Elvis 'went out and bought Moma a pink Cadillac.'

Elvis Presley had clearly come a long way in a short time. Circumstances had conspired to place him in the ideal position from which his music could reach the world. He had been signed to a major record company, and that company's investment was such that it was in their strongest interests to see it recouped. He had acquired one of the shrewdest, best respected and ablest managers and publicists in show-business. RCA's international connexions were world-wide: no market was not covered by them, either directly or through licensing. RCA's financial resources were considerable, and all Elvis had to do was deliver the goods. Nobody could have foreseen how soon or how triumphantly the goods were to be delivered.

# 3 Superstar

No sooner had Elvis Presley's first RCA recording sessions in Nashville been confirmed, and the release date set for the first single, than Colonel Parker arranged Presley's first television appearance, on the CBS network *Tommy and Jimmy Dorsey Stage Show.* This coup was made easier as the Dorsey ratings were fighting a losing battle against the *Perry Como Show,* networked by NBC (curiously enough, a part of RCA).

The classic recordings which emanated from the first RCA sessions, including the great performance of 'Heartbreak Hotel', demanded the widest possible exposure. The most potent medium was television, and Presley's appearance on the *Stage Show* gave a great boost to the Dorsey Brothers' ratings. He was rebooked immediately, and made such an impact that within weeks he was the talk of America. Show business moguls could not grasp the massive impact which his appearance had on the youth of America, or the unprecedented demand for his records which followed. Parents were shocked at Presley's apparently explicit sexual movements, to say nothing of the radically new music he performed.

Within weeks 'Heartbreak Hotel' became the biggest-selling single in the U.S.A. Presley's further Dorsey appearances were well-publicized, adding fuel to the blaze. The demand was remarkable, although many people thought that Presley was a nine days' wonder. There was pressure on RCA to issue an album quickly, to capitalize on the sudden demand before it evaporated. As Presley had only recorded a handful of songs for them there was not enough new material to fill an album. RCA turned to the Sun recordings which they had purchased, and their album was 'topped-up' by the inclusion of several such tapes. This decision was criticized: many felt RCA should have waited to get fresh Presley material, and that the inclusion of Sun recordings was an admission of lack of foresight. RCA replied that, having bought the Sun material, they had every right to issue it. Furthermore, one of the main reasons for signing Presley was the distinctive Sun sound, and it was logical to include examples on his first album. Whatever the pros and cons, the album became the classic rock'n'roll album, and was still selling, all over the world, a quarter of a century later.

The Colonel fixed up several important appearances at which Presley's magnetism as a performer – revealed during his last year at Humes High School – was demonstrated to a much wider audience. He appeared on television in California, but the incessant travelling and public appearances took their toll. Presley collapsed in Jacksonville, while visiting Florida, and was taken to hospital. He was warned to curtail his appearances, but Presley discharged himself the next day and continued the tour.

His live appearances made him a target for assault. Hundreds of screaming girls, raised to fever-pitch by Presley's appearance, frequently stormed the stage, trying to grab him and tear his clothes. But Presley said '. . . if they want my shirt, they can have it. After all, they put it on my back to start with!' His hotel rooms were besieged – but every appearance was not received with such enthusiasm. His act was too unusual and difficult for older audiences to grasp. The Colonel made a rare error of judgement when he booked Elvis to appear at the Frontier Hotel, Las Vegas, some weeks later. The performance was a disaster; the audience, made up almost exclusively of middle-aged, middle-class people, received Presley in stony silence.

But nobody could ignore the fanatical teen-age following which Presley generated within a few months, Hollywood – always on the look-out for new artists – became interested. Curiously enough, in the audience at the Frontier Hotel was the legendary Hal Wallis, who invited Presley to Paramount Pictures in Hollywood for a screen-test.

Stories surrounding this test are legion, and for some curious reason Presley was not asked to sing. However, on the strength of the test, Wallis offered Presley a three-film contract, and his screen debut was originally scheduled for *The Rainmaker* with Burt Lancaster and Katherine Hepburn. Presley was to play the part of a deranged youth but this was cancelled – perhaps because the image would have been wrong for him. The right part was not long in coming.

Meanwhile in Hollywood, Elvis appeared on the Milton Bearle Television show, which was seen by an estimated forty million viewers – over one fifth of the entire population of the U.S.A. This was on 6 June, and New York critics were in the minority in their scathing condemnation: '. . . an unutterable bore. . . he can't sing a lick. . . like watching a male stripteaser and a malted milk machine at the same time. . .' But this pasting from the press meant nothing to New York television. The new *Steve Allen Show* quickly booked Presley, and insulted the fans in the process; for Allen got Presley to sing his new hit 'Hound Dog' in evening dress to a droopy dog. Presley performed this against his better judgement, it appears, but the publicity generated was enormous.

The *Steve Allen Show* clashed with the well-established *Ed Sullivan Show* — Sullivan had earlier declared Presley would never appear with him. The ratings for Elvis's appearance on the *Steve Allen Show* caused Sullivan to change his mind. Presley had demonstrated his audience-pulling power, and suddenly became the hottest property in show-business. Sullivan booked Elvis, but stipulated he was to appear from the waist up, so that his suggestive movements would not be seen. Fifty-four million people tuned in, a record which stood until the Beatles appeared on the same show eight years later.

Quite apart from his music, it was clear that Elvis's appearance was also beginning to affect young American fashion. His long slicked-back hair, with casual out-door clothes worn on most occasions, and the collar turned up at the back; passions for fast cars, pool, pretty girls and his generally aggressive stance all had enormous influence on young people. The Colonel soon 'sold' Elvis in many ways: bubble-gum cards, posters, pictures, books, magazines — one devoted exclusively to Elvis — all fanned the flame of Presley-mania, and created a visual image as strong and direct as the musical one.

This extension of promotion and publicity was also a deliberate attempt to soften up the public in readiness for Presley's imminent film career. By the time of Presley's first film, he would be as well-known visually as his co-stars, whoever they might be. Presley had withdrawn from *The Rainmaker,* and although he still had the Paramount contract, his first film was for Twentieth-Century Fox. This was finally titled *Love Me Tender,* but its working title was *The Reno Brothers.* Presley sang the title song from the film on the *Ed Sullivan Show.* The producer of *Love Me Tender* was David Weisbart — a shrewd choice, for he had produced James Dean's most successful film *Rebel Without a Cause,* which reflected the youthful, inarticulate rebelliousness of the young generation a year or so earlier.

Presley's success was *not* inarticulate. He broke off filming to return to Tupelo, where the town had created an 'Elvis Presley Day', giving him the freedom of the township and a gift of five thousand dollars. With his growing fortune, Elvis naturally wished to secure the future for himself and his parents. Later in 1956 be bought a green-and-white ranch on Audubon Drive, on the outskirts of Memphis. He had a swimming-pool installed (mainly for show, as he was not a keen swimmer), and a garage for his three cars.

At the end of October Elvis appeared on the *Ed Sullivan Show* again, three weeks before *Love Me Tender* was premièred at the Paramount Theater on Broadway. It was simultaneously released at 550 cinemas, and within days proved a financial success. By the beginning of December 1956, Presley had begun work on his second film, *Loving You*

— his first under the Paramount contract. He returned to Memphis for Christmas, dropping by the Sun Recording Studios to look up Sam Phillips and other old friends. Also present were Carl Perkins, Johnny Cash and Jerry Lee Lewis, and Phillips actually recorded five numbers by this star-studded quartet. Although contractual problems must be labyrinthine, it ought to be possible to find a way of releasing this outstandingly important session after a quarter of a century.

By this time everything Presley did was news. The film studios had to cope with hundreds of letters every day, thousands of phone calls, and incessant demands from the press for interviews and preview shots of the film. Elvis Presley received the most intensive publicity of any star at this time, and it says much for his strength of character that he was able to withstand this so well, and to remain at heart the same polite, reserved and charming person he had always been.

His acting did not show the same creative force as his singing: Presley was not another James Dean. However, nobody in show-business could ignore his enormous earning-power, which, thanks to RCA's world-wide connexions, had spread to many countries. In May 1957 Elvis began his third film, the MGM production of *Jailhouse Rock.* This was a tougher proposition: up at 6.30 each morning, the day's shooting did not finish before 6.00 in the evening — and in the film, Elvis had to drive an excavator and dance, as well as play the most demanding of the roles he had undertaken for the screen.

The result was an unqualified success — by far the best of his films so far. It has clearly stood the test of time, not least for the remarkable *Jailhouse Rock* sequence, which became an important visual image for rock music. Presley received $250,000 for the film, plus fifty per cent of the profits, and with the money he bought another residence to replace that on Audubon Drive. This bigger property was in Whitehaven, a suburb of Memphis. It became part of the city itself in 1969, and was always an exclusive residential district.

The new property, which comprises thirteen-and-a-half acres, was called Graceland. It had been built before World War II by Dr Thomas Moore, who named it after his wife's aunt, Grace Toof, from whom the Moores had inherited the land. Graceland was No. 3764, Highway 51 South. Presley paid $100,000 for it — which in 1957 was a high price for such a property.

At the end of September 1957, Presley returned to Tupelo for a charity concert in aid of the *Elvis Presley Recreational Center*, and then flew to Hawaii for concerts in the Honolulu Stadium. This was his first visit outside mainland America, apart from a tour in Canada, and he became very attracted by Hawaii. On his return to Graceland, Presley received his papers from the Memphis Draft Board, for induction into the United

States Army for two years' compulsory national service. Presley was due to appear before the Draft Board (effectively his call-up day) on 20 January 1958, but he applied for a deferment as he had begun work on his fourth film, *King Creole,* another Paramount picture. The deferment was granted until 24 March.

*King Creole* was finished in time, and is one of Presley's best films: his acting ability is clearly revealed. The director, Michael Curtiz, respected and experienced in Hollywood, had made a considerable name for himself at Warner Brothers' studios, and the addition of stars such as Walter Matthau, Dean Jagger and Carolyn Jones enhanced the appeal of this remarkable film. The story, loosely based on the best-selling novel *A Stone for Danny Fisher,* by Harold Robbins, was superior to those of Presley's earlier films. When the film was released, in May 1958, it was well received, even by critics who had panned Presley's earlier film appearances.

But by then Presley had joined the United States Army. On 24 March he reported for induction at Memphis Draft Board No. 86. He was accompanied by his parents and his friend Lamar Fike. Presley stepped forward when his name was called (the step signified his acceptance of induction) to become Private Presley 53310761. With his fellow draftees, he boarded an army bus for Fort Chaffee, Arkansas, for basic training.

After the six weeks training, during which he was required to live in the camp, Presley was transferred to Fort Hood, where his specialist Army training commenced. For this, a soldier was permitted to live out of camp, if his family lived within easy travelling distance. Presley rented a bungalow at Killean, a small nearby town, to which his family moved so that he could join them early in May.

Despite his army service, Presley was in high spirits. He knew that his fourth film had achieved great success, and sales of his records — by then he had achieved something like ten consecutive number one records — actually increased when he joined the army.

Once again, a change in Presley's life found him able to cope. A year or two before his phenomenal rise to stardom left him — by all accounts — very much unchanged as a person. Now, thrown into a completely different environment, surrounded by publicity, he again demonstrated his level-headedness. The army authorities were concerned at Presley's call-up. Some feared he would throw tantrums and become emotionally disturbed at the authority he would have to submit to. Others felt he should become part of the Army's special services corps, reserved for those with skills as sportsmen, entertainers or artists, who had an opportunity to continue their calling in a military setting — representing the army in sport, entertaining troops or using their skills to benefit their fellow-soldiers. Clearly, Presley could have joined them, but he did not: he asked for no special treatment, and became a much-liked trainee soldier. After ten weeks, he was granted a week-end pass, and the opportunity was taken by RCA to take him to Nashville for recording sessions on 10/11 June. The result was one of his best sessions, and several major hits.

But family troubles now began to concern Presley. By the beginning of July, Gladys Presley was clearly unwell. It was decided she should return to Memphis by train, where she was admitted to the Methodist Hospital. Four days later, hepatitis was diagnosed. By 11 August, her condition had deteriorated badly. On compassionate leave, Elvis flew to Memphis — a brave step, as he had a deep fear of flying. He began a round-the-clock vigil with his father, but early in the morning, 14 August 1958, Vernon broke the news to him that his mother had died of a heart attack, brought on by the hepatitis. By a melancholy coincidence, the father of Presley's friend and bodyguard, Red West, died eight hours later.

We have seen how close was the bond between Elvis and his mother. It is not difficult to imagine the shock and deep distress her untimely death caused him. Many years later, friends close to Presley claimed that he never got over her death.

By the beginning of September, he had been transferred to the Third Armoured Division, for posting to West Germany as part of the U.S. contribution to the NATO forces stationed there. On 26 September he went by train to Brooklyn Naval Yard, New York, to join the troopship *U.S.S. General Randall.* They sailed to Bremerhaven, West Germany, after Presley had given the obligatory interviews, duly taped by RCA and issued as a record, and photo-calls.

On the dockside, whilst saying farewell to his family, he decided on the spur of the moment to invite them to follow him to Germany to live there for the duration of his posting. A few weeks later, Vernon, with his mother Minnie Presley (then in her mid-sixties), Red West and Lamar Fike, followed Elvis to Germany. Elvis was stationed at Freiburg, and the family at first stayed at the Grünewald Hotel in Bad Nauheim. Later, they moved into a house on Goethestrasse. Shortly afterwards Vernon met Davada (Dee) Stanley, the wife of Sergeant Bill Stanley. Mrs Stanley's three sons were all under the age of six. The Stanleys became great friends of the Presley family.

Elvis settled in well to his duties in Germany. He became a marksman, was promoted, and his fame did little to disrupt his army life. His fan-mail, however, was prodigious, averaging 10,000 letters a week. Many of the letters were addressed simply to 'Elvis, Germany'. He received no special treatment from the Army authorities, he got on well with the Germans, and by all accounts came to enjoy army life. One activity the army introduced him to was karate, and he soon developed a passion for it which he retained for the rest of his life. Red West reports that from time to time Elvis and his fellow-soldiers were given tablets to keep them alert during manoeuvres. This was Presley's first encounter with stimulants.

Meanwhile relations between Dee Stanley and her husband had become strained, and after several months as welcome visitors to the Presley household, the couple split up and were divorced. Vernon Presley and Dee became very close friends.

Elvis had meantime met Captain Joseph P. Beaulieu, and his 14-year-old adopted daughter, Priscilla. Priscilla was apparently mature for her age, both physically and mentally, and it was not long before Elvis began to call at the Beaulieu home with greater frequency.

Presley's film career had been so successful that plans were being laid for the first film on his return to civilian life, based on his army adventures. Paramount Pictures began filming location shots for the film in Germany, using a stand-in, for it was decided that under no circumstances would he commence filming whilst he was still in the army. This meant that on his discharge, the film could be completed quickly, to capitalize on the publicity generated by his return to civilian life.

At the beginning of 1960, the unit to which Presley was assigned decided to throw a farewell party for their famous soldier. By an extraordinary coincidence it was arranged and organised by Captain Marion Keisker — the very same Marion Keisker who had worked for Sam Phillips at Sun Records in the early 1950s, and who had been instrumental in pushing Elvis's name. Some years later, she left Memphis, joined the U.S. army, was promoted to the rank of Captain, and posted to Germany.

The party took place on 1 March 1960. Two days later Elvis returned to Fort Dix, New Jersey, via Prestwick in Scotland (for an hour's change of flight — the only time Presley set foot in the British Isles).

On 5 March, Elvis Presley was discharged, and returned with his family to Graceland. He was now free to resume his career, and in April appeared with Frank Sinatra on his networked television show, the *Timex Special.* But Elvis had already been back in the recording studios and on the film sets. His first priority in Hollywood was to finish *G.I. Blues,* the final title of his army film.

It is clear that whoever was responsible for handling Elvis Presley's public image whilst he was in the army had done an outstanding job. The Colonel, of course, takes much of the credit; his publicity skills ensured that Presley's discharge received enormous coverage. The discharge itself was not particularly newsworthy — Presley could not remain in the army for ever — but the decision not to allow much material to be released during his two years away meant that Presley was not over-exposed. But he had been unable to develop his musicianship during his service, and if RCA had put poor material 'in the can' in order to keep the public happy whilst he was away, the result might well have done irreparable damage to the singer's long-term career.

Furthermore, people saw that Presley had been prepared to do his service along with everyone else, with no special favours asked or granted. In a sense, this was even more difficult for him, as anyone who is famous in the services has to be better than everyone else, to show they are the *same* as everyone else. Presley had been a good soldier, and this led to a change of heart on the part of those members of the older generation to whom he represented a dangerous figure before his call-up. For middle-class America, Elvis Presley had matured into a good, all-American boy.

Presley's homecoming was in marked contrast to the reception he had been accorded by middle-class America four years before. In 1956, Billy Graham said 'from what I've heard, I'm not sure I'd want my children to see him'; but in 1960 the State of Mississippi passed a resolution welcoming Presley back, citing him 'a legend and inspiration to tens of millions of Americans and hence he reaffirms an historic American ideal that success in our nation can still be attained through individual initiative, hard work, and abiding faith in one's self and in the Creator'. The train which carried him from New Jersey to Memphis was mobbed all the way, with Presley being called upon to appear on the platform, at whistle-stops, as if he was a Presidential candidate. The police escort from the central Memphis station to Graceland was immense, and for most of the day Memphis was reduced to a gigantic traffic jam.

A few weeks later, Elvis went to Nashville for his first post-Army recording session. This was extensive and highly successful, although it demonstrated a softer approach, not as raunchy and revolutionary as in 1956-58. His April appearance with Frank Sinatra, in which they sang duets, emphasized this comparative lack of aggression, a point reflected in the *Billboard:* '. . . the expected dynamite was, to put it mildly, a bit over-rated. . '

Presley resumed his career with *G.I. Blues,* and his next post-Army single 'It's Now or Never' meant that Presley now appealed to middle-of-the-road stations and radio shows. He had found a new audience among listeners who previously would not have heard their favourite show play a Presley single. *G.I. Blues* shows a different Presley than seen in *Jailhouse Rock* and *King Creole.* He appeared with children and puppets, and was more of an all-round entertainer. This aspect of Presley's developing career could have been beneficial, but it did not in fact work out that way.

On 3 July 1960, Vernon Presley and Dee Stanley were married. Elvis did not attend the ceremony, claiming that his appearance would have caused a riot, and spoilt the occasion for his father and step-mother. Perhaps Elvis's attachment to his mother's memory was too strong — and in addition he was busy completing *G.I. Blues.* As soon as this was finished, he returned to the Twentieth-Century Fox studios to make the most remarkable film of his career. This was *Flaming Star,* in which he played a half-breed. There were only two songs in the film, the first over the credits, and the second within minutes of the start of the story, and this lack of singing is said to have upset many fans who expected another musical. However, what they got was an acting role of astonishing promise from Elvis.

The immense commercial success of *G.I. Blues,* allied to Presley's current chart hits, possibly led to a serious miscalculation by Fox. *Flaming Star* — completed quickly, but betraying no signs of haste — was rushed out by Christmas, 1960. The public had not been told what to expect, and consequently the film was not the success it deserved to be. Fox had already contracted to make one more Presley film, but they made no further films after that. The comparative lack of success of *Flaming Star* also led to a back-pedalling on any role which demanded more acting than singing ability from Presley. This was a tragedy, since *King Creole* and *Flaming Star* showed that Presley had considerable acting talent.

The years 1960-65 saw Elvis Presley consolidate his wealth, but not his musical character. The years at Graceland with a crowd of like-minded friends — who came to be dubbed the 'Memphis Mafia' — led to a certain indolence in his life-style which at times went too far. At other times his generosity became legendary: the cars and lavish gifts he showered on sometimes the most casual acquaintances were countless, yet his contributions to charities and deserving causes were almost always made anonymously. It is only since his death that such donations became known.

During 1961 Dee Presley suffered a miscarriage. She and Vernon had no children. The same year Elvis invited Priscilla Beaulieu to spend Christmas at Graceland with the family. Her father, by then promoted to major, had been transferred to Travis Air Force Base, near San Francisco. Priscilla moved in with Vernon and Dee, in January 1962, to finish her last eighteen months' high-school education at the Immaculate Conception High School in Memphis.

Later in 1961 Presley was invited to appear at the Royal Command Variety Performance in London before Queen Elizabeth II. He did not accept it is said, because Colonel Parker insisted that Presley be presented to Her Majesty. Such a condition was out of the question, but what was surely not pointed out to the Colonel was that stars appearing in the show are almost always presented to the Royal party before the performance. If Presley had accepted, there is every chance he would have met the Queen; but he inadvisedly refused, and was never again asked.

From 1961 to 1968, Elvis Presley made twenty-one more feature films, none of which compares with the best of his previous screen work. The succession of films, and the accompanying sound-track albums, led to less and less work in the recording studio. For over two years, from January 1964 to May 1966, Presley recorded nothing but soundtracks for a succession of films. They went from bad to worse, a flagrant waste of his talent.

Presley's creative life during these years fell into the routine of an average of three films a year, some made as quickly as in sixteen days. These years saw the rise of a new generation of rock-inspired artists; it is no surprise that Presley's influence declined considerably.

RCA must have been concerned at the continuing fall-off in sales of Presley albums. The sessions they persuaded Elvis to undertake in Nashville in May 1966, to make a new religious album, was Presley's first major studio visit for three years. There is no doubt that the success of the resulting album was both welcome and long overdue. But it was some time before he returned to the studio again, although the subsequent changes in his film-making (a slowing-up in the number of films made, and a greater musical quality in the songs used) was wholly beneficial.

However, Presley was not entirely immune to the changes in popular music. He admired the Beatles, and hosted a party for them in Hollywood on 27 August 1965. Photographers were forbidden, but it is known that the five played and sang together. It is by no means inconceiveable that this unique session was recorded. If so, it is as important as that made at the Sun Studios with Carl Perkins, Johnny Cash and Jerry Lee Lewis in December 1956. A tape of even one song by Elvis Presley and the Beatles would represent riches indeed.

# 4 The Last Decade

In February 1967 Elvis Presley bought a ranch near Walls, DeSoto County, Mississippi, just across the state line, ten miles south of Graceland. He named it Circle G, and stocked it with thoroughbreds. Throughout his life, Presley retained a strong affection for animals, as befitted a 'country' boy. At Graceland in the early 1960s, Presley had a small collection of fine horses stabled behind the mansion, as well as a collection of peacocks on the lawns. In addition, his pet dog, Muffin, endeared himself to Presley, although many friends and visitors report that he was a bad-tempered animal. Perhaps the most remarkable pet was Scatter, a chimpanzee, who had some curious habits: he drank neat bourbon, was trained to use the bathroom, and had his own tailor-made clothes. He was a great favourite with the 'Memphis Mafia'. After only a few months expenditure on the Circle G ranch had exceeded $500,000, but by then Presley had a more important event on his mind.

At 9.41 a.m. 1 May 1967 Elvis and Priscilla Beaulieu were married in a private suite at the Aladdin Hotel, Las Vegas. A justice of the Nevada Supreme Court, Judge David Zenoff, performed the private ceremony, with only a few witnesses. The couple flew to Hollywood for Elvis to complete his current film, *Clambake.* Two days later they returned to Memphis, where they held a big party for friends and members of the staff who had not attended the wedding. Shortly after his marriage, Elvis bought a large house in Los Angeles, reputedly at a cost of over $400,000.

Nine months to the day after the wedding, Priscilla gave birth to a daughter, Lisa Marie. This was naturally a happy time for Presley, although the assassination of Dr Martin Luther King at the Lorraine Motel, Memphis, on 4 April distressed him.

RCA studio sessions in Nashville in September produced several important recordings, especially 'Guitar Man' and 'Big Boss Man', and shortly negotiations were afoot to bring to fruition another important event in Presley's life. This was a television spectacular, to be screened by NBC; the first Presley special, and the first time he had appeared before an audience (albeit via telerecording) since his engagements in Hawaii in 1961.

The director chosen for the television show, Steve Binder, was anxious to make not merely a photographic record of Presley singing a selection of his hits. He wanted to recapture the excitement of early rock'n'roll alongside big production numbers (in one Presley's name appeared in lights twenty feet high). This was a moment of truth for Presley — and he knew it. He admitted to several friends that he was very nervous about appearing before an audience again, and was anxious about his ability to engender the old excitement. From his first dramatic entry, in an all-black leather outfit, although his hands were visibly shaking, the chemistry worked. He was once again the magisterial performer, the incomparable rock artist. As the performance continued, he relaxed noticeably. He became at ease, humorous — although he was still the shy boy from Tupelo — even faintly self-deprecatory.

This successful television programme put Presley back in the forefront of popular music in the U.S.A. His future did not lie in making more of the pappy films of the previous years. Although Presley was getting one million dollars per film, the Colonel commanded $100,000 a performance for him; so ten performances would make the same money in less time. Furthermore, the live shows led to albums, a lucrative sideline to such engagements.

By the beginning of 1969, Presley's professional and personal life had changed markedly for the better. Married, and a father, he was much in demand for live-shows at the most exclusive and expensive venues. This was something short of the gigs of popular rock bands of the late-1960s, but it was a significant step in the right direction. Most important, Presley was able to sing, and not merely cavort in front of a camera. This increased freedom led him to expand his repertoire significantly: he included many songs by young musicians and singer-songwriters.

In March 1969 Presley's best film for several years — *Charro* — was released. Although this is not in the *Flaming Star* class — Presley's acting, being somewhat stiff — it was a clear attempt at more significant work. By this time, Presley had changed recording venues too: he held an extended recording session in January and February 1969 at the American Studios, Memphis. This was the first time he had made recordings — other than those for films — since 1956 outside an RCA studio. The chance to record in his adopted home city was clearly beneficial. The songs are, by and large, a fine collection, and brilliantly performed, including one of the finest performances from him for many years: the classic 'In The Ghetto' which again demonstrated his finely-tuned response to contemporary rock music.

However, Presley was still contracted for the last of his formula-films, an innocuous piece entitled *Change of Habit,* whose title was more significant than many realized. In July, the film completed, he began exhausting rehearsals for another demanding event: a month-long engagement at the International Hotel, Las Vegas. This time, there was no chance to re-do anything that went wrong: every show was live, in front of a packed audience at the hotel's Showroom Internationale. The result was a resounding success, and not only financially. Presley gave two shows a night, seven days a week, for a month, during which more than 100,000 people saw him perform.

A return engagement was booked for January 1970, during the traditionally 'slack' season. This went against most established yardsticks for live shows. It was only five months after his previous appearances, and was to take place during a traditionally bad month for business. But a week before he opened, fifty-eight performances — all but seven of the twenty-nine days — had been sold out. Three days later Presley and his entourage travelled to Houston for a series of performances at the giant Astrodome, in front of 44,500 people for each of the twelve shows. Presley's fee was $1,200,000.

The tremendous interest generated by these appearances led naturally to their extension. It was clear the public wanted no more of the Presley films, but cinema could do more than television to create atmosphere. What better way of reaching millions of people than by a full-length, colour, spectacularly-recorded documentary on Presley, issued as a feature-film? To direct such a film, the Oscar-winning Denis Sanders, whose *Czechoslovakia 1968* had catapulted him to the forefront of his profession, was chosen. The result was a fine film, which did its subject proud.

Early in 1971, rumours began to circulate concerning Presley's marriage, and his alleged drug-taking. Whilst the peripatetic nature of his profession places strains on those involved, problems between Presley and his wife were probably exaggerated. It is no secret that Priscilla did not take kindly to the 'Memphis Mafia', equally, she was not liked by Presley's bodyguards. In a book published shortly before Presley's death, his ex-bodyguards claimed Presley was by this time a 'walking drugstore', but against this should be set the claims of others, equally close to him, who strenuously denied such abuse, pointing to Presley's frequent, outspoken criticism of drugtakers. In any event, at the White House in 1971, President Nixon created Presley a member of the Federal Drug Enforcement Bureau. But it is not difficult to believe that, from time to time during his demanding concert tours, Presley sought the help of stimulants.

In May 1971 Presley undertook another extensive recording session in Nashville, which produced his classic blues recording 'Merry Christmas Baby', as well as material of less interest. There were also three songs for which he accompanied himself on the piano, a rare glimpse of his keyboard talents. Presley's life now settled down to a succession of concert engagements along the lines of super-cabaret, and this led him to neglect recording work. From time to time his concerts would be recorded, and bootleg versions of many of them have flooded the market in the U.S.A.

At the beginning of 1972, Presley entered an unsettled and tragic period of his life. In January the ten-mile portion of the four-lane US Highway 51 running past Graceland was officially named Elvis Presley Boulevard. During an engagement at the Las Vegas Hilton, Presley was introduced to a bodyguard called Mike Stone. Stone was a karate expert, which interested Presley. Shortly afterwards Priscilla Presley began taking karate lessons from Stone. On 31 March Stone's wife entered a divorce petition against her husband, and on 5 June it was granted. It was clear to friends that Mike Stone and Priscilla's association had become very close indeed, and later in the year Elvis and Priscilla announced that they had separated. At about this time Elvis met Linda Thompson, the reigning Miss Tennessee, and they became close friends.

Presley's most important engagement of the 1970s was *Elvis: Aloha from Hawaii* live television special on 14 January 1973, beamed direct to millions of viewers in many countries, and taped for future release. A double-album was quickly released in quadraphonic — and became the first million-selling quadraphonic recording. A second MGM documentary, *Elvis on Tour,* was then made and released.

In October 1973, Elvis and Priscilla were divorced in Santa Monica. Although Elvis was deeply upset by the end of his marriage, both parties always maintained they retained the greatest affection for each other. Early in 1974, Vernon and Dee Presley separated. Meanwhile Elvis embarked on an extensive series of tours, possibly to prevent his brooding over the sad events. This presented a substantial problem for RCA: with their major artist constantly on tour it was difficult to get him to learn new material to record. There was no reason, after the flop of the Memphis live album, to continue the policy of live recordings, with their attendant technical problems and great cost. By the end of 1975 it is likely that Presley was inclined to take up studio work again, although it was difficult to pin him down to dates. A single session in 1975, and two in 1976 — the last two taking place at Graceland — required much over-dubbing and cosmetic engineering to make them suitable for release, which reflected Presley's current difficulties.

Presley celebrated his fortieth birthday in 1975. By this time he had already undergone several stays in hospital for the treatment of various conditions which disturbingly, became more frequent. Rumours began to circulate concerning his weight problem. He had always been big, but now he was getting fat. Frequently he had to crash-diet to make his bulging figure presentable for live concerts. In August 1975 he was back in the Baptist Hospital, after breaking off a two-week engagement at the

Las Vegas Hilton. At this time Vernon suffered a serious heart attack.

On New Year's Day 1976, Presley played before the biggest crowd of his career, over 60,000 people, at a concert in Pontiac, Michigan. Shortly afterwards he invested in a new company, Presley Center Courts Inc., to develop the growing market for racquet-ball, a sport in which he had become interested. This was the first time he allowed his name to be used for a business venture. Later the same year he left the company, which was renamed, but early in 1977 he was sued for $150,000 by his ex-business associates. During 1976 his bodyguards Red West, Sonny West and Dave Holder were fired by Vernon. Presley's personal secretary, Becky Yancey claimed this was over their alleged rough handling of Presley fans, which led to embarrassing and costly lawsuits. Towards the end of 1976, Elvis met the attractive twenty-year-old Ginger Alden, who became a constant companion.

Elvis Presley's troubles increased when on 21 March 1977 he cancelled an appearance at Baton Rouge, Louisiana, and flew back to Memphis, suffering from what his personal physician, Dr Nichopoulos, said was fatigue and intestinal influenza, with gastro-enteritis. Ex-president Nixon telephoned the hospital to inquire after Presley. Two months later, Vernon and Dee were divorced.

In spite of these troubles, a major television show from CBS was taped in June 1977. Elvis continued touring, apparently fully-recovered. It was planned to issue an album to coincide with the screening of the show, after the tour ended on 26 June in Indianapolis.

A further series of concerts was planned to begin in late August, and on the sixteenth Presley and his entourage were preparing final arrangements. At two-thirty in the afternoon his friend Joe Esposito found Elvis Presley lying on the floor of his bathroom/dressing-room. Dr Nichopoulos was called and tried to revive Presley, both at Graceland and in the ambulance on the way to the hospital in Memphis. But his efforts were in vain, and Elvis Presley was pronounced dead at three-thirty.

By five o'clock, a thousand fans had gathered outside the Graceland gates. An hour later there were three thousand, and by six-thirty almost twenty thousand. The following day, a Wednesday, thousands filed past his body. Over two hundred policemen and a medical team of 120 were on hand to control the crowd and to treat the many fans overcome by heat and emotional stress. On Thursday, with over 2,000 mourners standing vigil outside Graceland, a car smashed into the crowd at four in the morning killing Juanita Joan Johnson and Marie Alice Hovarter, and critically injuring Tammy Baiter. The driver, Treatise Wheeler, aged eighteen was charged with multiple offences connected with the accident.

The pathologist's report declared that Presley died of cardiac arrythmia — an irregular heart-beat — he was laid to rest in a mausoleum at Forest Hills Cemetery, Memphis, close to his mother's grave.

In the days following his death, the population of Memphis was swelled by an estimated 200,000 visitors, an astonishing demonstration of the extent of his following. President Jimmy Carter, in a eulogy unprecedented for a rock singer said:

> Elvis Presley's death deprives our country of a part of itself. He was a symbol to the people of the world of the vitality, rebelliousness and good humor of this country.

# PART II

# THE MUSIC

# 5 The Sun Recordings, 1954-5

The story of how Elvis Presley came to make these recordings is told in Chapter 2. Because Sun's owner Sam Phillips did not keep detailed records, information about the sessions is sketchy. But Phillips considered a number of the recordings were not good enough to be released. This was because they were inconsistent. To some Presley fans this may sound like heresy; but Phillips was no fool: his judgement was sure, and his enthusiasm for Presley was only fired when the singer found what Phillips was looking for. This was not always achieved, and Phillips tended to release only material which followed this new path.

The other material was not useless. But Phillips knew what he was doing: the technical quality of the recordings issued is remarkably fine. He was a great record producer, at a time when record-producing had not assumed the importance it did later. The distinctive, pure sound of the Sun recordings influenced many later performers and producers. Phillips also recognized that the emergent rock music was the most potent force in popular music at that time; so he held back those titles which did not contribute to the progress of rock. These songs, although good of their type, were not so innovative or important as the early Presley rock tracks.

6 July 1954. *Venue:* Sun Studios, Memphis.
*Titles recorded:* 'Blue Moon', 'Blue Moon of Kentucky', 'I Love You Because', 'That's All Right, Mama'.

It is not certain if all these songs were recorded at this session. However it is clear that from the very first, Presley's unique voice and style were fully-formed. 'Blue Moon', the Rodgers and Hart song from 1934, receives a totally unique performance. Presley's high-register voice exerts a hypnotic fascination. The accompaniment is simple, but effective: gently picking on acoustic guitar and bass, with a hazy sound-image that both mirrors the song, and provides the perfect background to Presley's singing. 'Blue Moon Of Kentucky' is very different in tempo. Presley's voice is still in its highest register, but the song is transformed into a fast rockabilly style. Bill Black's bass work is breathtaking, and this performance doubtless influenced later singers such as Don Cole. A take of a simpler version, also done at these sessions, exists but, has never been released commercially. It was released on a pirate record

'I Love You Because' also exists in two versions: the first released is the more straightforward. It begins with clear whistling, and is sung without pretension. Sam Phillips did not issue this, but it was included on Presley's first RCA LP two years later. A longer version was released by RCA in 1974; with an extended middle section — spoken, not sung, by Presley — it is probably the better performance, but too long for one side of the normal ten-inch 78-rpm in 1954.

'That's All Right, Mama' was Presley's first genuine rock recording. It was also his first hit, and the song which made a great impact in Memphis. Elvis, Scotty Moore and Bill Black had never played together before. Elvis is in magnificent voice — full of fire, riding the music with great power.

With these songs, Presley began his recording career, and it is interesting to consider why they are so unusual. In the first place, their recording quality is outstanding, with no allowances necessary for their age or the lack of stereo. On this evidence alone, Phillips was a creative record producer, getting down on the tape just what he and his musicians wanted. Secondly, the musical fusion of black music and country music — both mainstream elements in music of the South — is wholly successful. Earlier attempts to mix these elements were unable to break away from the instrumental make-up of the classic jazz or blues bands. This meant singers were limited to brass or saxophones and piano backing. With Presley's first recordings, these instruments vanished. With Presley's embracing of the blues the harmonies tended to fall more prominently on the rhythm guitar. The piano bass had to be replaced by a more prominent bass-line (either string-bass or bass-guitar). These instruments, therefore, were highlighted in a new way; for in the blues, harmony and beat were more important than in country music, which tended to rely on melody and figuration. The absence of the saxophone and the later addition of a small drum section completed the classic make-up of the rock band: drums, bass guitar, rhythm guitar and lead guitar. From the Beatles to the Sex Pistols this formation remained the basis for rock music. The family of three guitars provided a natural musical unity. But above all it transferred up an octave the main lead instrument. With baritone or tenor singers, lead instruments in the same register could only cut loose when the singer was silent — otherwise they got in each others' way. By transferring the melody to the lead guitar both could be heard simultaneously, without getting in each others' way.

September 1954. *Venue:* Sun Studios, Memphis.
*Titles recorded:* 'Good Rockin' Tonight', 'I Don't Care If The Sun Don't Shine', 'Just Because'.

Details of this session are sketchy. 'Good Rockin' Tonight' is one of the most important of Presley's Sun recordings. As the title implies, it is early rock, but is of more than historical interest. For the first time, the versatility of Presley's voice is revealed on disc: strong, rich, and deep, yet capable of a wide range of timbres. The progress since the July sessions is startling — particularly when one realizes that this high-energy music was created by just three people — without drums.

'I Don't Care If The Sun Don't Shine' is unusual in including bongoes — possibly played by D.J. Fontana, who had been a member of Presley's stage band for some time. The song is similar to the faster version of 'Blue Moon Of Kentucky', but less innovative. 'Just Because' was not released by Sam Phillips, but surfaced two years later on RCA; D.J. Fontana is probably the drummer on this track. Phillips's reluctance to issue it is understandable, for Presley's performance is predictable. The song is a fast, soft rocker, memorable for its outstanding guitar solo.

December 1954. *Venue:* Sun Studios, Memphis.
*Titles recorded:* 'Harbour Lights', 'You're Right, I'm Left, She's Gone', 'Milkcow Blues Boogie', 'You're A Heartbreaker'.

There is considerable doubt that 'Harbour Lights' was recorded at these sessions: its use of all-acoustic guitars lends weight to July 1954 being the probable date. The recording was also rejected by Phillips, and first appeared only in 1976. Its main interest is that it is early Presley, although the song later became a hit for the Platters. Presley's voice sounds raw, and comes and goes in disconcerting fashion, as if he was moving around the microphone. It exposes his inexperience, which also points to the earlier dating.

The title of 'I'm Left, You're Right, She's Gone' has always been something of a mystery. This is how it is always referred to, but in the song Presley mainly sings 'You're Right, I'm Left, She's Gone', which makes more sense as the title. Whatever the title, the addition of D.J. Fontana on drums gives a more solid backing, and the result is one of the beefiest Presley performances so far. This record was a moderate hit in Britain three years later, which says something for its undated sound; but it stands to one side of the rock mainstream, since it has a greater country feel than rock enthusiasts like.

'Milkcow Blues Boogie' is one of Presley's most important Sun recordings. It begins slowly, and very well, before Presley stops and says: 'Hold it fellas. That don't *move* me. Let's get real, real gone for a change!'. He then launches into a faster version, with a fine lengthy guitar solo, before the song fades out. This was the first Presley recording to adopt this trick. In 'You're a Heartbreaker', Presley's voice takes on a different quality: it is lower in pitch, and seems flawed by phasing and echo, which produce a washy and sibilant result.

January/February, 1955. *Venue:* Sun Studios, Memphis.
*Titles recorded:* 'Baby, Let's Play House', 'I'll Never Let You Go', 'Mystery Train'.

'Baby, Let's Play House' is a medium-fast rock number enlivened by raw and gutsy guitar work. Presley's repetition of 'Baby, baby, baby' are very exciting, and probably influenced Gene Vincent. With 'I'll Never Let You Go', we encounter one of the Sun recordings which resists pigeon-holing. It is very slow, wafted by acoustic guitar shakes and a soft bass line. Presley's voice is haunting: high, and veering on falsetto, until the end, which is faster. 'Mystery Train' is rock music, a fine fast number.

July 1955. *Venue:* Sun Studios, Memphis.
*Titles recorded:* 'I Forgot To Remember To Forget Her', 'Tomorrow Night', 'Trying To Get To You'.

This last Sun session is not particularly memorable. 'I Forgot to Remember to Forget Her' is good early Presley; but his country roots are to the fore. The essence of his earlier rock records is absent. 'Tomorrow Night' was withheld by Phillips and RCA for ten years, until March 1965 when Chet Atkins supervised a new backing track for Presley's original vocal line. As the early Sun takes were not multi-tracked, the original backing had to be obliterated. Despite all this cosmetic surgery, the result is quite good, but it cannot be judged as an example of early Presley. Atkins was doubtless responsible for larding the voice over with echo. However, something of the excitement and passion of the early Presley shines through, qualities which were generally lacking at the time when Atkins resurrected the track. 'Trying To Get To You' also remained unreleased by Phillips, but was put out by RCA in April 1956, on Presley's first album.

# 6 The Early RCA Recordings, 1956-8

10/11 January, 1956. *Venue:* RCA Studio, Nashville.
*Titles recorded:* 'Heartbreak Hotel', 'I Got a Woman', 'I'm Counting On You', 'I Was The One', 'Money Honey'.

By the time Elvis Presley had signed with RCA, his musical style had been forged into a distinctive form which was soon to take the world by storm. He was ready to go — and now he had the resources of one of the most important recording organisations in the world behind him. It is significant that Elvis Presley remained loyal to RCA for the rest of his life.

In the studio with him for this session were colleagues from the Sun days, as well as musicians with whom Elvis Presley had not previously worked. He knew Scotty Moore, Bill Black and D.J. Fontana, but Chet Atkins (a distinguished guitarist and manager of the RCA Nashville Office) and pianist Floyd Cramer were newcomers. Also, three singers, Gordon Stoker and the Speer brothers, Ben and Brock, were booked to add backing vocals — a new departure for Presley. The result must have exceeded the dreams of everybody taking part, for 'Heartbreak Hotel' became one of the legendary rock performances. For many people, this *is* Elvis Presley, and it continues to excite and fascinate listeners.

'Heartbreak Hotel' is a classic performance, yet when it is analyzed it appears so simple that one cannot recall a time when one did not know it. It is all the more effective for being so restrained. This may seem surprising in view of Presley's early image, but the beat is held back; the smouldering intensity and wounded defiance is conveyed entirely by the voice. 'Heartbreak Hotel' is a basic blues, with a syncopated throb. The key, E minor, fits Presley's voice like a glove, and when the bass guitar enters before 'Heartbreak' in the line '. . . down at the corner of Lonely Street at Heartbreak Hotel . . .' the interest quickens, leading to the second time, with quiet, insistent drums and guitar. Floyd Cramer's piano is ideal: it is impossible to imagine this song without his phrases high on the piano pattering like sad rain. The whole performance is outstanding.

'I Got A Woman,' a fast, bouncy number, also begins with Presley alone, with a slurred 'weell'; but soon the rhythm has him moving around the microphone: his voice comes and goes as he moves this way and that, turning his head to encourage the other musicians. This was the first song Presley recorded for RCA. It has simple but effective guitar breaks, and an infectious feeling of musicianship. The sudden slow ending is brilliantly judged. 'I'm Counting On You' is a ballad, but Presley is still moving around, and the occasional syllable is lost. Like most ballads of the period, this chugs along over a triplet beat; but Cramer's piano variations make the rhythm unpredictable. At no point can these musicians be taken for granted: there is always something interesting going on. 'I Was the One' is another ballad and the biggest sound on any song from these sessions. Presley's voice comes over more clearly here: it is full of inflections, from a plummy staccato to a sneering falsetto. At the time these recordings were made, there was no singer to compare with Presley for range and instrumental use of the voice. 'Money Honey' was recorded immediately after 'Heartbreak Hotel', and the sense of achievement in the earlier number had tumbled over into this performance. This is *real* rock'n'roll. Later, in 1956, Gene Vincent and the Blue Caps had a world-wide hit with 'Be-Bop-A-Lula', but Vincent's number was clearly influenced by Presley's 'Money Honey'. Cramer shows his prowess again: delicate glissandos, fast and insistent, flick from the top of the piano, punctuating Presley's deeply rhythmic performance, which is further enhanced by easy-paced guitar work.

30/31 January, 1 February, 1956. *Venue:* RCA Studios, New York City.
*Titles recorded:* 'Blue Suede Shoes', 'I'm Gonna Sit Right Down And Cry', 'Lawdy, Miss Clawdy', 'My Baby Left Me', 'One-Sided Love Affair', 'Shake, Rattle and Roll', 'So Glad You're Mine', 'Tutti Frutti'.

Ten days after completing his first RCA session, Elvis Presley was in RCA's New York studios to record eight more songs. Chet Atkins, Floyd Cramer and the singers were absent, and Cramer was replaced by Shorty Long. Some cuts from this collection are in the same class as the first sessions.

'Blue Suede Shoes', with its driving rhythm, is a classic rock'n'roll record. The barely-controlled power of Presley's performance is made all the more enthralling by deliberate mispronunciation of some consonants. This gives the song a quality of bravado — a couldn't-care-less attitude — but it is clear that every quaver is sincerely meant by Presley. Scotty Moore's guitar is remarkable: he 'bends' chords flat to tilt the song in the rhythm-and-blues direction, and his guitar licks in verse 2 build the energy, until by the third verse it really burns.

'I'm Gonna Sit Right Down And Cry', another fast number, is punched along by a walking bass and insistent chord clusters from the piano. Presley is very close to the microphone, but the guitar solo is poor, and the song fails to ignite. 'Lawdy, Miss Clawdy' begins with fast piano chords — unusual, in view of the slow pulse. This is a genuine performance — a change from the spliced perfection of some artists — but there is hesitation in Presley's voice. I suspect he had not thoroughly absorbed the song. In 'My Baby Left Me', however, the message is faithfully reflected in the pitch of Presley's vocal line, which produces a whining effect, underpinned by an insidious beat. A very good rock number can be found in 'One-Sided Love Affair'. Presley is in bouncy voice, with a 'hup' quality of humour and toe-tapping zest. 'Shake, Rattle and Roll' is a classic performance, which shows Presley's voice barely controlling its explosiveness. Other members of the band join Presley for the title each time it occurs, and the piano provides a major part of the texture. The chunky guitar solo is chordal, betraying the blues roots. Another fabulous take is 'So Glad You're Mine', especially in the original mono version. Later electronic interfering makes Presley's voice harsh and strident, but the original tapes show him in clean voice. The 'ooh-ee's simply tingle with life, echoed by good guitar work. Finally, 'Tutti Frutti', which is another incomparable performance. Presley's vocal work is sensational; anybody who wants to be a rock singer should study each inflection of this recording. The fierce beat is sustained with solid power; above it the guitar flickers intermittently until it breaks out in the fiery solo. The ending — a genuine early touch of echo — is quite astonishing.

11 April, 1956. *Venue:* RCA Studio, Nashville.
*Title recorded:* 'I Want You, I Need You, I Love You'.

Some problems must have surrounded this session, for this was the only song recorded. The result almost tells us as much, for in some transfers the first published take (itself spliced) subjects Presley's voice to severe mutilation. Although good recordings were by no means rare, this was still 1956, and some techniques were in their infancy. Presley is stuck back on a hefty wall of rhythm-and-echo. There is no light and shade in this ballad, but the alternative take, issued twenty years later, lets us hear Presley more as he was. As he made a mistake in the title in this alternative take, it was not issued at the time.

2 July, 1956. *Venue:* RCA Studios, New York City.
*Titles recorded:* 'Any Way You Want Me', 'Don't Be Cruel', 'Hound Dog'.

Presley sings 'Any Way You Want Me' with ringing power in the original recordings, although later 'stereo-transcriptions' lacerate the ears. It is difficult to describe this song; perhaps 'smoochy-rock' gets nearest. But Presley's performance is outstanding. At the end, the way in which he sings the word 'heart' is totally sincere; the sort of moment to make one want to play the song over and over again. 'Don't Be Cruel' is a classic cut, but it is more dated than other performances. Maybe the 'happy' inflection of Presley's voice has less appeal than his characteristic menacing form; and the song itself lacks grit. It remains, however, one of Presley's best recordings. 'Hound Dog' is truly sensational, with a pull that packs as big a punch decades after it was recorded. This is the young rebel revealed, rooted deep in the blues soil. Presley's 'Hound Dog', like 'Heartbreak Hotel' and a few others, is the essence of rock'n'roll. It is the pull of conflicting harmonies which give this song its aggressive quality; the song is in C major, the major chord of which (and on which Bill Black's bass line is based) is C, E and G. Presley erupts into the song with his never-to-be-forgotten opening in E flat. This sets up tremendous tension against the E natural in the bass, Presley spits the words with contempt. Gordon Stoker, the singer from earlier sessions, is joined by Neal Matthews, Hoyt Hawkins and Hugh Jarrett, to form the Jordanaires; their singing adds great impact. Later in the song they clap, against solid drumming and inspired guitar licks.

August/September, 1956. *Venue:* Twentieth-Century Fox Studios, Hollywood.

*Titles recorded:* 'Let Me', 'Love Me Tender', 'Poor Boy', 'We're Gonna Move'.

This came before the 'soundtrack-album' concept, and the songs for Presley's first film were very different from those by which he achieved notoriety. This is just easy-paced country-music, which fits the film's *locale* very well.

'Let Me' is pure country music. The song is hardly outstanding, but Presley's performance is so good that people could well be converted after hearing it. The title track, 'Love Me Tender', is a gentle, slow-moving ballad, beautifully sung. The delayed entry of the word 'tender', when it first appears, is a magical touch, as is the close harmony of the backing vocals (the Ken Darby Trio) and their wistful final solo notes from the guitar.

'Poor Boy' is another good number, but contains too much of a 'squeeze-box' effect, 'We're Gonna Move' is not, as might be expected, a rock number. The move in the title is a move of house.

September 1/3, 1956. *Venue:* Radio Recorders Studios, Hollywood.

*Titles recorded:* 'Any Place Is Paradise', 'First In Line', 'How Do You Think I Feel?', 'How's The World Treating You?', 'Long Tall Sally', 'Love Me', 'Old Shep', 'Paralysed', 'Playing for Keeps', 'Ready

Teddy', 'Rip It Up', 'Too Much', 'When My Blue Moon Turns To Gold Again'.

After recording the songs for his first film Elvis remained in Hollywood to make these recordings. Although his standard band was not used for the film, they played for this three-day session. The recording quality of 'Any Place is Paradise' is not good, for an exaggerated echo has ruined the song. 'First In Line' is a long ballad but again the words are inaudible, owing to excessive echo. 'How Do You Think I Feel?' is not so swampily recorded. This fast number is one of the poorer tracks of Presley's early career. 'How's The World Treating You?' is much better: a sentimental ballad, with the Jordanaires much in evidence. Presley appears to sing this well, so far as one can judge through the wall of 'electronic hash.

The technical 'enhancement' does not matter in 'Long Tall Sally', a number which was soon to be a smash hit for Little Richard. Presley's performance has a raw, earthy, high-energy output. It is a classic, driving rock song, staggeringly performed. It plays for only one minute forty-nine seconds, but what dynamite is packed in! By contrast 'Love Me' is a slow, sentimental number. Presley makes the most of its pathos, by a natural break and fractional hesitancy. Only after it is over does one realize the song itself is mediocre, but Presley turns it into true art. The same can be said of 'Old Shep', the song that meant so much to him as a boy. The material is finer than 'Love Me', although it is possible to take exception to the sentiment. In its way, this is a classic performance, though it has little to do with rock'n'roll. With 'Paralysed', we are back with the fast rockers, but the voice is almost lost. The energy of the song is the thing, and that is fully realized. 'Playing for Keeps' is a gently moving number, the lyrics of which are above average; and Presley makes the most of them.

'Ready, Teddy' — another Little Richard number — also gets a high-energy performance. This is a classic recording: Presley's voice tingles with vibrant life, and the beat drives along as fast as possible. The original mono tape is far preferable to 'stereo enhancement', which reduces the tight impact to infernal noise. 'Rip It Up' became an international smash for Bill Haley and the Comets. The hard rhythm of this performance is muted by echo on Presley's voice and the surrounding acoustic, but nothing can mask the 'throwaway' style essential to this classic rock number. The Jordanaires feature prominently in 'Too Much', a medium-tempo shuffle, which is blues-based but thankfully has not been subjected to later studio hashings to the same degree as others from this session. Every word is crystal clear. The togetherness of Dudley Brook's piano and Scotty Moore's guitar is beautifully judged. The engineers appear to have been up to their tricks on 'When My Blue Moon Turns to Gold Again', which is similar to 'Too Much', but Presley's voice is spoiled by echo, and poor balancing with the Jordanaires, who smother him. A pity.

12/13 January, 1957. *Venue:* Radio Recorders Studios, Hollywood.
*Titles recorded:* 'All Shook Up', 'Got A Lot O' Livin' To Do', 'I Beg Of You' *(not passed for release — re-recorded 23 February),* 'I Believe', 'Mean Woman Blues', 'Peace In The Valley', 'Take My Hand, Precious Lord', 'Tell Me Why', 'That's When Your Heartaches Begin.'

Presley's three appearances on the *Ed Sullivan Show* for CBS-TV culminated on 6 January 1957 with a performance of the religious song 'Peace In The Valley'. The public response was so strong that little time was lost in getting Presley into the studio to make a commercial recording of it. As Presley's previous chart success had been with rock numbers, 'All Shook Up', was chosen as his next single. Further songs were recorded to fill out the *Loving You* album, although the performances used in the film were not those recorded here. 'Tell Me Why' was not released for eight years, so this important session appeared piecemeal.

'All Shook Up' shows the early Presley at the height of his powers. This is a classic cut, brilliantly sung, a lesson to all aspiring rock'n'roll singers, who should study every beat of Presley's performance. Note, too, Presley's use of the *back* of the guitar, almost as an additional drum. The medium-fast tempo of this rocker — Presley's first undisputed No. 1 hit in Britain — is not punched out regardless. The sustained chords of the Jordanaires, the delicate touches from Moore, Black, Fontana and Brooks prove that basic rock'n'roll is not all sound and fury. 'Got A Lot O' Livin' To Do' featured in *Loving You,* and influenced another white rock star, Jerry Lee Lewis. But Presley's suggestive 'c'mon baby's is even more smouldering than Jerry Lee's. Presley's voice is amazingly wide-ranging, as the final bars degenerate into scat singing of careless abandon. 'I Believe', the early 1950s Frankie Laine monster-seller, was included for the *Peace In The Valley* collection, issued as an EP. Presley's performance, though sincere, is stiff, and, as the first song recorded at the session, should have been re-made at the end, after everybody had played themselves in. 'Mean Woman Blues', also included in *Loving You,* is a rock classic by Claude Demetrius. Jerry Lee Lewis cut a timeless version of this, backing his world-wide hit, 'Great Balls of Fire', and by comparison Presley falls between two stools. On the one hand, the use of the Jordanaires detracts from the man-to-woman nature of the number, but their later clapping is just right. Presley's guitar licks are tremendous — something absent from Jerry Lee — but Dudley Brooks's piano good as it is, has not the clattering boxiness of Lewis. A fine Presley performance, although the revival atmosphere ultimately spoils it.

'Peace In The Valley', the main reason for the sessions, is a religious blues number. This is a remarkable recording: with no extraneous background effects, one can judge the quality of Presley's voice. He sings with great sincerity. His voice has great reserves of strength, yet is supple, and used with intelligence. The same is partly true of 'Take My Hand, Precious Lord', but the use of electronic organ adds a distinctive new tone-colour to the sound. Dudley Brooks plays this instrument with delicacy, and Presley, returning to his musical roots in a gentle revivalist number, is completely convincing. 'Tell Me Why', which was not released until 1965, is largely a country ballad. It stood outside the mainstream of Presley's success at that time, and was probably felt to lack commercial appeal. The performance, though, could hardly be improved upon. Neither could 'That's When Your Heartaches Begin', a slow song, with a wide-ranging melody. Presley sings with magisterial power phrasing and breath-control and the difficult business of talking a middle section in a slow song is carried off perfectly.

19 January 1957. *Venue:* Radio Recorders Studios, Hollywood.
*Titles recorded:* 'Blueberry Hill', 'Have I Told You Lately That I Love You', 'Is It So Strange', 'It Is No Secret'.

A feature of the previous session was Presley's recording of material from other singers; in 'Blueberry Hill', he continued this. As Presley recorded his version, Fats Domino's inimitable recording was becoming a world-wide smash hit. Presley's performance is lower-powered than Domino's, although Presley is in magnificent voice. Dudley Brooks's piano is distinctive and stylish; but as Domino was his own pianist, his version has the edge over Presley. 'Have I Told You Lately That I Love You?' is another familiar number, but Presley's performance is not outstanding. 'Is It So Strange' is not in the same class: the words are trite. 'It Is No Secret' became the fourth song for the *Peace in The Valley* EP. Presley's restrained emotion, against a throbbing background, is most effective.

23/24 February 1957. *Venue:* Radio Recorders Studios, Hollywood.
*Titles recorded:* 'Don't Leave Me Now', 'I Beg Of You', 'I Need You So', 'Loving You', 'One Night', 'True Love', 'When It Rains, It Really Pours'.

This is a mixed bag, and the release was as haphazard as the collection. 'Don't Leave Me Now' helped fill out the *Loving You* album: a slow predictable ballad, with a faintly 'bluesy' feel, it is well performed. 'I Beg

Of You' is something else: a medium-tempo 'soft' rocker, with the Jordanaires adding a distinctive background. Presley's voice is in good shape; he trumps a previous ace by his treatment of the word 'hold' in 'hold my hand' — he erupts suddenly on a long pitched growl, in true blues-shouter style.

'I Need You So' is a sentimental ballad, sung with great emotion, but lacking commercial appeal. A different proposition is 'Loving You', the title song of Presley's second film. This is another ballad, but not so sentimental. Apart from Presley's purely-delivered melody, Brooks's contribution is the most important: his piano is stylish, apart from some out-of-character chords. The song ends magically. 'One Night' is another classic: a slow rocker, Presley's voice takes on a 'constricted' quality, which forces its way through the music. Presley's timing is held back until the break 'Been too lonely too long' which is climactic in the best sense. Cole Porter's score for *High Society*, was one of the most distinguished composed for the screen. The song 'True Love', was a major hit for Bing Crosby and Grace Kelly and is a simple waltz. Presley gives a marvellous performance, outstandingly well sung, perfectly in tune, superbly phrased, with some telling Porter harmonies. A surprising success. 'When It Rains It Really Pours', a blues power song is very different musically, yet it remained unreleased for eight years.

February/March, 1957. *Venue:* Radio Recorders Studios, Hollywood.
*Titles recorded:* 'Hot Dog', 'Lonesome Cowboy', 'Party', 'Teddy Bear'. In addition three previously recorded titles ('Loving You', 'Got A Lot O' Livin' To Do' and 'Mean Woman Blues') were redone for the film soundtrack of *Loving You.*

This session was to lay down tracks for Presley's second film, *Loving You.* The three additional titles were not issued on disc, as they had already been recorded by RCA. Of the others, 'Hot Dog' is a fast 'train' number, with a locomotive whistle effect. The song is feeble, but Presley does something remarkable with it. Scotty Moore's guitar manages to quarry gold from the dross, and the fade-out is well managed. 'Lonesome Cowboy' is another inferior song, but 'Party' is better: a good up-tempo number with distinguished guitar breaks, but (at 1:27″) it is too short. The gem of the set is 'Teddy Bear'. Its cheeky style extends to exaggerated slurring of words, and extending certain phrases beyond their usual length, catching up by shortening others. The voice has echo around it, but it works well. A classic of its kind.

May 1957. *Venue:* MGM Studios, Hollywood (Culver City).
*Titles recorded:* 'Baby I Don't Care', 'Don't Leave Me Now', 'I Want To

Be Free', 'Jailhouse Rock' (two versions, only the first issued commercially), 'Treat Me Nice' (unissued — re-recorded the following September), 'Young and Beautiful'.

This batch of songs was for Presley's third film, *Jailhouse Rock*. 'Baby I Don't Care' and 'Don't Leave Me Now' are contrasted: the first is a great rocking number, one of Presley's most infectious performances, 'Don't Leave Me Now' is different from that recorded the previous February in a studio session. Here it is more violent, aided by a recording quality which puts an added strain on Presley's voice. In the film Presley sings yet another version of this number, with simple accompaniment but no backing vocals.

'I Want To Be Free', despite the distinguished lyricist and composer (Lieber and Stoller), comes across poorly. The title track is another matter. This is a classic Presley recording and the film sequence is startling. Another Jerry Lieber-Mike Stoller number, the chords which grab the attention at the start, and punctuate the song, are among the most famous sounds in rock'n'roll. Dudley Brooks's piano, high on the keyboard, is another never-to-be-forgotten sound, and the natural rock beat, with real bounce between the beats, is the epitome of controlled fire. The fire comparison continues with the burning guitar licks; but against this exciting instrumental sound, Presley's voice personifies youthful rebellion, through the power of music. This performance is a true rock classic, and it is sobering to realise that within a short time Presley had committed to disc half-a-dozen or so of the most innovative statements in popular music this century. Now we have become used to the styles which evolved from this music, it is difficult to imagine how original this music was, and how it differed from other popular music of the mid-1950s. *Jailhouse Rock,* both as a film and a song, was a milestone. 'Young and Beautiful' is, by contrast, slow and sentimental, with the piano used not as a percussion instrument, but as a gentle tone-colour, supported by soft wire-brush strokes on the drums and stylish close-harmony from the Jordanaires.

5/7 September 1957. *Venue:* Radio Recorders Studios, Hollywood.
*Titles recorded:* 'Blue Christmas', 'Don't', 'Here Comes Santa Claus', 'I'll Be Home for Christmas', 'My Wish Came True', 'O Little Town Of Bethlehem', 'Santa Bring My Baby Back To Me', 'Santa Claus Is Back In Town', 'Silent Night', 'Treat Me Nice', 'White Christmas'.

The titles give the reason for these sessions: Elvis's first Christmas LP, and his first album of religious material. In the event, the religious content is minimal, but the celebration of Christmas is there. 'Blue Christmas' is a slow ballad, the Jordanaires chromatic chord slides give the song a strange feel, but Presley is here at his best although absent from the middle eight, when the song sags. 'Don't' is another slow ballad, but incomparably better. Presley's voice is in commanding shape, and his breath-control effortless, as he rides high in full power. Contrast is provided by 'Here Comes Santa Claus', a children's Christmas song, with a humorous lyric. Presley tantalizes: his timing varies, though the song does not warrant such artistry. 'I'll Be Home For Christmas' is a slow ballad, with quiet drumming by D. J. Fontana. Presley sings the first line of verse two very well but his last phrase is hardly recognizable. Another slow ballad, 'My Wish Came True', is similar to 'Don't', but not so successful. The Jordanaires gospel-harmonies take the spotlight. The setting of 'O Little Town Of Bethlehem' is more well-known in the United States than in other English-speaking countries, and is a genuine performance in which only the electronic organ tends to obtrude. 'Santa Bring My Baby Back To Me' is worlds away: here we are in the mainstream of rock, and the result is a classic. A fast ostinato kicks the song into life, and the bravado of Presley's singing extends to verse two, which he begins flat, and verse three which, on repeat, is given a totally different vocal treatment. In short, this performance is a lesson in how to sing rock'n'roll: Presley inflects the most straight-forward lyrics with subtle undertones. 'Santa Claus Is Back In Town' is a classic blues-based number, proving again that Presley had an instinctive feel for the blues, but could also suggest double-meanings without incurring the wrath of moral-protecting public figures.

'Silent Night' reveals another facet of Presley: it is a version of undoubted sincerity, and it would probably be more highly regarded if released by any other singer. One of the problems that beset Presley was that those who identified him with the blazing earthiness of rock could not accept that he could also sing a hymn with reverential calm. Every word in his performance is crystal clear and the only criticism is his splitting of the word 'Saviour' into two syllables.

'Treat Me Nice' is a complete contrast. It was not used on the Christmas album, but appeared in *Jailhouse Rock.* It is a bouncy number, with magical piano from Dudley Brooks. Worth a mention is the solid bass line, and the way in which Presley's voice dovetails perfectly with the Jordanaires in the baritone register. The final number, 'White Christmas', is the famous Irving Berlin song, unforgettably recorded by Bing Crosby. As in 'True Love' Presley is genuine enough, but one senses the song is not really in his blood. The Crosby version remains the all-time classic performance.

January 1958. *Venue:* Radio Recorders Studios, Hollywood.
*Titles recorded:* 'As Long As I Have You', 'Crawfish', 'Danny', 'Dixieland Rock', 'Don't Ask Me Why', 'Hard Headed Woman',

'King Creole', 'Lover Doll', 'New Orleans', 'Steadfast, Loyal And True', 'Trouble', 'Young Dreams'.

This session put down the songs for Elvis Presley's next film, Paramount Pictures' *King Creole.* The songs are a fine mixture, with some classic material. 'As Long As I Have You' is a slow ballad, which Presley sings well within his power, but with full voice. The pianist adds too much colour, with his wide-spread phrases. The calypso style of Harry Belafonte had become a world-wide phenomenon the previous year with his string of smash hits, 'The Banana Boat Song, 'Island In The Sun', 'Coconut Woman' and 'Mary's Boy Child'. In *King Creole* (the film) 'Crawfish' clearly shows his influence. It is a street-call song, similar to the 'Strawberry Woman's Song' in Gershwin's *Porgy and Bess.* But Presley embraces this different material successfully. 'Danny' was recorded for inclusion in *King Creole,* but dropped from the film, and remained unreleased for over twenty years. It was finally issued on *A Legendary Performer* Vol 3. It is easy to see why it was dropped, for it would not have added to the film. It is slow with full backing vocals — Presley gets rather lost in the texture. In 'Dixieland Rock' however, one's worst fears are realized: it falls between two stools, the only point of interest being the insistent opening rhythm. 'Don't Ask Me Why' is more sure of itself; a slow throbbing ballad, well sung.

'Hard Headed Woman' is breathtaking in its surges of power. The use of brass, in true New Orleans style makes sense, and the underlying rhythm is more interesting. The song is enlivened by shouts of 'Oh Yeah' from the Jordanaires, and there is a orchestral break which galvanizes Presley into using his voice wordlessly, for all the world like a lead baritone sax. The final 'ah-ah-oo' leaves one gasping, but all the way through, Presley has driven the song forward in unstoppable fashion. If 'Hard Headed Woman' is a classic of its kind, then so is 'King Creole'. The menacing bass guitar builds an atmosphere of high tension, which is taken up by Presley. Only when his voice rises on the fourth line of each verse does it appear that the caged tiger is about to escape. The guitar work by Scotty Moore is outstanding. Moore's acoustic guitar adds much to 'Lover Doll', a gentle, medium-bounce number; but the song is not memorable. Nor is another jazz-rock fusion, 'New Orleans', which highlights the problem. Fast rock and New Orleans jazz do not mix. There is good trumpet work but the result remains a mere curiosity. 'Steadfast, Loyal And True' stands apart; for it is in essence a school song put in for the story line, and not for its musical qualities. 'Trouble' is more interesting. This is a slow medium-tempo blues-based number, full of threatening gestures and a brooding, menacing quality, a testament to rebellious youth. Presley breaks his voice, like a yodel, as though to escape from the surroundings, and the doubling of the tempo by the drums is imaginative. The Creole Jazz ending is startling, but works, and Presley's final whispered, 'Yeah!' still shows defiance. Compared with this classic recording, 'Young Dreams' is best forgotten: a formula song, feeding on commonplace material.

1 February, 1958. *Venue:* Radio Recorders Studios, Hollywood.
*Titles recorded:* 'Doncha' Think It's Time', 'My Wish Came True' *(not issued),* 'Wear My Ring Around Your Neck', 'Your Cheatin' Heart'.

This was the last session Presley recorded before he joined the U.S. Army, and it may have been difficult, for one of the songs remained unissued, and the others were all taken many times. 'Doncha' Think It's Time' and 'My Wish Came True' were both attempted on 23 January 1958, but nothing came of them. (Although it is possible something from takes of 'Doncha' Think It's Time' was used on the issued version, which basically comes from the 1 February session.)

The result is almost a parody of Presley. After forty takes, someone should have decided it was time for something else. 'Wear My Ring Around Your Neck' also disappoints, but for different reasons: here the recording is at fault, with Presley in the background, submerged beneath the powerhouse noise and hard-driving rhythm of this fast rocker. It is almost impossible to believe that this song was recorded in the same studios, by the same musicians, a matter of days after similar material ('Hard Headed Woman', 'King Creole') had been successfully captured on tape. The same is true of Hank Williams's great number, 'Your Cheatin' Heart': the performance is disappointing and should have been remade.

10/11 June, 1958. *Venue:* RCA Studios, Nashville.
*Titles recorded:* 'A Big Hunk O'Love', 'A Fool Such As I', 'Ain't That Lovin' You Baby', 'I Got Stung', 'I Need Your Love Tonight'.

Compared with the unsatisfactory recordings made earlier in 1958, the dynamism returned here with redoubled force. 'A Big Hunk O'Love' is a classic rocker. Presley is at the top of his form. Although the recording is smothered with echo, it is in keeping with the song. 'A Fool Such As I', a medium 'walk' number, is very different, with the Jordanaires better integrated. Ray Walker took over from Hugh Jarret as bass singer in the Jordanaires for these sessions, and his low C's are astounding. The recording is better, too: a fatter sound which tends to bury Presley on occasion, but classic qualities shine through. 'Ain't That Lovin' You Baby' is a marching-tempo song constructed along the lines of 'Heartbreak Hotel', but with a happier message, with Presley letting his hair down.

Another classic cut is 'I Got Stung': the vitality is remarkable, with the song driving along in top gear.

Another classic cut is 'I Got Stung': the vitality is remarkable, with the song driving along in top gear. Even Presley gets a little lost in the general *melée*, but when he surfaces the magic is blazing through, as he kicks the rhythm along. Finally (although it was the first to be recorded) 'I Need Your Love Tonight' is another classic rocker. It is fast, but not frenetic, with Presley's voice little short of amazing: all the earlier qualities are there, and most importantly his control of vocal technique. Hank Garland's surging guitar work is especially fine.

# 7 From Nashville to Hollywood, 1960-66

20/21 March 1960. *Venue:* RCA Studios, Nashville.
*Titles recorded:* 'A Mess Of Blues', 'Fame and Fortune', 'It Feels So Right', 'Make Me Know It', 'Soldier Boy', 'Stuck On You'.

The first sessions after Presley's Army discharge continue where he left off twenty-one months before. The band was virtually the same, the venue was the same, but the recording techniques had improved enormously. Stereo, previously seldom used in popular music recordings was now a matter of course and the greater fidelity brought a more natural sound and a more creative approach to recording. Pop and rock

'A Mess Of Blues' is a classic Presley recording: curiously his voice sounds different from other numbers at the same session. He sings with his tongue further back in his mouth. But Presley is fully in front, giving each workd its due; he drives the song forwards, matching the lyrics and giving urgent shape to the number. The final falsetto is a master-touch. With 'Fame and Fortune', the tempo seems too slow so that the overall effect is droopy. 'It Feels So Right' is unusual. It has a slow powerful pulse, which Presley throws out at the top of his register. 'Make Me Know It' is in medium-fast rock tempo; Presley's performance makes something interesting out of less than top-drawer material — and the fine recording helps. 'Soldier Boy', a natural choice for Presley's first session after his army service, is moderately slow: this came before the 'protest songs' of the early 1960s, but is sung with real intensity. Another fine performance is 'Stuck On You'. This has a rock tempo, more gentle than the rockers of the 1950s. It is attractive, and beautifully recorded with everything balanced and clear. Presley sings in a relaxed manner, totally in command, and this recording has achieved classic status.

3/4 April, 1960. *Venue:* RCA Studios, Nashville.
*Titles recorded:* 'Are You Lonesome Tonight?', 'Dirty, Dirty Feeling', 'Fever', 'Girl Next Door Went A'Walking', 'I Gotta Know', 'I Will Be Home Again', 'It's Now Or Never', 'Like A Baby', 'Reconsider Baby', 'Such A Night', 'The Girl Of My Best Friend', 'The Thrill Of Your Love'.

The first sessions after Presley's army discharge had gone well, possibly better than many would have thought, and it was clear he was as dynamic as ever. This session reinforced that view, for Presley now recorded some of his greatest performances and his biggest-selling individual record. 'Are You Lonesome Tonight?' marks a startling change of direction: it is a slow-moving ballad, gentle, caring, beautifully sung, with the kind of voice Presley had already shown on 'Silent Night' — natural, unforced, dead in tune, and totally distinctive. This classic song is enhanced by the extended 'talking' section in the middle — a difficult procedure to bring off, but here, surrounded by echo, it succeeds. This single sold over five million copies. In 'Dirty, Dirty Feeling' a fast bouncy musically dated number, Presley sounds like one of his favourite singers, Bobby Darin. 'Fever', is incomparably better. Presley's performance is totally restrained and full of subdued but insistent strength, outstandingly recorded. The 'Girl Next Door Went A 'Walking' is also unusual: to judge by Presley's perfectly-proportioned performance, he liked it. Another good popular number, but which now sounds faded, is 'I Gotta Know', a medium-tempo bounce. Again, the beat is infectious, and Presley is having a high old time against the vocal counterpoint of Ray Walker. 'I Will Be Home Again' is a sop to the venue: a classic recording of its type, this slow ballad, sung in duet with Charlie Hodge, has limited appeal outside Nashville enthusiasts.

With 'It's Now Or Never' we come to one of Presley's greatest performances. This song sold around ten million copies as a single, and is an English version of the Neopolitan song, 'O Sole Mio'. After a gentle introduction Presley's first, stirring top E, strong and manly, sets the scene, and the ensuing singing, abetted by Floyd Cramer's graceful piano, adds to the atmosphere. The steady beat is just right and the climax, with Presley soaring up to an incredible top G sharp, is pure magic. Another very fine performance is 'Like A Baby' which is helped by the controlled backing. Boots Randolph's saxophone solo is memorable; dirty and bluesy, oozing with sexual undertones.

In spite of the major successes of 'Are You Lonesome Tonight?' and 'It's Now Or Never', a possibly more lasting example of Presley's genius is to be found in 'Reconsider Baby'. This is a basic blues, not contaminated by other types of music or commercial pressures. It is clear that he was a blues singer of importance. It is tragic that he never cut a blues album, but performances such as this give a tantalizing glimpse of what might have been. This is a classic blues performance; timeless and awe-inspiring in its power and emotion. Boots Randolph's contribution is staggering and everyone on this take struck musical sparks from the others. This track is a refutation of those who do not recognize what a phenomenal artist Presley was.

Vastly different material is found on 'Such A Night' — a curious choice, for it had been a world-wide hit for Johnnie Ray a half-dozen or more years earlier. Presley's performance is disappointing: had he recorded this number *before* he went into the army, then he would have made a better job of it. Presley had trouble recording this, which accounts for the nature of the standard release. On *A Legendary Performer,* Vol 2, two false starts are included, where he has difficulty getting the beat right. 'The Girl Of My Best Friend' is a very good song of its day, which has also stood the test of time. A medium-bounce tempo, the lyrics are far from mundane, and the Jordanaires backing contributes to Presley's tale of woe. The song is distinguished, and superbly recorded.

27-28 April and 6 May 1960. *Venue:* RCA Studios, Hollywood (April) and Radio Recorders Studios, Hollywood (May).
*Titles recorded:* 'Big Boots', 'Blue Suede Shoes', 'Didja Ever', 'Doin' The Best I Can', 'Frankfurt Special', 'G.I. Blues', 'Pocketful of Rainbows', 'Shoppin' Around', 'Tonight Is So Right For Love', 'Tonight's All Right For Love', 'What's She Really Like'. N.B. *The session on 6 May was to re-record the songs which were unsuccessful in April.*

These sessions were to lay down the tracks for Elvis Presley's first film after his army discharge, *G.I. Blues.* Two songs with almost identical titles, 'Tonight Is So Right For Love', and 'Tonight's All Right For Love' were necessary, as the first was unable for copyright reasons to be released at that time in Europe. The film deals with U.S. Army life in Germany as part of N.A.T.O., which Presley had experienced during his service. 'Big Boots', however, is a lullaby to a dozing child, and is well sung in Presley's quiet manner. The use of celeste in the backing is just right, but the song is over before it has got going. 'Blue Suede Shoes' is good, but it lacks the rawness of the performance of January 1956. 'Didja Ever' is an 'army'-type song. It has add-on lyrics to a tune which is basically on 'open' notes, which are to those of a bugle call. The use of a baritone tuba is another big plus, but it is Presley's performance which grows in strength with each line.

'Doin' The Best I Can' is a slow ballad, written by Doc Pomus and Mort Shuman. Presley sings this well and with sensitivity. But it is last on the *G.I. Blues* album, which thereby comes to an end on a sorrowful note. 'Frankfurt Special' (always spelled 'Frankfort') is a tremendously successful song, a fast 'train' number, kicked into life by Presley's tight entry, 'Is this train the Frankfurt Special?'. From that opening it drives forward, each verse rising by a semitone from the previous one. 'G.I. Blues' itself moves to a march rhythm, the Jordanaires 'Hup, two, three, four', and is a successful mixing of a blues-beat with the march, but with little independent life. The same cannot be said of 'Pocketful of Rainbows', which is very attractive: soft, with gentle percussion, and quiet accordion and guitar work. Presley sings this to perfection, as he also does 'Shoppin' Around', a medium-fast rocker with strong country bias. 'Tonight Is So Right For Love' uses the *Barcarolle* from Offenbach's opera *The Tales of Hoffmann* whereas 'Tonight's All Right For Love' takes a tune from Johann Strauss's *Tales From the Vienna Woods* as its basis. The Offenbach tune stands up better to this treatment than the Strauss. 'What's She Really Like?' is a catchy number, of medium-bounce tempo, sung in appropriately easy-going style. In *A Legendary Performer* Vol 3 a faster take of 'Frankfurt Special' is issued: it is preferable to that used in the film, but the speed was probably too fast for the set. This collection of songs for *G.I. Blues* constitutes one of the best for a film made by Presley. His next film — and his next recordings — were vastly different.

8 August 1960. *Venue:* Twentieth-Century Fox Studios, (?) Hollywood.
*Titles recorded:* 'Britches', 'A Cane And A High-Starched Collar', 'Flaming Star', 'Summer Kisses, Winter Tears'.

These four titles were recorded for Presley's next film a dramatic Western, *Flaming Star,* in which he gives the finest acting performance of his career. In the event, owing to the dramatic nature of the film only two songs were used, the title song (played over the opening credits) and 'A Cane And A High-Starched Collar'. Curiously enough, only the title song and 'Summer Kisses, Winter Tears' were issued before 1976, when 'A Cane And A High-Starched Collar' was released on Vol. 2 of the *Legendary Performer* series. 'Britches' did not appear until 1978, on Vol. 3 of the same series.

It is not surprising that the songs have a country, almost hill-billy flavour to them. 'Britches' is a medium up-tempo number, with a pretty tune, enhanced by Presley's 'Yo-de-o-de-o' refrain. It is short, only 1:39", but attractive. 'A Cane And A High-Starched Collar' is sung almost at the start of the film, at a family dance-gathering, before a horrifying murder plunges the story into a black atmosphere, from which it never escapes. The issue on Vol. 2 is fascinating, because it starts with take two — announced — and lets us hear the breakdown, Presley's comments, and the announcement of and complete take three. Presley may have had some trouble with the words in take one — which we do not hear — and in take two he breaks down in laughter at the line 'I'll be your darling Jenny'. On the complete take, the accordionist messes up his chords, so these faults (which could have been easily edited out) possibly prevented the earlier release of the song.

'Flaming Star' itself is striking — it has a Red-Indian feel (as befits the story — Presley plays a half-breed). It uses low unpitched drums as an ostinato. This song recalls the musical atmosphere of Johnny Preston's big hit of early 1960, 'Running Bear', also with a Red-Indian background, and was possibly influenced by it. The stereophonic recording enables us to hear the wide and deep backing. 'Summer Kisses, Winter Tears' which *was* issued at the time, although not used in the film, has an air of nostalgia about it. But is too based on formulas to have independent life.

October, 1960. *Venue:* Twentieth-Century Fox Studios (?), Hollywood.
*Titles Recorded:* 'Forget Me Never', 'In My Way', 'I Slipped, I Stumbled, I Fell', 'Lonely Man', 'Wild In The Country'.

These recordings were to tape the songs for Elvis Presley's next film, *Wild In The Country.* This film too shows more of Presley's acting than his singing, but the music does feature more prominently than in *Flaming Star.*

'Husky Dusky Day', used in the film, was never issued commercially: it was recorded on the sound set, not in a studio, and of those listed above, 'Forget Me Never' was not used in the film. It is a gentle softly swaying song with a quiet acoustic guitar accompaniment. It is a haunting number. 'In My Way' is similar: slow, accompanied by acoustic guitar. The recording is strange: there is a distracting buzz. 'I Slipped, I Stumbled, I Fell' is a hard rocker, spoiled by echo: there is no 'air' around Presley or the instruments. 'Lonely Man' is very fine indeed. It has great emotional appeal, and Presley's performance is one of the best of his career. A neglected song, it deserves to be better known. 'Wild In The Country', another gentle number, is heard over the credits in the film, where its hypnotic movement creates the film's atmosphere.

30/31 October 1960. *Venue:* RCA Studios, Nashville.
*Titles recorded:* 'Crying In The Chapel', 'His Hand In Mine', 'I Believe In The Man In The Sky', 'If We Never Meet Again', 'I'm Gonna Walk Dem Golden Stairs', 'In My Father's House', 'Jesus Knows Just What I Need', 'Joshua Fit The Battle', 'Known Only To Him', 'Mansion Over The Hilltop', 'Milky White Way', 'Surrender', 'Swing Down, Sweet Chariot', 'Working On The Building'.

As can be seen, this session was set up to make a new religious album. The result is remarkable: one can understand that his church upbringing had given Presley a deep love and reverence for these songs. The charge of sentimentality can be levelled against a few of these items, but Presley's sincerity is never in doubt. 'Crying In The Chapel' — the most successful of these recordings, not released for five years — veers near these waters, but the pulse is slow, with harmonies (superbly realised by the Jordanaires) that carry the beat. It is sung by Presley with tenderness and a fine feeling for the words. In 'His Hand In Mine', Presley sings beautifully against the vocal backing. Although the instrumentalists are unknown, it is possible the distinctive piano stylist is Floyd Cramer. The tasteful arrangements on most of the songs recorded are best shown in 'I Believe In The Man In The Sky', a medium-fast religious song and 'If We Never Meet Again', in 3/4 time — a slow song with fetching melody. But the song cannot escape the charge of stiffness, which cannot be said of 'I'm Gonna Walk Dem Golden Stairs', a fast revival number. Presley sings below full power, but enough to keep the song moving. The waltz *tempo* is apparent in 'In My Father's House'. Presley, the Jordanaires and Millie Kirkham blend, with a lovely quality to Presley's voice. Ray Walker takes a verse to contrast, and the diction and phrasing of all singers are exemplary. The harmonies, a feature of these sessions, are heard to excellent effect in 'Jesus Knows Just What I Need', a slowish medium-tempo song. Unusually, the piano has a gently insistent 'oom-pah' part. In complete contrast, the spiritual 'Joshua Fit The Battle', is fast and bouncy, with soft, swift piano and drums. The Jordanaires shine here. 'Known Only To Him' returns to slow 3/4 time, an expressive song, performed with great tenderness. 'Mansion Over The Hilltop' lacks distinction, although it is effective enough. It is the Jordanaires who shine in 'Milky White Way' (the first song recorded at the sessions) against Presley's relaxed, balanced solos.

The enormous success of 'It's Now or Never' demanded a follow-up, and 'Surrender' attempts to repeat the formula. The Neapolitan song, 'Come Back To Sorrento' is transferred to bossa-nova rhythm, with fast guitar chords. It does not quite come off — although Presley sings the arrangement to perfection, with a dazzling top B flat full of powerful head-tone. The arrangement of 'Swing Down, Sweet Chariot' is in fast, close-harmony style. Presley threads through the intricate vocal tapestry effectively here and in 'Working On The Building', a bouncy revival number. Presley leads without shouting and the second verse begins with Presley in duet with a descant. The Jordanaires clapping adds to the growing religious fervour.

12/13 March 1961

*Venue:* RCA Studios, Nashville.

*Titles recorded:* 'Gently', 'Give Me The Right', 'I Feel So Bad', 'I Want You With Me', 'I'm Comin' Home', 'In Your Arms', 'It's A Sin', 'Judy', 'Put The Blame On Me', 'Sentimental Me', 'Starting Today', 'There's Always Me'.

A new album was the reason for these sessions, and 'Gently' sets the overall tone. It is remarkable for Presley's soft vocal line, as well as guitar work which threads its way against his voice. There are some nice harmonies and a quiet, superbly balanced, bass line. 'Give Me The Right' is not top drawer material: a slow, heavy ballad with a surprisingly free saxophone solo from Boots Randolph. 'I Feel So Bad' is quite different, with phrases from guitar and piano propelling it. 'I Want You With Me' is a standard rock number of its time, and Bobby Darin also made a fine recording of it, on his best-forgotten album. *For Teenagers Only.* What makes the Presley track less appealing is the recording. Presley gets lost in the general uproar. With 'I'm Comin' Home', a Charlie Rich number, driven with fast drumming, Cramer's piano is still not well-balanced. 'In Your Arms' has Presley's voice better balanced, but the Jordanaires and Millie Kirkham have too much echo. This time, Boots Randolph is too distant! But as the song is not up to much, this is no greater disaster. The slow, delicate number, 'It's A Sin', begins with a soft falsetto from Presley — a good example of his ability to handle this tricky part of the voice. Poor balancing spoils 'Judy', where the guitar never stops, and is so far forward that it overshadows the song. It is difficult to hear Presley while this clatter is going on just behind him. 'Put The Blame On Me' is a good arrangement, a good performance — though it is a mediocre number.

'Sentimental Me', is a better song — slow, with a gently throbbing beat. Presley gets round this one, but it lacks conviction. 'Starting Today' is much better: Floyd Cramer's gentle, haunting piano is ideally balanced. This is a really beautiful song, delicately performed by Presley and the Jordanaires. Finally, 'There's Always Me' is a superb performance: the opening is magical, with much achieved with little effort. A fine track, of which any singer would feel proud.

21/23 March 1961. *Venue:* Radio Recorders Studios, Hollywood.
*Titles recorded:* 'Almost Always True', 'Aloha-oe', 'Beach Boy Blues', 'Blue Hawaii', 'Can't Help Falling In Love', 'Hawaiian Sunset', 'Hawaiian Wedding Song', 'Island Of Love', 'Ito Eats', 'Ku-u-i-po', 'Moonlight Swim', 'No More', 'Rock-A-Hula-Baby', 'Slicin' Sand'.

These tracks make up the songs for Elvis Presley's next film, Paramount Pictures' *Blue Hawaii.* A succession of Hawaiian songs provided a challenge: the distinctive sound of Hawaiian music places constrictions on songwriters, and variety is not always achieved. 'Almost Always True' is a situation song, of a *frère-Jacques* construction. It has a long saxophone introduction from Boots Randolph, but is not memorable for anything else. Presley arranged the traditional Hawaiian song, 'Aloha-oe', which is well sung by him in Hawaiian. The strange thing is that all the backing vocals are on the left-hand channel; an unimaginative use of stereo. Little need be said about 'Beach Boy Blues', which appeared before Californian surfers became famous. It is a feeble song, indifferently performed. Much the same, is true of 'Blue Hawaii', but this undistinguished song is enhanced by unusual instrumentation, and Presley's soft high note at the end. 'Can't Help Falling In Love' can only be better; the melody is another classical theme, the 'Plaisir d'Amour' by Martini (*Il Tedesco*). This is sung with very good breath control by Presley: the breaks in the vocal line are natural and effective. 'Hawaiian Sunset' is the best of the Hawaiian-type numbers: it is well sung, with nice harmonies in the arrangement. Most striking is the unusual melody-line. The famous tune 'Hawaiian Wedding Song' is tastefully done, but less so is 'Island Of Love' written by the composers of 'Hawaiian Sunset' (Tepper and Bennett), who offer a watered-down version of that song.

In such surroundings, it was natural that a Belafonte-style number should surface and his influence is obvious in 'Ito Eats'. It even includes 'day-day' repeats, and the final line shows its indebtedness. There is, however, a relaxed feel, and the use of unpitched drums is effective. The slow, gently bouncing number, 'Ku-u-i-po', is also well sung, with fine use by Presley of his *mezzo-voce*. The song itself hardly merits attention, neither does 'Moonlight Swim', a gentle but innocuous number. 'No More' is a good song, which Presley seems to believe in, and enjoy singing. He doubtless got a lot of fun from 'Rock-A-Hula-Baby', an impossible fusion of Hawaiian and rock; a slick, fun piece. The nearest to a genuine rocker in the collection is 'Slicin' Sand', which is of the 'Blue Suede Shoes' variety, but it does not stand up on its own.

25/26 June 1961. *Venue:* RCA Studios, Nashville.
*Titles recorded:* 'His Latest Flame', 'I'm Yours', 'Kiss Me Quick', 'Little Sister', 'That's Someone You Never Forget'.

These sessions — spread over two days — produced only five songs, but included some outstanding hit material. 'His Latest Flame', a classic recording of a fine song by Doc Pomus and Mort Shuman, tells a story — like 'The Girl Of My Best Friend'. It is propelled by an original rocking beat, and the words are more important than in most rockers. Presley sings with power and ease. The piano part (presumably Floyd Cramer) adds the finishing touch. 'I'm Yours' is outstanding: a slow arrangement of this fine song. Floyd Cramer, this time on organ, adds a superb part. Cramer also appears on 'Kiss Me Quick', a medium bounce to a soft rock beat — but hardly hit material.

'Little Sister', is another classic Presley performance. There is a 'dirty' feel, a smouldering innuendo in Presley's voice, which is cut through by electric guitar phrases. This has a mesmerising effect, helped by the song being contained within a few notes. The final number, 'That's Someone You Never Forget' is excellent. It is slow, and moves with block harmonies: a haunting song, beautifully sung.

5 July 1961. *Venue:* RCA Studios, Nashville.
*Titles recorded:* 'Angel', 'A Whistling Tune', 'Follow That Dream', 'I'm Not the Marrying Kind', 'Sound Advice', 'What a Wonderful Life'. (NB 'A Whistling Tune' was not issued.)

These five songs, recorded under studio conditions by RCA, made up the sound-track for Presley's film, *Follow That Dream*, an innocuous vehicle enlivened by Presley (as Toby Kwimper) displaying judo skills. In the event, 'A Whistling Tune' was not used and turned up (in a different recording) in Presley's next film.

'Angel' has a slow, exotic atmosphere, with an attractive echo answer from Millie Kirkham. The song, however, is barely passable. The title song, 'Follow That Dream', is a happy song with an infectious bounce. 'I'm Not the Marrying Kind' is a quiet, bouncy number, with a slow introduction. It is effective in its restrained piano. Much the same is true of 'Sound Advice' but it is well undistinguished. The final song, 'What A Wonderful Life' is better, and Presley appears more moved by it, missing no trick to give point to the words.

15/16 October 1961. *Venue:* RCA Studios, Nashville.
*Titles recorded:* 'Anything That's Part Of You', 'For The Millionth And Last Time', 'Good Luck Charm', 'I Met Her Today'. ('Night Rider' was recorded at these sessions, but was unsatisfactory, and re-recorded the following March.)

RCA were looking for a new single and found one with 'Good Luck Charm'. 'Anything That's Part of You', a ballad, is one of the most underestimated Presley recordings. Floyd Cramer's piano is to the fore, and through it an acoustic guitar weaves delicate embroidery. Presley's performance builds to hypnotic effect. 'For The Millionth And Last Time' is undistinguished, and although set to a *cha-cha-cha* rhythm, is enervating. 'Good Luck Charm', was a big hit throughout the world, (No. 1 in Britain) but, heard from a distance of almost twenty years, does not stand up. It is a medium tempo bounce, elevated to hit status by the musicianship lavished upon it. Presley's genius as a singer stems partly from his ability to give a totally committed performance, bringing out the song's best qualities, so that one feels the song is better than it really is.

The same comments apply to 'I Met Her Today'. This ordinary ballad is so well sung that one listens to Presley's voice than to what he is singing about.

October/November 1961. *Venue:* Radio Recorders Studios, Hollywood.
*Titles recorded:* 'A Whistling Tune', 'Home Is Where The Heart Is', 'I

Got Lucky', 'King Of The Whole Wide World', 'Riding The Rainbow', 'This Is Living'.

These sessions provided the songs for Presley's next film *Kid Galahad*, about a boxer. 'A Whistling Tune' is precisely what it says: a catchy number, but little more. 'Home Is Where The Heart Is' is a good song, and Presley sings with great feeling for the vocal line. 'I Got Lucky' is unusual in that the drum follows Presley's vocal line. It is a happy song, but not particularly memorable. 'King Of The Whole Wide World' is outstanding; a good rock number, with chunky piano and burning saxophone. Presley's vocal range is quite fantastic — from a *mezzo-voce* in one octave to a powerful *fortissimo* in another, with only a fractional gap between. Tremendously successful, the song tingles with well-being. 'Riding the Rainbow' is another rocker, but not so good. It is lightly arranged, and the piano is featured, but it does not add up to much — neither does the final song, 'This is Living'. Another fast rocking tempo, with a strong boogie bass, Presley's duetting against the Jordanaires is well done, but it cannot rescue the song.

18/19 March 1962. *Venue:* RCA Studios, Nashville.
*Titles recorded:* 'Easy Question', 'Fountain Of Love', 'Gonna Get Back Home Somehow', 'I Feel That I've Known You Forever', 'Just For Old Times' Sake', 'Just Tell Her Jim Said Hello', 'Night Rider', 'She's Not You', 'Something Blue', 'Suspicion', 'You'll Be Gone'.

These sessions produced a new album and a single, but the songs are variable in quality, and none shows Presley at his greatest. The first song, 'Easy Question', is too innocuous, and the second, 'Fountain of Love' too uncertain in style, to be successful. This is not a criticism of Presley, who sings both numbers superbly, but of the material. 'Fountain Of Love' is an unsuccessful mixture. 'Gonna Get Back Home Somehow' is better: a fast, infectious number, whose variety of vocal colouring produces inimitable results. 'I Feel That I've Known You Forever', a slow waltz, builds to a finely controlled climax, but lacks power. The sentimental slow ballad, 'Just For Old Times' Sake' has the merits of a restrained arrangement and distinctive harmonies. Presley sings this with great feeling, but 'Just Tell Her Jim Said Hello' is disappointing. The arrangement is fussy: the triangle sounds like a nagging door-bell, and the recording is poorly balanced. The bass is too far forward, and the final chord cuts off as the song fades. 'Night Rider', a fast number, has dirty, raucous saxophone commentary, but is poor material. Presley sounds uncommitted in 'She's Not You'. 'Something Blue' is better, for this features an imaginative piano from Floyd Cramer. 'Suspicion', a fine number, which was a big hit for Terry Stafford in 1964, is not the outstanding performance Presley could have given. The final song, 'You'll Be Gone' is another unusual number: it has the flavour of a Mexican *beguine*, and is notable for stylish guitar work. There is too much echo around Presley's voice but one can appreciate his breath control. An under-rated recording.

March 1962. *Venue:* Radio Recorders Studios, Hollywood.
*Titles recorded:* 'A Boy Like Me, A Girl Like You', 'Because Of Love', 'Earth Boy', 'Girls! Girls! Girls!', 'I Don't Wanna Be Tied', 'I Don't Want To', 'Return To Sender', 'Song Of The Shrimp', 'Thanks To The Rolling Sea', 'The Walls Have Ears', 'We'll Be Together', 'We're Coming In Loaded'.

These songs constitute the numbers for Presley's film for Paramount Pictures, *Girls! Girls! Girls!*, and are the usual mixture of situation numbers, formula offerings, and outstanding songs. The songs featured in the majority of Presley's films for the next seven years or so are rarely noteworthy. The surprising thing is that, with so many second- and third-rate songs Presley was able to do anything. 'A Boy Like Me, A Girl Like You', is light-years away from the classic Presley recordings of the 1950s and the early 1960s. It is without any distinguishing characteristics. 'Because Of Love' is even worse: an instrumental backing so feeble and lacking in fibre that it sounds childish compared with Presley's sterling work on the vocal line. 'Earth Boy' is another formula song, but has a pinch of oriental flavouring. The title track 'Girls! Girls! Girls!' is a fast and bouncy number, and it has the virtues of fun and an extended Boots Randolph saxophone riff. 'I Don't Wanna Be Tied' recalls one of Presley's favourite singers — Bobby Darin. It would be good juke-box material, and has an unusual slow ending, but does not bear repetition. 'I Don't Want To' is good of its type, and will be familiar to those who know 'The Party's Over'. Well sung, this ought to have achieved success, and could still prove to be a posthumous hit for Presley. But 'Return To Sender', is a classic cut, an outstanding example of Presley's art at its best. The song is difficult to bring off, but the vocal tight-rope Presley treads is superbly done. Not for a second do the repetitions of the title seem too many, and the unusual words are commandingly put across. The beat is exactly right, and although nothing to do with rock, this is Presley at his best. 'Song Of The Shrimp' is very strange. This unusual song is beautifully written, clearly recorded, tastefully arranged and endearingly performed, giving an outstanding result. But it is still a song about a shrimp! 'Thanks To The Rolling Sea', another Darin-type performance, is a superior plot-song. Its use of drums gives it a 'chain-gang' feel. 'The Walls Have Ears' might have been effective on the screen, but heard by itself it is best forgotten. 'We'll Be Together' is also poor material, as is 'We're Coming In

Loaded'. The unusual arrangement, has a flickering bass line, but the song is feeble.

Autumn 1962. *Venue:* Hollywood.

*Titles Recorded:* 'A World of Our Own', 'Beyond The Bend', 'Cotton Candy Land', 'Happy Ending', 'How Would You Like To Be', 'I'm Falling In Love Tonight', 'One Broken Heart For Sale', 'Relax'. 'Take Me To The Fair', 'They Remind Me Too Much Of You'.

These were recorded for the MGM film *It Happened at the World's Fair*. This continues the formula of *Girls! Girls! Girls!* and the songs are of variable quality. 'A World Of Our Own' is pleasant enough, but mediocre, hampered by a wooden backing. 'Beyond The Bend' is another undistinguished song, and not even inventive guitar playing can rescue this. Although some admire this performance, it is sad that Presley performed this material. 'Cotton Candy Land' is a kind of oriental lullaby, beautifully done but with no life outside of the film. With 'Happy Ending' we are back to a fast rocker with an infectious beat, but the song has no guts. 'How Would You Like To Be' is a children's song enlivened by a military drum. The middle eight is in Polka-Dots manner, but the song is too long. 'I Am Falling In Love Tonight' is better material, a slow ballad with imaginative work from organ and piano. Elvis begins the song unaccompanied, dictated by the demands of the film; but it makes a very effective, compelling beginning. 'One Broken Heart For Sale' is a better number than most of the other songs. It is a fast bouncer in 'Return To Sender' style but it has a secondhand air. The song is marred by poor recording; the sound is tight and the acoustic has a squashed image. Perhaps the best number is 'Relax', which is dramatic yet quiet and dreamy, written in a style not unlike 'Fever'. There is a gently picking guitar thread against Presley's Darin-ish style. But the song tends to lose its way in the middle section. 'Take Me To The Fair' is hardly worth mentioning. Presley's singing is good in the final song 'They Remind Me Too Much Of You'. Again, the song does not quite make it; but with a fine piano contribution and Presley's superb phrasing the result is an object lesson to ballad singers.

22/23 January 1963. *Venue:* Radio Recorders Studios, Hollywood.

*Titles recorded:* 'Bossa Nova Baby', 'The Bullfighter Was A Lady', 'El Toro', 'Fun in Acapulco', 'Guadalajara', 'I Think I'm Gonna Like It Here', 'Marguerita', 'Mexico', 'There's No Room To Rhumba In A Sports Car', 'Vino, Dinero Y Amor'.

Eleven days after MGM handed over the song tapes for *It Happened At The World's Fair* to RCA, Presley was back in Hollywood to put down these titles for his next film. This was for Paramount Pictures, and was his second location film, *Fun in Acapulco.*

The Acapulco setting naturally demanded a collection of songs with local atmosphere. With one or two exceptions, the composers did not find inspiration in the Mexican location. It seems as though Presley was unhappy. He re-recorded a number of these songs, and an alternative take of 'Guadalajara', taped on 27 February 1963, is included on *A Legendary Performer* Vol. 3. The first song, 'Bossa Nova Baby', is something like the old Presley, and contrasts with the inferior material he had previously used in his films. This is a fast, modern record, notably because of its use of organ. There is a touch of rock about the song, together with a Bossa Nova feel which is magical. In spite of the fast pace, every word is crystal-clear and in its way this is a classic recording. The remaining songs are little more than aural wallpaper. 'The Bullfighter Was A Lady' is best merely imagined; 'El Toro' is feeble, and 'Fun In Acapulco' is distorted by the recording engineers. Elvis begins the song very loudly, which surprised the engineers. They turn down the volume, and do not adjust it, ruining the sound of Presley's voice.

There are no problems with 'Guadalajara', which is a curiosity. Presley sings it in Mexican Spanish, and very well, for his diction enables every word to be heard. The same cannot be said of 'I Think I'm Gonna Like It Here', another feeble number without the benefit of good orchestral backing. 'Marguerita' is a better song, and begins arrestingly with two trumpets. Unfortunately the engineers have compressed the sound, making it sound bland. The orchestration in 'Mexico' is its best feature; this is another forgettable number. A blind should also be drawn over 'There's No Room To Rhumba In A Sports Car', in spite of Presley's vain attempts to infuse life into it. The Mexican number 'Vino Dinero Y Amor' brings this poor collection to a close. It is a wild number, very fast, but as the backing consists of what appears to be the entire population of Mexico, it is difficult to appreciate.

26/27, May, 1963. *Venue:* RCA Studios, Nashville.

*Titles Recorded:* 'Blue River', 'Devil In Disguise', 'Echoes Of Love', 'Finders Keepers, Loosers Weepers', 'Long Lonely Highway', 'Love Me Tonight', 'Never Ending', 'Please Don't Drag That String Around', 'Slowly But Surely', 'Western Union', 'What Now, What Next, Where To', 'Witchcraft'.

These were required for a new album, but were issued in haphazard fashion. It may be that Presley's films, with their soundtrack albums, made RCA feel they were pushing out too much Presley material.

'Blue River' is very catchy, and contains a frantic guitar lick. It is not particularly memorable, but is superior to the previous film material.

'Devil In Disguise' is a very unusual song: the guitar and piano introduction is contradicted by the subsequent *cha-cha* rhythm, and when the chorus arrives the beat has changed to a fast pulse. A solid bass from Bob Moore joins in and the song takes off when clapping suddenly appears. 'Echoes Of Love' is a medium-tempo song with repeated phrases on piano and unusual use of vibes. Presley is relaxed and easy-going like the song itself, which is good pop but little more. 'Finders Keepers, Loosers Weepers', is humorous, but too flippant to bear repetition. The distinctive characteristic, apart from the medium bounce in Presley's voice, is Boots Randolph's saxophone. In 'Long Lonely Highway', a 'travel' song of blues extraction, there is an unusual catchy rhythm, similar to 'Devil In Disguise'. 'Love Me Tonight' is a slow ballad with a gentle piano which features prominently. Elvis is in good voice, and sings in a simple manner. A similar song is 'Never Ending', but it is not distinctive material. 'Please Don't Drag That String Around' is a good up-tempo number pushed along by a fruity saxophone line. In spite of its qualities, this song lacks an immediate hook, as one might expect from a number used as a fill-up in a film soundtrack. 'Slowly But Surely' is disappointing, apart from the guitar lick which opens it. 'Western Union' is a novelty number, designed to recapture the style of 'Return To Sender'. Like most such attempts it is a pale imitation of the original. 'What Now, What Next, Where To' despite its clumsy title, is one of the best numbers from these sessions. Presley is abetted by Floyd Cramer on piano, but the engineers have surrounded his voice with echo. The final song, 'Witchcraft', is a fast blues number. The opening is a standard bass line, but when Boots Randolph joins Presley, a great jive record results.

July, 1963. *Venue:* Hollywood.
*Titles recorded:* 'C'mon Everybody', 'Do The Vega' (not used in film), 'If You Think I Don't Need You', 'I Need Somebody To Lean On', 'Night Life' (also not used in film), 'Santa Lucia', 'Today Tomorrow And Forever', 'Viva Las Vegas', 'What'd I Say', 'Yellow Rose Of Texas'/'The Eyes Of Texas'.

These songs were for Presley's next film *Viva Las Vegas.* In Britain, the title was changed to *Love In Las Vegas.* This is one of the best collections of songs in a Presley film since *G.I. Blues,* three years before. 'C'mon Everybody' is not the same as the great Eddie Cochran number. It is a medium-fast song with good breaks. 'Do The Vega' shows the influence of the samba-type song 'La Bamba'. 'If You Think I Don't Need You' has a big-band backing, tight and hard-driven, with another outstanding saxophone break. This fine song deserves to be better known, as does the Doc Pomus/Mort Shuman number 'I Need

Somebody To Lean On'. In spite of filigree guitar work and gentle piano backing, there is too much echo on the voice, and the instruments are too far back. This song has a similar atmosphere to another under-rated number a few years before, 'Was There A Call For Me?' by Woody Harris and Marty Holmes. 'Night Life' is not in this class: it begins with a sinuous 'night-club' atmosphere from baritone saxophone and a mean electric bass. The change of key (to the supertonic) is standard formula, but effective. The Neopolitan song 'Santa Lucia' is a surprise choice, but Presley rises to the challenge. His strong baritone voice copes well with this classic, but he is no Caruso. As the song only lasts 1′ 11″, it is over before it has begun. 'Today Tomorrow And Forever' is another piece of classical music, this time Liszt's *Liebestraum.* In spite of the distinctive tune, this is ruined by out-of-tune singing from the Jordanaires at the end. Somebody in the studio agreed for at the end of the take you can hear a lone 'Yuch'!

'What'd I Say' is the great rhythm-and-blues hit for Jerry Lee Lewis of two years before. Presley returns to his roots with exciting singing. Unfortunately Presley's voice is harsh, and buried in the general uproar. This cannot be because he was tired, as it was only the second song recorded at these sessions. The final number (or rather numbers) is the 'Yellow Rose Of Texas'/'The Eyes Of Texas'. This is an average arrangement sung without conviction.

October, 1963. *Venue:* RCA Studios, Nashville.
*Titles recorded:* 'Anyone', 'Barefoot Ballad', 'Catchin' On Fast', 'Kissin' Cousins', 'Kissin' Cousins' (No. 2), 'Once Is Enough', 'One Boy, Two Little Girls', 'Smokey Mountain Boy', 'Tender Feeling', 'There's Gold In The Mountains'.

These songs were possibly recorded in October, but exact details are not available. They were for Presley's next film *Kissin' Cousins,* in which he plays two parts. The first song 'Anyone' is poor, a ballad well sung but undistinguished. The country style is more to the fore in 'Barefoot Ballad', with violin, banjo, and possibly a nose flute in the background. Presley's voice sounds unlike anything heard before, but it fits the song and the film. 'Catchin' On Fast' is a very good song, with drums featured prominently, although it is possible to be put off by the sudden ending. It is difficult not to be confused by the two versions of 'Kissin' Cousins'. 'Kissin' Cousins', No. 1 is an under-rated song. It has a bluesy feel, with sensational drumming. 'Kissin' Cousins' No. 2 is different: the playing is poor by comparison. Three mediocre songs included are 'Once Is Enough', in rockabilly style; 'One Boy, Two Little Girls', a gentle bouncy number, and 'Smokey Mountain Boy', which has a march rhythm and a whistling introduction. 'Tender Feeling', using the song

'Shenandoah', is a stylish arrangement with effective lyrics. It is well sung, and reminds us what a great natural singer Elvis Presley was. The final song, 'There's Gold In The Mountains' is enlivened by good piano and guitar work, but is undistinguished.

12 January, 1964. *Venue:* RCA Studios, Nashville.
*Titles recorded:* 'Ask Me', 'It Hurts Me', 'Memphis Tennessee'.

'Memphis Tennessee' and 'Ask Me' were both recorded at the big sessions held on May 26/27, 1963, but were unsuccessful. At this session they were re-recorded along with the third song. 'Ask Me' has Floyd Cramer on organ, which adds a distinctive tone colour, but detracts from Presley's voice. 'It Hurts Me' is a slow ballad, with Elvis more controlled than for some time. Parts of the song are almost whispered, and others are given at full power. The result is dramatic and compelling. There is another take issued early in 1979, without the Jordanaires, but the song is improved by the additional voices. 'Memphis Tennessee' was a hit in 1963 for both Chuck Berry and (in Britain) Dave Berry. It is a pity that Presley's previous recording in May was unsuccessful. This is a superb performance, with the right quality of restrained unhappiness.

24, 28 February and 2, 6 March, 1964. *Venue:* Radio Recorders, Hollywood.
*Titles recorded:* 'Big Love, Big Heartache', 'Carny Town', 'Hard Knocks', 'It's A Wonderful World', 'It's Carnival Time', 'Little Egypt', 'One Track Heart', 'Poison Ivy League', 'Roustabout', 'There's A Brand New Day On The Horizon', 'Wheels On My Heels'.

These songs made up the tracks for Presley's Paramount film *Roustabout,* and show a marked decline in quality. Whatever Presley thought of this material, he attempts to give the least worthy song the best chance. He cannot avoid sounding uninterested in 'Big Love, Big Heartache', 'Carny Town' (very poor) 'Hard Knocks' (quite undistinguished) and 'It's A Wonderful World' which has a fast tempo but a slow-moving voice part. 'It's Carnival Time' is based on the harmonies from Fucik's 'Entry of the Gladiators' (the theme song for every circus). 'Little Egypt' is a song about a belly dancer. 'Poison Ivy League' is a cynical view of college-eds. 'Roustabout' matches the freewheeling mood of the title and is another song in fast tempo with a slow melody. 'John Brown's Body' forms the harmony for 'There's A Brand New Day On The Horizon', and the final song 'Wheels On My Heels' is nothing to write home about.

July 1964. *Venue:* Hollywood.

*Titles recorded:* 'Cross My Heart And Hope To Die', 'Do Not Disturb', 'Do the Clam', 'Fort Lauderdale Chamber of Commerce', 'Girl Happy', 'I've Got To Find My Baby', 'The Meanest Girl In Town', 'Puppet On A String', 'Spring Fever', 'Startin' Tonight', 'Wolf Call'.

These songs constitute the soundtrack recordings for MGM's *Girl Happy.* They are better than those used for *Roustabout.* 'Cross My Heart And Hope To Die' has a jazz-feel in its introduction, but fails to live up to this opening. 'Do Not Disturb' is a slow song, so well sung it almost makes one forget the poor material. 'Do The Clam' begins with soft drums and guitar, and is a speciality dance number, effective in the film, but not on disc, in spite of the use of stereo distance. The unusually titled 'Fort Lauderdale Chamber of Commerce' is a good song, well put over. It is a 'plot' song with a *cha-cha-cha* beat, and the hook around the title is very effective.

In 'Girl Happy' there is a quality reminiscent of Jimmy Justice to Presley's voice, which may be due to the engineers. 'I've Got To Find My Baby' has a dramatic opening in fast shouting style. 'The Meanest Girl In Town' is a fast song characterised by unimaginative use of backing vocals. In 'Puppet On A String', the Floyd Cramer-like piano introduction is atmospheric, but the song is average. So is 'Spring Fever', a fast bouncy number, and 'Startin' Tonight'. Both have poor material and uninterested performances. The engineers take the same view, for the reverberation at the end of 'Startin' Tonight' is cut off suddenly. The final song, 'Wolf Call' is a good novelty number with a more committed performance, but once again the mixing sounds false and unnatural.

February, 1965. *Venue:* RCA Studios, Nashville.

*Titles recorded:* 'Animal Instinct' (not included in film), 'Go East, Young Man', 'Golden Coins', 'Harem Holiday', 'Hey Little Girl', 'Kismet', 'Mirage', 'My Desert Serenade', 'Shake That Tambourine', 'So Close, Yet So Far', 'Wisdom Of The Ages' (not included in film).

This collection was required for Elvis Presley's first film of 1965, the MGM studio production of *Harum Scarum* (titled *Harem Holiday* in Europe).

Although no-one would pretend Elvis Presley's films up to this time had made any significant contribution to the history of the cinema, with this film Presley's credibility took a sharp downward turn. Almost all the songs in this film are mediocre, and scarcely bear serious attention.

By chance, the first song 'Animal Instinct' is quite good, enlivened by fascinating touches from flute and percussion with the accent falling on the second beat. Although this song has merit, it was removed from the film! 'Go East, Young Man' has an attractive *cha-cha* backing, but is otherwise unremarkable. With 'Golden Coins' we touch rock bottom. 'Harem Holiday' has no melodic appeal, and the accompaniment is divorced from the melody. By far the best is 'Hey Little Girl', a rocking number with intriguing use of piano. This also gets a committed performance from Presley,

The film's Middle East setting enabled the arrangers to include appropriate orchestral backing in 'Kismet' (a slow *cha-cha*). The song is made more interesting by the use of an oboe (although it sounds sour), and two antique cymbals. 'Mirage' is another feeble song, and so is 'My Desert Serenade' which can be best described as oriental-rock. When one considers what George Harrison was shortly to achieve by fusing Eastern influences with rock, this song pales into insignificance. 'Shake That Tambourine' is in fast-rocker tempo, but is mediocre, and the last two, 'So Close, Yet So Far' and 'Wisdom Of The Ages' do not deserve to be heard more than once. This collection can only be regarded as bitterly disappointing.

May 1965. *Venue:* Hollywood.

*Titles recorded:* 'Beginner's Luck', 'Chesay', 'Come Along', 'Down By The Riverside'/'When The Saints Go Marching In', 'Everybody Come Aboard', 'Frankie And Johnny', 'Hard Luck', 'Look Out Broadway', 'Petunia The Gardener's Daughter', 'Please Don't Stop Loving Me', 'Shout It Out', 'What Every Woman Lives For'.

These sessions produced the songs for the second of Presley's three films of 1965, the United Artists' production of Frankie and Johnny. The first song 'Beginner's Luck', is in medium-slow tempo, and is a quiet, restrained number of great gentleness. Presley sings it to perfection and the result is streets ahead of what he had done recently. 'Chesay' is best appreciated by reference to the film, which explains the European feel of the number. For those who do not know it the effect is of a Russo-Greek gypsy drinking-song. The song begins slow, and gets faster and faster; it is very effective. Unfortunately the same cannot be said of 'Come Along' another undistinguished piece. 'Down By The Riverside'/'When The Saints Go Marching In', traditional material, is well sung with a good bounce, but Presley's performance lacks the conviction. 'Everybody Come Aboard' is razzamatazz, but the writer's attempt to capture the right atmosphere has led him to rely on formulas. In 'Frankie And Johnny' Presley seems uninterested. Although well done, it is not a considered performance, and one can only assume it was an off-day. 'Hard Luck' has a mouth-organ introduction to set the scene and Presley gives the most committed singing of the set. But even he cannot redeem the words (Toodle-Oo)! 'Look Out Broadway' is another plot number with Presley in duet with Donna Douglas. It almost becomes a trio with persistent Mr Bass-Man. Although the *Showboat* atmosphere is well caught, the song does not stand up. 'Petunia, The Gardener's Daughter' begins with a honky-tonk opening from the band, and a relaxed, improvised introduction by Presley against the piano. He also duets with Donna Douglas on this song, which offers a faded charm. 'Please Don't Stop Loving Me' is a formula number of poor quality. 'Shout It Out' is fast but unmemorable. As an example of what Presley could do with less than first-class material 'What every Woman Lives For' is one of the best; this slow ballad has a prominent blues piano backing. Presley sings it well, and tries to make it a better number than it is.

26/27 July and 2 and 4 August, 1965. *Venue:* Radio Recorders Studio, Hollywood.

*Titles recorded:* 'Datin'', 'Dog's Life', 'Drums Of The Islands', 'A House of Sand', 'Paradise, Hawaiian Style', 'Queenie Wahine's Papaya', 'Sand Castles' (not included in film), 'Scratch My Back', 'Stop Where You Are', 'This Is My Heaven'.

These songs form the soundtrack numbers for Presley's third film of 1965, *Paradise Hawaiian Style.* This is clearly an attempt by Paramount Pictures to repeat the success of *Blue Hawaii* (1961), but no way does this film approach the earlier one. The songs are well sung and played by the distinguished musicians assembled. The root cause of the problem is the undistinguished material which they had to work with. The first song, 'Datin'' is well projected by Presley and his backing musicians, but is poor. The next 'Dog's Life', is far better and gets a much more committed performance. Once can sense the interest in his voice from the arresting opening to the striking conclusion. 'Drums Of The Islands' is sung by the male voice chorus in unison with Presley, but it is let down by the material, as is 'House Of Sand' and 'Paradise Hawaiian Style' in which Presley shows signs of strain. With 'Queenie Wahine's Papaya' we encounter a plot song, but for all the unusual lyrics and instrumentation, and the tongue-twisting way the song accelerates, it remains indifferent. 'Sand Castles' (which was not included in the film) is probably the best of the lot; it has plenty of atmosphere, and this gentle song receives a fine performance from Presley. 'Scratch My Back' is better than most but is not worthy of Presley's talent — the same is true of 'Stop Where You Are'. This has an unusual, rhythmic opening, but the ending is trite. The final song, a slow ballad, 'This Is My Heaven' receives the best performance in the entire film. Presley lavishes all his artistry on it, but the song remains, sadly, rooted to the spot.

February 1966. *Venue:* unknown.

*Titles recorded:* 'Adam and Evil', 'All That I Am', 'Am I Ready?', 'Beach Shack', 'I'll Be Back', 'Never Say Yes', 'Smorgasbord', 'Stop, Look And Listen', 'Spinout'.

These sessions, which may have taken place in either Nashville or Hollywood, were to tape the songs for Presley's next film, *Spinout* (in Britain, *California Holiday*). There are some interesting touches in 'Adam and Evil': Mr Bass-Man is in evidence as the drums begin a fast and intricate beat. Presley sings in his 'teddy-bear' voice, but divorced from the film the song hardly bears repetition. 'All That I Am' is a slow *Bossa Nova,* with a Spanish-guitar opening, very well sung, as is 'Am I Ready?' a slow ballad, but manifestly not a good song. In 'Beach Shack' Presley returns to Belafonte-style material, in a light and airy song that recalls 'La Bamba'. 'I'll Be Back' is a feeble number of interest only to Presley fans, but in 'Never Say Yes' the engineers appear to have interfered with the natural balance. For some reason this fast rocker has a messy sound, and the track a confused feel.

'Smorgasbord' has Presley picking women as though they were courses on a smorgasbord — a novel twist — and the song has merit. In 'Stop Look And Listen' we have one of the better songs in the film, only let down by the electronic organ. Once more, Presley has a touch of Darin in his performance, and the surprise ending is very attractive. The original title track, 'Spinout' is undistinguished with another too-prominent organ part in the middle section.

# 8 Change of Habit

25 and 28 May 1966. *Venue:* RCA Studios, Nashville.
*Titles recorded:* 'By And By', 'Come What May', 'Down In The Valley', 'Farther Along', 'Fools Fall In Love', 'How Great Thou Art', 'If The Lord Wasn't Walking By My Side', 'In The Garden', 'Love Letters', 'Run On', 'So High', 'Somebody Bigger Than You And I', 'Stand By Me', 'Tomorrow is a Long Time', 'Where Could I Go But To The Lord', 'Where No-one Stands Alone', 'Without Him'.

This major session was a turning-point in Presley's career. The material drew from him performances of incomparable stature. Presley's following during the previous ten years had been among the most loyal of any singer. But a singer can only retain the respect of his fans by recognizing that they demand both a continuation of the songs which established his reputation and an acknowledgement that popular music is continuously evolving. So far Presley appeared unwilling or unable to sense the change in popular music that occurred with the arrival of the Beatles. The necessary change for Presley began with these sessions although he continued to make poor films, we can clearly see the improvement in the choice of material.

'By And By' has a bright 'Sunday morning' revival atmosphere. Presley does not shout, but *sings*, forcing the attention towards the attractiveness of the song, rather than its simple religious message. With 'Come What May' we encounter a song which was out of date even when it was recorded. It is a fast rocker, but the production, to a generation used to the sounds of Phil Spector, is raw and messy. In 'Down In The Valley' we have another revival shouter, a fierce rock blues song which makes a powerful impact — but the words are far from religious! Nothing could be more different than 'Farther Along', a restrained song in waltz time. Presley sings this in a sincere manner. Another surprising number is 'Fools Fall In Love'. This is fast, with hefty brass and big vocal backing, which Presley sings *mezzo-voce*.

In 'How Great Thou Art' we have one of Presley's finest recorded performances. It is sung almost throughout in his low register, with deep rumblings from piano, timpani and male voice singers. The overall effect is overwhelming. Presley brings a magical top F at the end. 'If The Lord Wasn't Walking By My Side' is a bouncy number, sung in strict missionary manner, but it is unlikely any of the preachers in the First Assembly Of God Church could have matched Presley's fire and brimstone. This revivalist style continues with 'In The Garden', a slow song with real Gospel feel. This is not raw and gutsy, but suitably reverent. In 'Love Letters', Presley revives the Ketty Lester hit of 1962. The result is a magnificent performance, featuring piano and organ, although it is difficult to accept this as a man's song. 'Run On' has a blues introduction and although not particularly memorable, is a successful kind of 'Gospel-rock'. Presley's performance is compelling, but in 'So High' the effect tends to rely more on the arrangement than on his singing. The arrangement is good; after a while, clapping adds the icing to the cake, but even this cannot rescue the number. A fine slow song, 'Somebody Bigger Than You And I' provides a welcome contrast, and for this Presley sings in his deep baritone register. His breath control and phrasing are outstanding, and the same is true of 'Stand By Me'. In this performance Elvis returns to the church of his youth, for he leads the choir in this magnificent version of a very moving song. In 'Tomorrow Is A Long Time' we enter a new, and completely different world. This was the first song by Bob Dylan that Presley recorded, and it gives a tantalising glimpse of what might have been, had he recorded an album of Dylan compositions, instead of being side-tracked into a succession of formula films. It is a superb performance, maintained over nearly 5½ minutes. It is softly insistent yet civilized and the half-lights of the backing contribute to Presley's restrained interpretation. This gradually exerts a hypnotic fascination. But this masterly performance was used as a fill-up to the album of Presley's recently-completed film *Spinout!* It sticks out like a Mozart quartet discovered beneath a pile of Austrian drinking songs. More superb singing, closer to the majority of songs recorded at this time, is to be found on the hymn-like 'Where Could I Go But To The Lord?' Presley does not force his tone, and sings well within himself. He adds a faint blues inflection, which gives the right ethnic touch. Another tremendous performance is 'Where No-One Stands Alone'. This is also a slow 3/4 song, which leads from an inexorable build-up to a thrilling climax. The way in which Presley sings this suggests that the words had personal significance. The final song, 'Without Him', is notable for the light backing, confined mainly to organ and piano, and is performed with burning sincerity, entirely without mawkishness.

10 June 1966. *Venue:* RCA Studios, Nashville.
*Titles recorded:* 'If Every Day Was Like Christmas', 'I'll Remember You', 'Indescribably Blue'.

These three titles completed the lengthy sessions of the previous month, recorded for the Christmas market. 'If Every Day Was Like Christmas' is not the usual innocuous number, but a surprisingly serious song partly written by Red West. 'I'll Remember You' is not to be confused with the song 'I Remember You', revived by Frank Ifield in 1962. It begins with a too-fussy arrangement, although Presley sings with sincerity and conviction using superb breath-control and inflection in the lyrics. By far the best of these three is 'Indescribably Blue', a slow ballad which begins in Mediterranean style with tremulous guitar. This powerful song is sung appropriately. The solo female singer (possibly Millie Kirkham) adds a poignant touch, and Henry Slaughter on organ gives further instrumental colour. This is one of the most 'manly' performances Presley recorded.

June 1966. *Venue:* Hollywood.

*Titles recorded:* 'Baby If You'll Give Me All Your Love', 'City By Night', 'Could I Fall In Love', 'Double Trouble', 'I Love Only One Girl', 'It Won't Be Long' (not included in the film), 'Long-Legged Girl', 'Old MacDonald', 'There Is So Much World To See'.

These songs constitute the soundtrack recordings for Presley's next film, the MGM studio production of *Double Trouble*. Although by this time over-dubbing was standard practice, of Presley's soundtrack recordings this is one of the most 'produced'. The result lacks the feel of a standard studio recording, and the natural ambiance of undoctored sound. The songs do not show much advance over Presley's previous film material.

The first song 'Baby If You'll Give Me All Your Love' is a fast rocker, well sung, but of poor quality. The next, 'City By Night', is better: a medium tempo 'walking' blues, with imaginative use of brass. It is dramatic in its effect, and Presley sustains the menacing atmosphere with dark vocal quality. 'Could I Fall In Love' is another good song. One of its surprising features is the use of a string quartet, and it is possible that we hear Charlie Hodge in duet with Presley. 'Double Trouble' lacks coherent style; the backing is confused and messy, possibly the result of too much technical alteration. In 'I Love Only One Girl', the French folk song 'Après de Ma Blonde', is turned into a marching song, with unusual and not inappropriate effect. 'It Won't Be Long' is a totally forgettable number. 'Long-Legged Girl' begins in fierce stomping manner; it is well done, but lacks originality. With the old song 'Old MacDonald' Elvis lets himself go and gives a fun-filled performance. The final song 'There Is So Much World To See' falls between several styles, and fails. The arrangement is fussy and heavy, and although the lyrics are slick, the tune is poor.

28/29 September 1966. *Venue:* Radio Recorders Studio, Hollywood.
*Titles recorded:* 'Easy Come, Easy Go', 'I'll Take Love', 'The Love Machine', 'She's A Machine', 'Sing You Children', 'Yoga Is As Yoga Does', 'You Gotta Stop'.

A collection of mediocre songs, this set was recorded for Presley's next film, Paramount's *Easy Come, Easy Go.* There is an occasional flash of inspiration in the odd guitar lick during 'Easy Come, Easy Go' but there is an incessant and unbearable off-beat side drum. 'I'll Take Love' wallows in banality, and although Presley does his considerable best with this and 'The Love Machine', he cannot disguise his uncommitted performance. 'She's A Machine' is mildly interesting: it has a fast backing, but the vocal line is slow. A brilliant arrangement (featuring trumpets) also attempts to rescue 'Sing You Children', a fast Gospel-type number. 'Yoga Is As Yoga Does' scarcely deserves a mention, it is so badly recorded. 'You Gotta Stop' is more interesting; it has a slow introduction, and an unusual backing, once the frantic pace starts, with sudden breaks and fragmentary solos. Presley rises to this difficult challenge and rides the music, but it remains undistinguished.

21 February 1967. *Venue:* RCA Studios, Nashville.
*Titles recorded:* 'Clambake', 'Confidence', 'The Girl I Never Loved', 'Hey, Hey, Hey', 'A House That Has Everything', 'How Can You Lose What You Never Had?' (not included in the film), 'Who Needs Money?', 'You Don't Know Me' (specially recorded for disc).

Compared with *Easy Come, Easy Go* these songs for Presley's next film, United Artist's *Clambake,* are an improvement. But one must question the judgement of whoever was responsible for contracting Presley to record material of such low quality. The title song, 'Clambake', receives a fine performance and has an unusual bass line. It appears to be founded on 'Shortin' Bread'. 'Confidence' is a children's song, but is unlikely to appeal to any child. 'The Girl I Never Loved' is another example of a third-rate song well done. 'Hey, Hey, Hey' is a typical pop song of the mid-1960s. This uses formulas of the time, but is so well done it has its own validity. Unfortunately the recording is bad: Presley appears over-dubbed, and his first entry seems to come from another studio. 'A House That Has Everything' is a forgettable slow *cha-cha,* and 'How Can You Lose What You Never Had?' surely shows further interference by the technicians. It has an imaginative organ part, but Presley is ill at ease. 'Who Needs Money?' reflects the character of the song; everyone involved appears money-mad. Presley duets with Willie Hutchins on this fast number, but the song is dreary. Presley is heard to much better effect on the last song 'You Don't Know Me', a slow ballad, good and well sung. Once more the engineers must be faulted, as Floyd Cramer's fluent piano appears several miles away.

On 20 March 1967, Presley, with his usual coterie of musicians, arrived at the RCA Studios in Nashville. Something must have gone seriously wrong, for only one song, 'Suppose', was recorded, and this was never issued. Later in June, it was re-recorded for Presley's next film *Speedway.*

June 1967. *Venue:* Hollywood.

*Titles recorded:* 'Five Sleepy Heads' (not included in the film), 'He's Your Uncle Not Your Dad', 'Let Yourself Go', 'Speedway', 'Suppose' (not included in the film), 'There Ain't Nothing Like A Song', 'Who Are You?', 'Your Time Hasn't Come Yet Baby'.

These songs were for Presley's next film, MGM's *Speedway.* We have noted the change of direction in Presley's career emanating from the May 1966 sessions, but the songs for this film unfortunately do not carry conviction. 'Five Sleepy Heads' was cut from the film. It is a bedtime story, sung to Brahms's 'Lullaby'. Although the original tune is a distinct improvement over most of Presley's film songs, the arrangement does not work. 'He's Your Uncle Not Your Dad' is not worthy of Presley. 'Let Yourself Go', however, a mean blues-type song, is a good number by most standards, and is enhanced by Presley's performance, full of raunchy passion. An infectious, rocking rhythm is a characteristic of the title-track, 'Speedway' which results from outstanding drum work. The song drives, and there is a nice use of tambourine, but Presley's first entry is subdued and his voice never in focus. 'Suppose' (attempted the previous March in Nashville) is unusual: it is slow and darkly dramatic, well projected by Presley. An unusual feature of the backing-track is the double bass played with the bow. 'There Ain't Nothing Like A Song' again has Presley too far back. For a fast-moving song put over with drive and gusto, this is a serious technical fault, and even the presence of Nancy Sinatra for a few lines does not redeem it. 'Who Are You?' is worse: a slow samba, it is very poor material. 'Your Time Hasn't Come Yet Baby' can only justify its soft, bouncy existence by the story of the film.

10 and 12 September 1967. *Venue:* RCA Studios, Nashville.

*Titles recorded:* 'Big Boss Man', 'Guitar Man', 'High Heel Sneakers', 'Just Call Me Lonesome', 'Mine', 'Singing Tree', 'We Call On Him', 'You Don't Know Me', 'You'll Never Walk Alone'.

This unusually varied group of songs was not recorded with any definite project in mind, but includes some of the most important songs Presley recorded for years.

A good example is 'Big Boss Man.' This is given a superb performance by all concerned and the overwhelming impression is of a powerfully-driven song. The guitar-work, possibly by Jerry Reed, is outstanding, and there are imaginative touches from Charlie McCoy's harmonica. The same is true of 'Guitar Man', which is a finely-driven country song, with Presley relishing the almost autobiographical lyrics. With 'High Heel Sneakers' (a hit in Britain for Tommy Tucker three years before), Presley's performance, to use the then-current jargon is more 'rocker' than 'mod'. The song does not stand up to this treatment, and although the atmosphere is subtle and erotic, its cleverness means Presley has little chance to get going. Presley is also ill at ease in 'Just Call Me Lonesome' and 'Mine'. The first is poor, for it lies too high. 'Mine' is a slow ballad, distinguished by Floyd Cramer's piano, but Presley's uncertainty can be noticed in a tremulous quality in his voice. No complaints can be levelled against 'Singing Tree', which is beautifully sung. Especially effective are the duet harmonies, but the song has no strength. 'We Call On Him' is a gentle number, but lacks distinction. In 'You Don't Know Me', Presley re-recorded a song which he had already taped for the film *Clambake.* The fine song was a hit for Ray Charles in 1962, and the re-recording is outstanding, with superb breath control from Presley, and the Jordanaires on top form. Apart from these virtues, Floyd Cramer's fine pianism is audible. Finally, 'You'll Never Walk Alone', an astonishing hit for Gerry Marsden (of Gerry and the Pacemakers) in 1963. Although Presley's performance is sincere, and possibly influenced by the Liverpool singer, the sound is out of focus and the result not compelling.

2 October 1967. *Venue:* RCA Studios, Nashville.
*Titles recorded:* 'All I Needed Was The Rain', 'Going Home', 'Stay Away', 'Stay Away, Joe'.

The above four titles were recorded for Presley's next film for MGM, *Stay Away, Joe.* Presley also recorded the song 'Dominic' which was never released. It is not known whether the performance was unsatisfactory or if it was never completed. The songs released show a vast improvement over Presley's previous film numbers. 'All I Needed Was The Rain' is a very good country-blues, soft, with a faintly moaning harmonica threading its way through a complex acoustic guitar pattern. This receives an exceptionally fine performance from Presley. If fault can be found, the song fades out too soon, breaking the spell. In 'Going Home' there is more interesting use of guitars. There was confusion in earlier pressings between 'Stay Away' and 'Stay Away, Joe.' This is understandable, but the songs are very different. The first, 'Stay Away', is an adaptation of the English folk song 'Greensleeves', but the words and arrangement do not come up to the haunting quality of the original.

This is a pity, for this could have become a big hit for Presley. He is more at ease in 'Stay Away, Joe'. All through this hill-billy stomp there is a genuine laugh in Presley's voice, which is quite infectious.

15 and 17 January 1968. *Venue:* RCA Studios, Nashville.
*Titles recorded:* 'Too Much Monkey Business', 'U.S. Male'.

Confusion surrounds this session. There were rumours that many more numbers were put down, but so far as can be ascertained these two were the only titles completed. 'Too Much Monkey Business' is a medium-fast rocker, which had already been a hit for Chuck Berry. It is a curiosity from Presley. Apparently he asked for new lyrics, but the flippant reference to Vietnam in January 1968 is in bad taste. In 'U.S. Male' Presley is again out-of-touch with contemporary thought. This is full of male chauvinism, and sung in a style which does not come off, although it became a hit.

March 1968. *Venue:* Hollywood.
*Titles recorded:* 'Almost In Love', 'Edge Of Reality', 'A Little Less Conversation', 'Wonderful World'.

These four songs are from Presley's next film, MGM's *Live A Little, Love A Little.* They are more successful than any of Presley's film recordings for a long time. 'Almost In Love', a medium-tempo *bossa nova*, has a fine arrangement, including strings, trombones and vibraphone. It is a surprisingly successful mixture, as this was not Presley's *mètier*. This song, which is not so well known as it ought to be, shows a new facet of Presley's musical personality. 'Edge of Reality' is another interesting number. It begins with a chromatic choral introduction, and the use of brass is noteworthy. 'A Little Less Conversation' has a rocking feel, typical of the best of the late 1960s. It is fast, with florid drumming, powerful brass and a heavy, active bass. Presley's performance is one of his best: there is a throb and arrogance in his singing which is irresistible. Given the right song, Presley was still capable of putting in a performance difficult to surpass. 'Wonderful World' suffers by comparison: it is a kind of fast waltz but not a great song, with a fussy backing.

# 9 The Return of the Master, 1968-9

After the television spectacular for NBC, recorded in June 1968, Elvis Presley's career seemed set fair to enter a new and vital phase. The success of the show, with its immensely wide-ranging material, demonstrated for the first time in many years Presley's command of the rock idiom. Here was no ageing star, brought out for teenagers of the 1950s who now found themselves the carpet-slippered, television-addicted parents of the late 1960s. Presley was a paradox on this show: he had not changed at all with regard to his earlier material, but he had changed with regard to his stage presence and choice of material.

27/29 June 1968. *Venue:* NBC Studios, Burbank, Los Angeles.
*Titles recorded:* 'All Shook Up', 'Are You Lonesome Tonight', 'Baby What You Want Me To Do' (2 versions), 'Big Boss Man', 'Blue Christmas', 'Blue Moon Of Kentucky' (not released), 'Blue Suede Shoes', 'Can't Help Falling In Love', 'Don't Be Cruel' (not released), 'Guitar Man' (2 versions), 'Heartbreak Hotel', 'Hound Dog', 'If I Can Dream', 'It Hurts Me' (not released), 'Jailhouse Rock', 'Lawdy Miss Clawdy', 'Let Yourself Go' (not released), 'Little Egypt', 'Love Me', 'Love Me Tender', 'Memories', 'Nothingville', 'One Night', 'Santa Claus Is Back In Town' (not released), 'Saved', 'That's All Right' (not released), 'Tiger Man', 'Trouble' (2 versions), 'Trying To Get To You', 'Up Above My Head', 'When My Blue Moon Turns To Gold Again' (not released), 'Where Could I Go But To The Lord?'

This extended series of recordings were to tape Presley's NBC-TV Spectacular, an hour-long show which marked Presley's comeback. The television film was well done, and makes fascinating viewing. But divorced from the screen, the soundtrack album is in many ways the most disappointing Presley issue. In spite of the large number of titles recorded, it is best to deal with them in order of appearance on the record, as they often occur in medleys lasting only a few bars. Furthermore, they are strung together with linking dialogue which makes it difficult to pick out individual songs.

The main drawback is the atrocious quality of the recording. It is almost unbelievable that in 1968 these recordings were made only in mono. For those interested in Presley's speaking voice, the record contains many examples of him chatting to the audience.

Generally speaking, the songs make up a selection of Presley's hits of the previous dozen years, and the album begins with a fine version of 'Trouble' which originally appeared in *King Creole*. In this new version, the opening New Orleans riff is cut out, and Presley's singing is not as eruptive as earlier. This segues into 'Guitar Man', which appears as a recurring theme on the record. This gets a tremendous performance full of dark surging qualities from Presley; and the orchestra, helped by squealing high trumpets, is fabulous. It is a different story with, 'Lawdy Miss Clawdy', full of extraneous noise and atmosphere, where it is difficult to appreciate Presley through the screams, bumps, slurps and bad balancing. This segues into 'Baby What You Want Me To Do' which is an edited version of a lengthy take in the film (part of the long guitar solo is included on *A Legendary Performer* Vol. 2) but the confused sound has all the attraction of a home-movie. The album moves into a medley of 'Heartbreak Hotel', 'Hound Dog' and 'All Shook Up', but the technical disaster goes from bad to worse. In 'Heartbreak Hotel' Presley's voice, full of power and conviction, is all but drowned in applause. 'Hound Dog' is also well performed, with powerful orchestral brass, but the recording is bass-heavy, and the sound is made worse by an extraordinary recording fault. This is an apparent electrical feed-back on the note B Flat. This note gets louder and louder, and blares through 'All Shook Up'. The result is an unmitigated disaster; no self-respecting artist should lend his name to this.

The last three songs on side 1 are little better: 'Can't Help Falling In Love' suffers from poor balance and overpowering over-dubbed strings later. 'Jailhouse Rock', one of the rawest songs Presley ever recorded, fares better in these circumstances, but Don Randi's stodgy organ playing draws back the rhythm. Presley can do nothing to lift this song, and the final section degenerates into a welter of noise. 'Love Me Tender' is not fit to be compared with his earlier version.

On side 2 we enter a different world. 'Where Could I Go But To The Lord' was the first song recorded on 28 June. It appears that the engineers had been listening to the previous day's disasters, for the sound is much better; it is clean and clear, and the backing musicians seem more committed. Presley's voice, now we can hear it, is in good shape; the only criticism being that acoustically he is set a little too far back. This segues into a fine, sincere performance of 'Up Above My Head' which in turn leads into 'Saved'. This is a brilliant performance of a staggering gospel-rock number by Lieber and Stoller, which gets better as it proceeds up the scale. In 'Blue Christmas' we are back to the confusion of 27 June, with both song and performance lost in acoustic gloom. 'One Night' starts in ludicrous fashion, but Presley turns this sonic dross into vocal gold. 'Memories' is a fine song, well performed, with a shimmering orchestral tapestry in the background. The crude recording techniques are not too obvious here. In 'Nothingville' a haunting atmosphere is created, full of dark and lonely foreboding. Presley gives a marvellous performance, but it is over too soon! It segues into 'Big Boss Man', where the drawbacks of the orchestra ought to have stopped the release of this take. Presley is very good, but the NBC orchestra is badly out of synchronization. Curiously enough, Presley revives 'Little Egypt', from *Roustabout,* and the dozen or so bars of this funny little song contrast with the reprise of 'Trouble' and 'Guitar Man', which are little more than reminiscences. The record ends with 'If I Can Dream', which was Presley's current hit. This slow beefy ballad was clearly *not* recorded at the sessions which produced the earlier confusion, for it is well recorded, with Presley's voice full of power and gravel. It is extraordinary that he used this style of singing, for his voice is almost unlike anything in the earlier part of his career. The song moves to a powerful climax, with a slow brass build up which makes a fine ending to an uneven and exasperating record.

Of the other songs recorded in these sessions, but issued on later LPs, it is better to deal with them in alphabetical order. 'Are You Lonesome Tonight?' comes from the poor sessions of 27 June, and is only interesting for the atmosphere and rapport between the singer and the audience. The extended instrumental version of 'Baby What You Want Me To Do?' also appears on *A Legendary Performer* Vol. 2 where it 'highlights Elvis on lead guitar'. This is the only merit on the take. In 'Blue Suede Shoes', the poor recording has undeniable drive. The second verse is much better, for at last Presley can be heard, and the guitar is not so obtrusive. 'Love Me' is another messy piece of work, for all its atmosphere. 'Tiger Man' attempts to recapture the early days of rock'n'roll, but the recording is so dismal that the performance has no significance. 'Trying to Get to You' is a great improvement, for Presley is much better balanced.

July 1968. *Venue:* Possibly Hollywood.
*Title recorded:* 'Charro'.

This is the only song in Presley's next film, the National General Pictures' *Charro*. The film, hardly one of Presley's compelling performances, shows a desire to tap Presley's under-used acting ability. The title song, heard over the credits, is unusual and dramatic, with a big orchestral backing used sparingly by the arranger, Hugo Montenegro, whose use of strings, piano and horns in the early part, is striking. Montenegro was then enjoying an international hit with his theme from the Clint Eastwood film, *The Good, The Bad and The Ugly*. But 'Charro', for all its qualities, feeds on the more commonplace characteristics of the earlier tune. It is an unusual song which gives a tantalizing glimpse of Presley's feel for the big dramatic ballad, something largely denied him up to this time.

October 1968. *Venue:* Hollywood.

*Titles recorded:* 'Almost', 'Clean Up Your Own Backyard' ('Aura Lee', 'Sign Of The Zodiac' and 'Swing Down, Sweet Chariot' were also recorded at these sessions, but were unsuccessful, and have not been released.)

These songs were for the film soundtrack of Presley's next film *The Trouble With Girls*, for MGM. In the event only 'Almost' and 'Clean Up Your Own Backyard' were released on disc. 'Aura Lee' and 'Sign Of The Zodiac' were probably recorded on the film set. 'Almost' shows poor over-dubbing, for Presley is not well balanced with the instruments. A very obtrusive piano begins the song, and tends to smother Presley later. 'Clean Up Your Own Backyard' is quite different. This is a good number, with a gentle but solid beat, and receives a superb performance from Presley. Every inflection can be heard and savoured, and the over-dubbing of brass and female vocals enhances the gospel feel of the song.

13/23 January 1969. *Venue:* American Studios, Memphis.

*Titles recorded:* 'A Little Bit Of Green', 'Come Out' (not released), 'Don't Cry Daddy', 'From A Jack To A King', 'Gentle On My Mind', 'Hey Jude', 'I'll Be There', 'I'll Hold You In My Heart', 'I'm Movin' On', 'Inherit The Wind', 'In The Ghetto', 'Long Black Limousine', 'Mama Liked The Roses', 'My Little Friend', 'Poor Man's Gold' (not released), 'Rubberneckin'', 'Suspicious Minds', 'This Is The Story', 'Wearin' That Loved On Look', 'Without Love', 'You'll Think Of Me'.

These extended sessions, which took ten days, together with the following sessions in February (spread over six days), produced a new batch of material, which was intended to capitalize on the success of the album of the TV Special. Although that album left much to be desired from the technical viewpoint, these recordings, the first Presley made in Memphis since the Sun days fifteen years before, show a great advance. The material is generally speaking good, as are the natural, yet imaginative, recordings. For once it is possible to listen with pleasure, without having to make allowances for inferior material or inadequate engineering.

'A Little Bit Of Green' displays a restrained yet insistent beat. Curiously, this is not one of the best songs from the sessions. 'Don't Cry Daddy' is a difficult song: it can be seen as a mawkishly sentimental, but

Presley's performance is musically worthwhile. It is a very morbid song, but it is possible to imagine that Presley believed in it. Just over seven years earlier, Ned Miller had a hit with 'From A Jack To A King', but it is difficult to see what was in Presley's mind by using it at this late stage. Presley chews over this song like a dog gnawing away at a meaty bone. The original vocal line may not have been up to much, but Presley's alterations make no sense. But Presley reveals unsuspected depths in the lyrics of the Dean Martin hit 'Gentle On My Mind'. Presley is rugged as opposed to the bland sophistication of Martin. Presley's bass-work is fascinating, as is the rest of the backing. But also remarkable is the restrained use of female voices, Presley's seriousness, and the result is a very fine performance. In 'Hey Jude' Presley turns to the Beatles. Just as the 'Gentle On My Mind' performance is different from that generally known, so 'Hey Jude' is so unlike the original as to make it a different song. He performs it in a high voice, as though half-whispering to a friend, but this strange atmosphere exerts a fascination. 'I'll Be There' is unusual, in that Presley vocalizes for much of the time, almost in a bluegrass way. The song is hardly a world-shaker, but it is pleasant enough. A notable feature of the instrumental backing is the varied and colourful arrangement, which almost makes the song sound better than it is. 'I'll Hold You In My Heart' has dated. The recording is not well balanced, for the drumming is too far forward and obtrudes on Presley's plastic singing. But what breath-control! 'I'm Movin' On' is superb. The performance is delicate, yet solid, and the strength and tenderness of 'travel' country-based music is fully revealed. The jangly piano and solid, driving brass is quite hypnotic in its build-up and growth. 'Inherit The Wind' is another fine performance, but the vocal quality seems strained. This was the first song recorded on 16 June, and the stiffness is noticeable.

When we come to 'In The Ghetto' we encounter a classic Presley recording. It is essentially a protest song and nobody listening to this performance can remain unmoved. Every word is crystal clear, and Presley's manly voice has both authority and tenderness. The subject of the song is the plight of those who live in ghettoes, and the bare, insistent, unchanging harmonies mirror this, as the singer is trapped by their pull.

With 'Long Black Limousine' we enter an unusual atmosphere. Solemn bells intone this morbid funeral song. In spite of the dark tragedy behind the number, the drumming and bass-line are both superb, and Presley feeds off them and to them. His voice is in great shape; he takes quite extended phrases in one breath, and the song shows a fine use of recording technique.

'Mama Liked The Roses' is a female equivalent of 'Don't Cry Daddy'.

Presley is doubtless sincere but this has to be listened to with indulgence. 'My Little Friend' is a weak song and, although the arrangement is good, Presley's voice sounds a little querulous. Unfortunately the over-dubbing of strings is not good, for the playing is poor and out of tune. 'Rubberneckin' is a fun song, sung by Presley with an attractive 'tight' quality. The brass playing is good and the infectious atmosphere urgent and zappy becomes very infectious. 'Suspicious Minds' became one of Presley's signature tunes, for he recorded four versions. This, the first, became a major hit for him towards the end of 1969. The song is outstanding, and the fast yet menacing atmosphere is ideally caught. The later versions are live, but there is no doubt that the clean nature of this first version enables more to be heard. 'This Is The Story' is a strange song. It has a 'still' introduction, modern, yet with hardly a change of tempo or harmony. The string over-dubbing is poor, as on 'My Little Friend'.

'Wearin' That Loved On Look' is outstanding. It opens in rhythm-and-blues slow style, with, Presley in staggering voice. He admired the Welsh singer Tom Jones, and there is more than a hint of Jones in Presley's performance. Apart from Presley's magnificent singing, the instrumentation deserves mention. The organ — way on the right hand channel — is imaginatively used, and the drumming subtly attractive. Rich contributions from the backing vocals and a clangy piano, together with a thumping bass-line make the whole thing irresistible. Tom Jones recorded *Without Love* sometime after Presley and went on to have a big hit with it; so in this instance he returned the compliment. It is a sentimental song, sung with great conviction by Presley. It is a pity this was not released as a single, for it could easily have been a hit for Presley. In the last song, 'You'll Think Of Me', there is a strangely disconnected opening, which gradually builds to the basic tempo. The song, which lasts almost four minutes, is long for the material, but Presley manages to hold it together through the layers of sound.

17/22 February 1969. *Venue:* American Studios, Memphis.

*Titles recorded:* 'After Loving You', 'And The Grass Won't Pay No Mind', 'Any Day Now', 'Do You Know Who I Am', 'If I'm A Fool', 'It Keeps Right On A-Hurtin' ', 'Kentucky Rain', 'Memory Revival' (not released). 'Only The Strong Survive', 'Power Of My Love', 'Stranger In My Own Home Town', 'The Fair's Moving On', 'True Love Travels On A Gravel Road', 'Who Am I?'.

This is a mixed collection of the same quality as the previous month's sessions. 'After Loving You' is an example of Presley at his best. The song holds no surprises for those who know 'Blueberry Hill', but Presley creates something passionate and dark from second-rate material.

Amazingly, he makes it work — and does so alone, for the backing offers no help. Only a great performer could have achieved this, but the song is not allowed to fade out naturally; it is snipped off before the end by the engineers. 'And The Grass Won't Pay No Mind' is another excellent performance. This Neil Diamond song features some fine string writing. Presley sings with delicacy, in a restrained and intimate manner. The song is difficult, ranging over two octaves. At first Presley appears to have trouble with the lowest notes, but overall this is a fine performance. 'Any Day Now' is another fine song, with music by Burt Bacharach. Typically, the melody has unusual contours, and the arrangement produces strange sonorities from the orchestra: now an oboe solo, now a few bars of solo violin, now the deep and solid brass sound. Presley gives a staggering performance: powerful, wide ranging, full of expression. Another unusual song is 'Do You Know Who I Am?' This is not a typical ballad, for it has unconnected changes of key (which make it difficult to sing), but Presley rises to the challenge. Another interesting feature is the occasional use of a string quartet. 'If I'm A Fool' is a straightforward country song, with a soft feel about it. This kind of material is easy to dismiss; but it should be remembered that songs of this type were close to Presley's heart. Familiarity is apparent in a Johnny Tillotson number 'It Keeps Right On A-Hurtin''. Presley turns in a moderate performance, which is well recorded. 'Kentucky Rain' is sung with passion and conviction, but as it is a despairing number the effect is enervating. Presley enters into the spirit of the song, and it is doubtful if he ever sounded more miserable on record. 'Only The Strong Survive' is a dramatic song from the Gamble-Huff stable. This is one occasion where Presley appears unfamiliar with the material, for the performance is too slow. 'Power Of My Love' is worlds away. It is remarkable in that it is both old-school rock'n'roll and in 3/4 time. Solid and raunchy, Presley's performance is irresistible: full of sly innuendoes and *double-entendres*. There are a few singers who can manage this, yet it stems from the Presley of 1954/1955. It is explosive, breathy and rich, with an extraordinary ending. 'Stranger In My Own Home Town', a Curtis Mayfield number, begins with a superb orchestral opening. The big orchestral backing is fused with basic rhythm-and-blues. Presley moves around the music, like a collector savouring his possessions; and this electrifying performance is an outstanding example of Presley's art. 'The Fair's Moving On' is akin to the Eartha Kitt song 'The Day That The Circus Left Town'. Both are in slow 3/4 time, and Presley puts it over clearly and simply; but he cannot disguise the song's lack of distinction. 'True Love Travels On A Gravel Road' is full of fire, with a wide-ranging vocal line, well arranged and recorded; but in the last analysis not out of the top drawer. 'Who Am I?' is a straightforward song, restrained and sincere. It is also well arranged and features more organ than other tracks: Presley sings it simply and appealingly.

5/6 March 1969. *Venue:* Universal Studios, Hollywood.
*Titles recorded:* 'Change Of Habit', 'Have A Happy', 'Let's Be Friends', 'Let's Forget About The Stars', 'Let Us Pray'.

These songs were for Presley's last feature film, Universal Pictures' *Change of Habit*. They contain an unusual song, 'Lets Forget About The Stars'. It could not have been recorded then, as it is in mono.

'Change of Habit' is a beefy number with a funky bass line. It is possibly too long, lasting 3¼ minutes, but in its favour are Presley's committed performance, a light and airy piano part, and an infectious rhythm. 'Have A Happy' shows an unwelcome return to the standards of Presley's least attractive earlier films. 'Let's Be Friends' was not included in the film, and is undistinguished. In spite of its strange background 'Let's Forget About The Stars' is feeble, and Presley appears bored and ill at ease with this unworthy material. The final song 'Let Us Pray', a surprisingly fast rocking number, is helped by staccato drumming and Presley's light voice. Although some commentators dismiss this, possibly Presley was more involved in this number than the others.

# 10 On Stage, 1969-74

Beginning with the live performances of August 1969 at the International Hotel, Las Vegas, Presley was able to rid himself of the succession of mediocre films. Although it was nine years since he last performed in public, any doubts he may have had were swept away by the tremendous success of the engagements. Return bookings were obligatory and naturally RCA wished to record them on disc. What few people seemed to realize was that what makes a fine concert (variety of material, to show the performer's range of abilities) does not necessarily make a fine record, where the purchaser would expect to find songs of a similar nature. This is not to say that all the songs must be the same; but the album has to have its own identity. Listening at home is different to being at a concert.

Presley's success as a live performer was partly because his concerts were carefully chosen, and rehearsed to perfection. On *'Sergeant Pepper's Lonely Hearts Club Band,* two years before, the Beatles had demonstrated the total-concept album, whereby the forty minutes' playing-time are used to make musical statements which themselves add up to a total greater than the individual songs. In time the album as a mere collection of songs became a thing of the past. With Presley's ability and resources, it is a tragedy that the record buying public were denied for years a Presley studio album as carefully put together and rehearsed as his live concerts.

To the record buying public in foreign countries, the constant flow of similar Presley material was exasperating. The millions of followers outside the U.S.A. had no chance to attend his live performances; their needs were completely ignored on discs.

One technical disadvantage of a live recording is that there is no opportunity to correct mistakes. For safety's sake, RCA tended to record two performances on the same day. The better performance got released; but for every released track from these live performances there was at least one unreleased. Since Presley's death, the number of unauthorized albums has risen to around fifty, and many of these used tapes which were rejected by RCA. However, in spite of the fact that RCA often possessed two or more performances of the same song, there might well be flaws in each of them which would prevent their release on a commercial album. Consequently, there would appear to be little point in listing all the titles which were recorded at these sessions, when a great many of them have not been released, and probably will not be released in the future. For the sake of clarity, only songs which *have* been released are listed and discussed.

22/26 August 1969. *Venue:* International Hotel, Las Vegas.
*Titles released:* 'All Shook Up', 'Are You Lonesome Tonight?', 'Blue Suede Shoes', 'Can't Help Falling In Love', 'Hound Dog', 'I Can't Stop Loving You', 'In The Ghetto', 'Johnnie B. Goode', 'My Babe', 'Mystery Train/Tiger Man', 'Runaway', 'Suspicious Minds', 'Words', 'Yesterday'.

The majority of these recordings were issued on the first album of the two-record set 'From Memphis To Vegas, From Vegas To Memphis'. 'All Shook Up' was the first song released from these performances, being taped at the evening performance on 22 August. This is a fine performance, with Presley's 'plummy' voice suiting the song, although this could be due to his nervousness. This is clearly the case in 'Are You Lonesome Tonight?'; but once he begins singing (after a hesitant spoken introduction) the magic of the performance overrides any tension. This is a good version of this classic number, and only the faintly hysterical backing singers detract, by being too closely balanced. 'Blue Suede Shoes' is disappointing. Presley seems uneasy, but James Burton's guitar work is outstanding. 'Can't Help Falling In Love' is better; a fine performance. 'Hound Dog' is a poor parody. It sounds as if the engineers have cut from an introduction (possibly 26 August) to a performance on another day (possibly 22 August). Presley's voice is too far back, and he is nervous. 'I Can't Stop Loving You' is good enough, but Presley sounds as if caught on an off night. The audience interruption at the end adds its own excitement. 'In The Ghetto' is reported to have been recorded immediately after 'I Can't Stop Loving You', but the result is superior. James Burton's guitar spins 'Johnnie B. Goode' into life, but this is from a batch of songs which place Presley's voice too distant in image. Presley's voice suited 'My Babe' very well. This dark song receives a formidable performance; and in the 'Mystery Train/Tiger Man' medley Presley is helped by the band, who are in good form.

'Runaway' was a major hit for Del Shannon in 1961, since when it has become a classic rock number. Presley had never performed it before. However much he may have admired the song, his voice is not at its best and his 'hammy' use of the microphone causes his voice to fade out at odd moments. The strain continues in 'Suspicious Minds'; this is faster than the earlier studio performance and may have been too high for

Presley at this time. It is also too long. The Bee Gees' number 'Words', which followed 'Suspicious Minds' in the show, is far better. It is slightly faster than the Bee Gees' version, and shows Presley receptive to influences; he gives a superb performance, free from strain and tension. Mention must be made of James Burton's astonishing guitar work, and fine backing musicianship from pianist Larry Muhoberac in Lennon and McCartney's 'Yesterday'. In the show Presley followed this with 'Hey Jude', but this was cut out before release.

16/19 February 1970. *Venue:* International Hotel, Las Vegas.
*Titles released:* 'Let It Be Me', 'Polk Salad Annie', 'Proud Mary', 'Release Me', 'See See Rider', 'Sweet Caroline', 'The Wonder Of You', 'Walk A Mile In My Shoes'.

Following the success of the August appearances, Presley returned in February for another series. The material released shows that RCA was anxious to find fresh numbers, although at the same time they recorded many songs Presley had done before. 'Let It Be Me' is a fine Gilbert Becaud song; it receives a hymn-like performance, with a massive sound backing. This is hardly hit material, but Presley clearly enjoyed it. 'Polk Salad Annie' is fabulous; Presley speaks over the 'till-ready' introduction, during which James Burton's guitar flicks malevolently until it catches fire. This is a marvellous song and it receives an hypnotic performance; there is more than a hint of James Brown's influence.

In 'Proud Mary', a hit the previous year for Creedence Clearwater Revival, Presley turns in a solid version, with fine backing from the band. This song shortly became a rock classic, and Presley included it in a number of shows. Three years before, Englebert Humperdinck's 'Release Me' first entered the British charts, to remain in the Top 50 for fifty-five consecutive weeks. This oozing melody is not well done by Presley. His voice sounds raw and his blues-tight shouting in the top register adds nothing to the cloying melody. 'See See Rider' became a favourite of Presley and he frequently included it in his live shows. It is a marvellous performance, full of power and dark strength, and the hard-driving guitar work from James Burton is fine. A studio performance probably would have enhanced 'Sweet Caroline'. This fine Neil Diamond song is well sung by Presley, but is too fast for the song to 'breathe' as it should. It preceded 'Release Me' in performance on 18 February; Presley's voice had probably not yet settled for the performance. 'The Wonder Of You' is outstanding. This is the only song released from the performance of 19 February and became a No. 1 hit for Presley in the summer of 1970. (In some charts it was Presley's first No. 1 hit in Britain for five years.) The strain in this case is appropriate, and the conviction and power of the performance are overwhelming. 'Walk A Mile In My Shoes' is unusual, not least in regard to the lyrics; but Presley gives a subtle performance. It is impossible not to be delighted by this example of popular music at its best.

4/8 June 1970. *Venue:* RCA Studios, Nashville.
*Titles recorded:* 'Bridge Over Troubled Water', 'Cindy, Cindy', 'Faded Love', 'Funny How Time Slips Away', 'Got My Mojo Working/Keep Your Hands Off', 'Heart Of Rome', 'How The Web Was Woven', 'I'll Never Know', 'I Really Don't Want to Know', 'I Was Born About 10,000 Years Ago', 'I Washed My Hands In Muddy Water', 'If I Were You', 'It Ain't No Big Thing', 'It's Your Baby, You Rock It', 'I've Lost You', 'Just Pretend', 'Life', 'Little Cabin On The Hill', 'Love Letters', 'Make The World Go Away', 'Mary In The Morning', 'Only Believe', 'Patch It Up', 'Sound Of Your Cry', 'Stranger In The Crowd', 'Sylvia', 'The Fool', 'The Next Step Is Love', 'There Goes My Everything', 'This Is Our Dance', 'Tomorrow Never Comes', 'Twenty Days and Twenty Nights', 'When I'm Over You', 'You Don't Have To Say You Love Me'.

This series of recordings is one of the most interesting of Presley's career because of the consistency of material and the quality of recording. For the first time in years people could hear Presley in a natural acoustic, singing material of remarkable range and sympathy.

'Bridge Over Troubled Water', the classic Simon and Garfunkel song, was released on the mainly live 'That's The Way It Is' album, when the final bars of a live version were spliced onto the studio recording to give the illusion of a live show. This fails on two counts: first the audience, had it been a live show, would not have refrained from applause once they realized what the song was; and secondly the sound-image changes suddenly on the last chord. It is impossible to believe that *two* pianos were used at the sessions — but there are two on the final tape, one on each channel. This would not matter much, were it not that they are neither in tune, nor in tempo. In spite of this meddling, Presley's outstanding *singing* is not disguised. This is a fabulous version, burning with sincerity and power, and finding depths in the song not revealed by the composers. It is a pity Presley's great version has been tampered with in this way.

'Cindy, Cindy' is worlds away; crude and lacking commitment. The heavy arrangement is notable in 'Faded Love', a standard country number. 'Funny How Time Slips Away' is different again. Singing without strain, Presley is the arch-stylist, at times stepping back to allow other musicians their day in the sun. 'Got My Mojo Working' is sensational; it is cut in after the song had begun, but whoever had the presence of mind to switch on the tape machine deserves a medal. Presley is enjoying himself to the hilt and urging the other musicians to do likewise. One hopes there are more tapes of this kind. Different again is 'Heart of Rome', almost Neapolitan, well done in every respect. However the song itself does not merit attention. The same applies to 'How The Web Was Woven', a medium-slow ballad, with a softly-insistent beat. Another change of material is found in 'I'll Never Know', a beautiful ballad which never manages to take flight, but which deserves to be better known.

'I Really Don't Want To Know' is another slow ballad, in waltz tempo. This is not as heavily arranged as some of the other songs. 'I Was Born About 10,000 Years Ago' was first cut into pieces and used as linking material for the 'Elvis Country' album. It was later issued *in toto*, and the result is a fine track — fast, brilliantly imagined, and full of delightful touches. The only drawback is the lyric, which is too parochial.

'I Washed My Hands In Muddy Water' has a similar feel; a toe-tapping number which Presley sings in great style. 'If I Were You' is good, commercial Nashville with acknowledged influences from the 1960s. Presley makes the most of less-than-compelling lyrics in 'It Ain't No Big Thing'. 'It's Your Baby, You Rock It' also falls into this category, with Presley adopting his 'Tom Jones' manner; and although 'I've Lost You' is a powerful ballad, its qualities are not best revealed here. This is strong stuff, but something of the tragedy is lost. The version recorded two months later in Las Vegas is better.

'Just Pretend' and 'Life' are similar: massive, slow and uninspired in both material and execution. These were recorded towards the end of the 6 June session; perhaps Presley was tired. 'Little Cabin On The Hill' is a happy country song, with brilliant harmonica work by Charlie McCoy. Presley gives an irresistible performance, which almost disguises the forgettable material. In 'Love Letters' Presey recorded a second version of the Ketty Lester hit which he recorded brilliantly in 1966. The first version, so good in every way, is eclipsed by the later take. Colonel Parker's earlier artist, Eddy Arnold, had a big hit in 1966 for RCA with 'Make The World Go Away', but Presley's version does not compare. Presley seems uninterested.

'Mary In The Morning' lacks subtlety. The song is over four minutes long and although parts are outstanding, the backing is over-done, shattering the fragile song. 'Only Believe' is a religious song of insufferable boredom, and 'Patch It Up' was better recorded later in August. Here the recording is badly balanced, reducing to inaudibility the efforts of many musicians, to ensure that the 'beat' comes through. 'Sound Of Your Cry' is an unusual ballad, which Presley sings particularly well, but the song alone could never have made it. 'Stranger In The Crowd' has a fast rhythm, masterfully built into a catchy beat. 'Sylvia' is not in the same class, although it has imaginative touches, including a string quartet. Presley is too far back to 'tell', and gets lost in the sound.

'The Fool' is strangely compelling; fast, with a bluesy feel, half-sung by Presley in a threatening moody manner. Charlie McCoy's harmonica is again worthy of note. 'The Next Step Is Love' is another fascinating track, the essence of Presley at his most 'laid-back'; everything is so casual it has almost a Perry Como influence. 'There Goes My Everything', a country waltz, was a big hit for Engelbert Humperdinck in 1967; but this recording repeated Presley's success as of March 1971 when his version entered the charts. So far as the United Kingdom was concerned, where it reached number six, it was again a hit. Presley's breath-control is amazing, as whole stretches are sung with one breath; and the recording quality too is fine. 'This Is Our Dance' is another fine song, and could prove a posthumous hit for Presley, should this masculine, gentle, romantic style become popular again. 'Tomorrow Never Comes' is another beautiful song, performed with sincerity and consistency of voice. The wide image of the recording is remarkable — the side-drum comes so far from the left that the player could be in the next studio! 'Twenty Days and Twenty Nights' is a slow ballad with strings and brass over-dubbed. Once more, the arrangement is impressive, as is Presley's performance; but the song lacks distinction.

'When I'm Over You' is weak; but 'You Don't Have To Say You Love Me' — the 1966 Dusty Springfield hit — is quite different. Although naturally beefier than Ms Springfield's treatment, Presley appears to have been subjected to phasing by the engineers, for his voice is sibilant and unnatural. A pity, for this is a very good performance.

13/15 August 1970. *Venue:* International Hotel, Las Vegas.

*Titles recorded:* 'Bridge Over Troubled Water' (not released), 'I Just Can't Help Believing', 'I've Lost You', 'Patch It Up', 'You've Lost That Loving Feeling'.

These recordings were used in the documentary film *That's The Way It Is,* and show Presley's genius as a live performer. 'Bridge Over Troubled Water' has not been issued; if it is anything like the other recordings, it must be outstanding. In 'I Just Can't Help Believing' Presley is enthralling: he is in good voice, relaxed yet powerful, and the orchestration is all that could be desired. In particular, his singing of the word 'girl' at the end of the first verse is almost unbelievable. In its way, this performance is a classic. So is 'I've Lost You', in which another fine performance of a haunting song is enhanced by marvellous orchestral backing. In particular, Ronnie Tutt's drumming and the fine piano of Glen Harding deserve mention, as well as the anonymous oboe player. 'Patch It Up' is in fast rocker style, enlivened by middle-register keyboard work and rhythmic clapping. This is a good song with plenty of drive, but it is not so fine a performance. It goes on too long, and the ending is inconclusive. With 'You've Lost That Loving Feeling' we have both the virtues and disadvantages of live recordings. This classic song, a double hit (in 1965 and 1969) for the Righteous Brothers, and for Cilla Black (in 1965), is staggeringly performed by Presley. Unfortunately the audience recognize the song (and then applaud their recognition) eight bars after it has begun. The atmosphere, carefully built up and magically created, is completely broken. This is a pity for the orchestration is fabulous — expecially low pedal Ds on trombones; but later Presley lowers the temperature by half singing, 'I'd get down on my knees for you — if this suit was not too tight!'

22 September 1970. *Venue:* RCA Studios, Nashville.
*Titles recorded:* 'Rags to Riches', 'Snowbird', 'Where Did They Go, Lord', 'Whole Lotta Shakin' Goin' On'.

For some reason 'Rags to Riches' has only been issued in mono on LP — surely it was recorded in stereo? However, the single version in mono was a hit for Presley in 1971, but lacks a definite Presley image. It is a slow ballad, suitably beefy, but not one of Presley's best. 'Snowbird' is well arranged and recorded, and sung in fine country style. 'Where Did They Go, Lord?' has a sombre opening to its dark, prayerful character, abetted by sudden flashes from the guitar.

The fine rocker, 'Whole Lotta Shakin' Goin' On', is updated by fluent drumming — *not* accenting the off-beat — and the constant pulse of the bass. Sam Phillips would have approved. This is enhanced by Charlie McCoy's organ-playing, which dates it somewhat; but the result is so infectious, so exhilarating, that criticism is silenced.

15 March 1971. *Venue:* RCA Studios, Nashville.
*Titles recorded:* 'Amazing Grace', 'Early Morning Rain', 'For Loving Me', 'The First Time Ever I Saw Your Face'.

These sessions should have been longer, but after one day Presley contracted an eye infection, and the remaining sessions were cancelled. This is a pity, for these four titles are excellent, and the following sessions could have developed into a first-class collection of material.

'Amazing Grace' was one of the remarkable successes of the early 1970s. Earlier in the year Judy Collins had a major international hit with the traditional lament, and the following year the Band of The

Royal Scots Dragoon Guards repeated the success, eclipsing Miss Collins. At the same time, her version was re-issued and succeeded in becoming another hit the second time around, only fifteen months after it had first entered the charts. It is one of the great melodies, and it was natural that Presley should be attracted by it. It was probably the Judy Collins version which led Presley to include female voices, but the result is not an entire success, for they obtrude too much. It would have been better had he sung it in an uncluttered arrangement. 'Early Morning Rain' is by Gordon Lightfoot; this begins with fine acoustic guitar and receives a marvellous performance from Presley. It is warm and intimate capturing exactly the spirit of the song. It is enhanced by excellent harmonica work by Charlie McCoy, and is a classic performance, 'For Loving Me' is another delicious performance; it is beautifully recorded, with Presley in full command. This is Nashville at its best, a wholly musical realization of the song. McCoy's harmonica and James Burton's guitar give additional lustre to Presley's performance.

'The First Time Ever I Saw Your Face' became a big hit for Roberta Flack the following year. This is a song which everyone admires and many singers perform, yet which was not a hit when it first appeared. It is surprising that Presley's was not the hit single. But it was the first song recorded, and the result is stiff and inflexible. The song needs a fluent, plastic performance and its best qualities are not apparent here.

15/21 May 1971. *Venue:* RCA Studios, Nashville.

*Titles recorded:* 'An Evening Prayer', 'A Thing Called Love', 'Don't Think Twice, It's All Right', 'Fools Rush In', 'He Touched Me', 'Help Me Make It Through The Night', 'Holly Leaves And Christmas Trees', 'If I Get Home On Christmas Day', 'I'll Be Home On Christmas Day', 'I'll Take You Home Again, Kathleen', 'I'm Leavin'', 'It's Only Love', 'It's Still Here', 'It Won't Seem Like Christmas', 'I've Got Confidence', 'I Will Be True', 'Lead Me, Guide Me', 'Love Me, Love The Life I Lead', 'Merry Christmas Baby', 'Miracle Of The Rosary', 'O Come, All Ye Faithful', 'On A Snowy Christmas Night', 'Padre', 'Seeing Is Believing', 'Silver Bells', 'The First Noel', 'The Wonderful World Of Christmas', 'Until It's Time For You To Go', 'We Can Make The Morning', 'Winter Wonderland'.

This major recording session, during which no less than thirty titles were recorded, made a welcome return to the studio for Presley. A glance at the titles will show that one of the ideas behind the sessions was to put together a new Christmas album; but the first song 'An Evening Prayer' was released the following year as part of a sacred album 'He Touched Me'. We have noted before that Presley's performances of religious

Elvis with his parents 1937

*Previous page.*
The Young Singer c. 1956

Aged 11

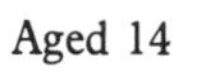

Aged 14

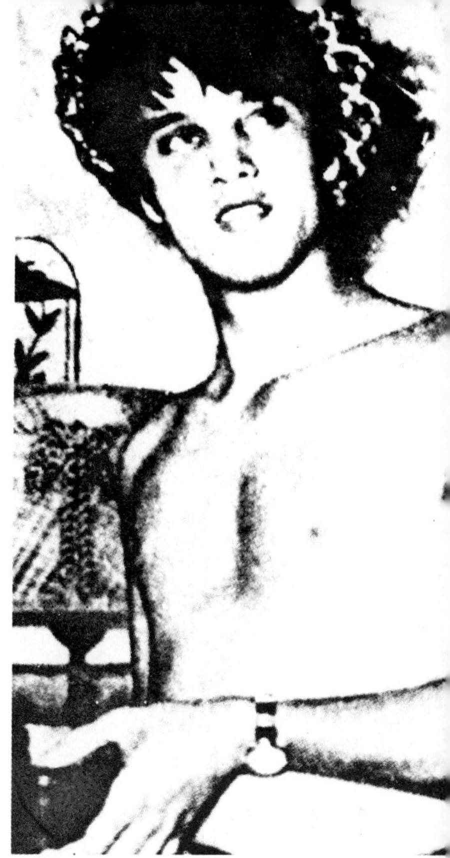

Aged 15

Aged 16 in High School Cadet Uniform

With his parents c. 1956

An early shot on stage

A *real* Hound Dog! 1956

An early publicity shot 1956

In his first film *Love Me Tender* 1956

With Wendell Corey in *Loving You* 1957

An unusual still from *Jailhouse Rock* 1957

On the set of *G.I. Blues* 1960

A publicity shot from *Kissin' Cousins* 1963

For the fans! 1967

Wedding Picture May 1, 1967

From *The Trouble With Girls* 1969

After the return 1970

A studio shot 1970

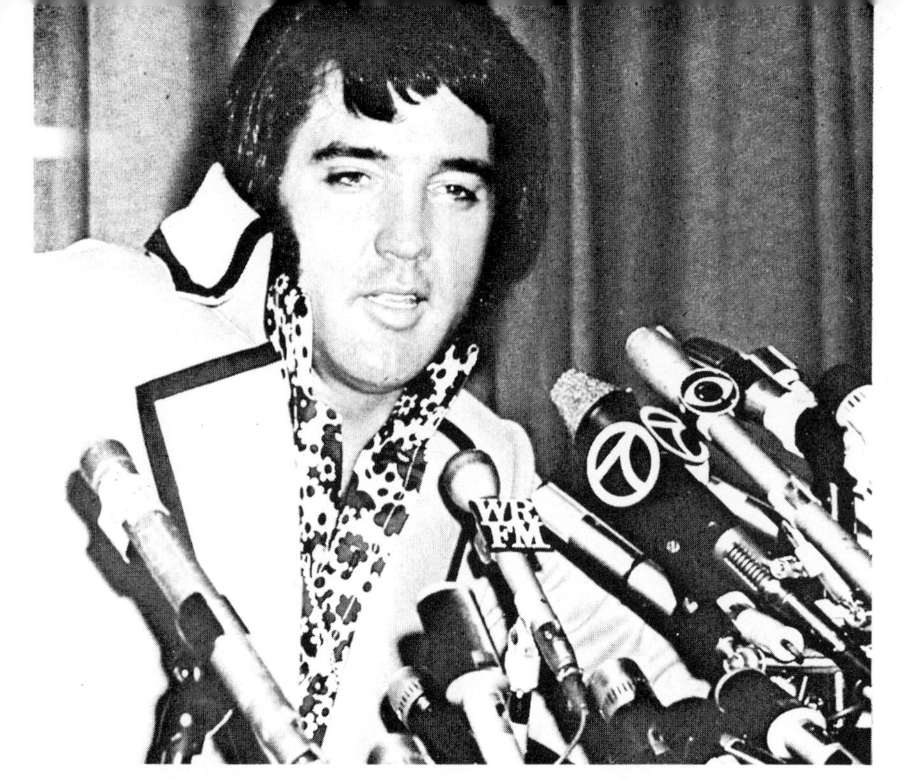


Press Conference 1971

A fine action shot from the later years c. 1974

With J. D. Sumner and The Stamps

On Stage

songs are marked by a deep and genuine sincerity, and 'An Evening Prayer' is no exception. Every word is crystal clear, and the performance is very moving, especially the concluding 'Amen'.

'A Thing Called Love' is a curious mixture of country material, above a walking bass, married to a Christmas-cake arrangement; the result is unsuccessful. Towards the end of the session on 16 May Presley put down a version of Dylan's 'Don't Think Twice, It's All Right', which lasts over eight minutes. For release it was cut to less than three minutes. When one considers the quality of some of the other songs at these sessions (especially 'Merry Christmas Baby') it is to be hoped that the complete take of 'Don't Think Twice, It's All Right' will eventually be released. As it happens, the engineers have done their best. As the song suddenly fades in, the listener is catapulted into the fluid world of the session. As well as Presley's fabulous singing, James Burton's superb guitar work should be mentioned. One must hope the complete take will appear sometime. 'Fools Rush In', the Johnny Mercer number, does not show Presley at his best, but it was possibly included with an eye to the Las Vegas market. It is slick, clean, but antiseptic. 'He Touched Me', the title track of the religious album, had doubtless been in Presley's mind for a long time. It is the kind of hymn he had known from his youth, and the performance is effective and moving. In 'Help Me Make It Through The Night', the classic song by Kris Kristofferson, Presley commits a rare error of judgement. The song, which is a cry for help, is sung by Presley in a beefy way which destroys the fragile melody-line.

'Holly Leaves And Christmas Trees' is feeble, as is 'If I Get Home On Christmas Day'. Presley seems uninterested, his lack of power in his top register is as if he could not be bothered. The similarly titled 'I'll Be Home On Christmas Day' is different. It is 'bluesy', and Presley forces his voice, to produce a sense of strain. The song is interesting and receives a more committed performance. 'I'll Take You Home Again, Kathleen' is fascinating, for this traditional song was originally recorded with Presley accompanying himself on the piano, the other instruments being over-dubbed. As Presley's piano playing here is uninteresting the procedure is justified.

'I'm Leavin'' is a remarkable performance of an unusual song. The title was in tune with the times and his performance is startling. Presley changes the quality of his voice to emphasize the despairing nature of the lyrics. This performance deserves to be better known. 'It's Only Love' is an attempt to produce a commercial number in the current style, but it fails. The material is not good enough, and Presley is unwilling to drive the song along. It is however a fascinating performance. 'It's Still Here' is another song accompanied by Presley on the piano. Presley here reveals himself a stylish and talented pianist, far from the chord-strumming which passes as piano-playing by some performers. It is a simple song, sensitively performed and the odd fluff in ensemble enhances its appeal. In 'It Won't Seem Like Christmas' we return to Yuletide material. Presley performs this 3/4 country song in a simple manner, making extensive use of his natural vibrato. 'I've Got Confidence' is in revival/gospel style. It ends as it begins to get going, and is not the success it could have been. 'I Will Be True' is the third number with Presley on piano, but the song lacks distinction. 'Lead Me, Guide Me' is more convincing, though the arrangement is so basic it can only be regarded as an album track. 'Love Me, Love The Life I Lead' is a number Presley might have heard Tom Jones sing, and its slow medium tempo gives full opportunity for Presley's powerfully straining emotion.

In 'Merry Christmas Baby' we encounter not only the finest recorded performance of these seven days but one of the greatest Presley performances committed to disc. It is a Blues, and once again his natural feel for this difficult medium is apparent. The Blues is a simple harmonic structure. This simplicity means almost any singer can *sing,* but only a handful can *perform,* the Blues. It is clear that Presley was one of this handful. It is a tragedy he never recorded a Blues album.

'Miracle Of The Rosary' is doubtless sincere, but it is the sort of religious song which would turn many people into atheists. It is in poor taste, and Presley sounds ill at ease. 'O Come, All Ye Faithful' is a beautiful performance, carefully arranged by Presley himself. The first verse is almost Lutheran in its four-part harmony, almost entirely unaccompanied; and in the second verse (with female descant) the cumulative effect is remarkable. The same cannot be said of 'On A Snowy Christmas Night' a slowish mediocre ballad, and 'Padre' also lacks distinction. 'Seeing Is Believing' is unusual: it is a driving rocker, but has a fervent religious message and the rhythm is so irresistible it could have become a major hit. 'Silver Bells', in contrast, did not even deserve to be recorded. 'The First Noel' is too high for Presley's voice. This forces him to strain which he attempts to disguise by exaggerating words, with the result that a simple carol is made unusually heavy (in the worst sense). 'The Wonderful World Of Christmas' is another uninteresting song but it is well-performed. 'Until It's Time For You To Go' became a classic hit for Presley and this performance is one of his best. He infuses each word with an added meaning.

'We Can Make The Morning', a straightforward ballad, is badly recorded, with Presley out of focus and uncertain. The final song, 'Winter Wonderland', has a baritone quality, but Presley is too heavy for this simple material.

8/9 June 1971. *Venue:* RCA Studios, Nashville.

*Titles recorded:* 'Bosom Of Abraham', 'He Is My Everything', 'I, John', 'Put Your Hand In The Hand', 'Reach Out To Jesus', 'There Is No God But God',

This session completed those begun the previous month. Two titles were recorded, 'I'll Be Home On Christmas Day' and 'Until It's Time For You To Go', in an attempt to improve on the May takes, but were not considered good enough to release. In the event, the earlier takes were issued. 'Bosom Of Abraham' was a disaster. It is ludicrously short — ninety seconds. Furthermore, when the song was released at Easter 1972 it was cut and pressed at $33\frac{1}{3}$ rpm, although labelled 45! It never stood a chance. 'He Is My Everything' marries new lyrics to the earlier double-hit tune, 'There Goes My Everything'. 'I, John' is a fast gospel number, with rousing female vocals. Presley sings with conviction, and the result is one of the best numbers in this style from him for some time. A revival feel is also prevalent in 'Put Your Hand In The Hand', a fine performance tingling with life.

'Reach Out to Jesus', and 'There Is No God But God' are both insistent religious numbers. The first rises to a *blitzkrieg* finish, but the second is more straightforward — even simple. Neither shows Presley at his greatest, but his sincerity is not in doubt.

16/17 February 1972. *Venue:* Hilton Hotel, Las Vegas.

*Titles issued:* 'American Trilogy', 'It's Impossible'.

This version of 'American Trilogy', one of at least four Presley recordings, was used for his single release. It is a fine performance of this successful fusion of three great songs 'I Wish I Were In Dixie', 'The Battle Hymn Of The Republic', and 'All My Trials'. It is done with tremendous conviction by Presley, and the single became a big hit for him in the U.K. in July 1972. 'It's Impossible', the surprising Perry Como hit of 1971 (his first for many years), is well performed, but the live recording suffers from poor backing sound. Other songs were recorded during Presley's shows at the Las Vegas Hilton, but are duplicated by alternative versions.

27/29 March 1972. *Venue:* RCA Studios, Nashville.

*Titles recorded:* 'Always On My Mind', 'Burning Love', 'Fool', 'It's A Matter Of Time', 'Separate Ways', 'Where Do I Go From Here?'.

Generally a fine collection of songs. 'Always On My Mind' is well sung, with an appeal which suits this excellent song, but it is eclipsed by 'Burning Love'. This superb rocker is sung in tremendous style, powerful and rich. There is magnificent drumming from Ronnie Tutt. Neither 'Fool' nor 'It's A Matter of Time' are in the same class, good as they are, especially 'Fool', where the arrangement is intriguing. 'Separate Ways' possibly reflects the state of Presley's marriage at this time, for he sings it with brooding sadness; but the arrangement is poor. 'Where Do I Go From Here?' is a fine performance of a mediocre song, with Ronnie Tutt saving the day instrumentally.

10 June 1972. *Venue:* Madison Square Garden, New York.
*Titles recorded:* 'All Shook Up', 'Also Sprach Zarathustra', 'American Trilogy', 'Can't Help Fallin' In Love', 'For The Good Times', 'Funny How Time Slips Away', 'Heartbreak Hotel', 'Hound Dog', 'I Can't Stop Loving You', 'Love Me', 'Love Me Tender', 'Never Been To Spain', 'Polk Salad Annie', 'Proud Mary', 'Suspicious Minds', 'Teddy Bear'/'Don't Be Cruel', 'That's All Right', 'The Impossible Dream', 'You Don't Have To Say You Love Me', 'You've Lost That Loving Feeling',

These recordings were possibly made as a trial for the project which was to take place the following January in Hawaii and were issued on one album, 'Elvis As Recorded At Madison Square Garden'. When confronted with a number of similar live recordings it is not always useful to compare them. The different situations during each live performance mean that the individual gig is only a record of that particular time and place.

Although the titles are listed alphabetically above, they will be discussed in the order in which they appear. Apart from being a live performance, there seems no point for Presley to have re-recorded old material.

The album is not one of Presley's most memorable. With many of these titles, Presley made his reputation in studio recordings which became classics. With the problems of live recordings, there was no musical reason for this album and in no instance is the performance as good as the best of Presley's earlier versions.

As the album begins, the sound is harsh and constricted; but Presley is in excellent voice in 'That's All Right'. 'Proud Mary' is ragged at first and Presley is indistinct. 'Never Been To Spain' receives an outstanding performance. The Dusty Springfield hit 'You Don't Have To Say You Love Me' is straightforward, but over-powering. This segues into 'You've Lost That Loving Feeling' which receives a scrappy introduction from Presley. The voices overload the high frequencies, and although this is not flawless (Presley repeats the 'suit too tight' gag) it still exerts a tremendous feeling of passion. Feed-back tends to trouble 'Polk Salad Annie' intermittently, and the old songs which end Side 1 are variable. 'Love Me' is a simple performance, but 'All Shook Up', driven by superb drumming from Ronnie Tutt, is very fast. 'Heartbreak Hotel' lacks the quality of the original, and the final three, 'Teddy Bear'/'Don't Be Cruel' and 'Love Me Tender' are good, but add nothing to what we already have.

Side 2 begins with 'The Impossible Dream'. This would have benefited from a studio recording, for Presley is not well-balanced, and he takes time to get into his stride. There are also mistakes, which annoy on repetition. Presley gets a good top A at the end, but this is not one of his best. 'Hound Dog' begins humorously, and then we hear a very different version from the classic recording of 1956. The vocal line is completely altered, with funky flicks from James Burton's lead guitar, before the 'real' 'Hound Dog' returns. An unusual performance — but not to be taken seriously. 'Suspicious Minds' is not a good performance, but it gets better. 'For The Good Times' makes up for this: this is a performance without gimmicks. 'American Trilogy', is unfortunately, not serious enough. It begins as a send-up, but the cumulative power is overwhelming. 'Funny How Time Slips Away' is a throw-away performance until the final joke ending. Presley's now familiar closing numbers 'I Can't Stop Loving You' and 'Can't Help Fallin' In Love' are good enough, but, like the songs that ended Side 1, do not tell us anything new about the songs or the singer.

14 January 1973. *Venue:* Honolulu International Centre Arena, Hawaii.
*Titles recorded:* 'Big Hunk O'Love', 'Also Sprach Zarathustra', 'American Trilogy', 'Blue Hawaii', 'Blue Suede Shoes', 'Burning Love', 'Can't Help Falling In Love', 'Early Morning Rain' (not released), 'Fever', 'Hawaiian Wedding Song' (not released), 'Hound Dog', 'I Can't Stop Loving You', 'I'll Remember You', 'I'm So Lonesome I Could Cry', 'It's Over', 'Johnny B. Goode', 'Ku-U-I-Po' (not released), 'Long Tall Sally', 'Whole Lotta Shakin' Goin' On', 'Love Me', 'My Way', 'No More' (not released), 'See See Rider', 'Something', 'Steamroller Blues', 'Suspicious Minds', 'What Now My Love', 'You Gave Me A Mountain', 'Welcome To My World',

This session, recorded live in Hawaii, was a satellite show, beamed directly throughout the world. Within a few days a double album was released in JVC's CD-4 quadrophonic system, which became the first million-selling quadraphonic record. The songs are discussed in the order in which they appear on the album.

The show begins with the ubiquitous 'Also Sprach Zarathustra', the opening fanfare from Richard Strauss's symphonic poem of 1896, based on Friedrich Nietzsche's lengthy poem. This had been used by Stanley Kubrick for his film *2001* (1969) since when it became the standard opening for almost every rock act in existence. The arrangement used here does not feature Presley, but the use of voices is effective. When

Presley bursts on stage, the quadraphonic recording gives unbelievable realism and impact, the stereo mix being insignificant in comparison. Presley begins in great style, powerful but relaxed, and the band is brilliant. The drumming is magnificent, and the trumpets blaze through like a burst of sunlight. Presley's voice, however, lacks the last ounce of total command. In 'Burning Love', which follows, Ronnie Tutt's solid drumming dominates the music. Presley rides the song and it is almost impossible to keep still while listening to this performance. As with all great rock bands, the band fractionally anticipates the beat. The George Harrison number 'Something' is finely sung, but the arrangement is too fussy for the first part of the song. This tends to affect Presley's performance, which is not outstanding. The next song, 'You Gave Me A Mountain', receives a performance of consummate power. It is impossible to overpraise either the orchestra or the piano-playing of Glen Harding. 'Steamroller Blues' is very much in Presley's blood, but although he receives a fine accompaniment, it is too fast. For safety's sake, the previous day's rehearsal was also recorded. It would be interesting to compare this with the version recorded the previous day. Showing his breadth of repertoire, Presley tackles the Sinatra hit of 1969 'My Way', and gives a performance certainly the equal of Sinatra's. Presley is in superb voice, and produces a thrilling top G, unforced, yet full of power right at the end. Mention must also be made of the beautiful solo violin in the second verse. Both 'Love Me' and 'Johnny B. Goode' show an understandable drop in voltage: the first is relaxed, and the second casual. But by any standards, especially with the fine harmony singing and magnificent guitar, these are excellent performances. In 'It's Over' (not the Roy Orbison song), the only performance Presley recorded of this, one can hear him turn from the microphone early on. It is too relaxed, but there is another fine top G here, too. 'Blue Suede Shoes', which Presley first recorded seventeen years, before, is something of a self-parody, and in 'I'm So Lonesome I Could Cry' his voice lacks the finest sustained quality. It is a beautiful song, which would have benefited from a studio recording. 'I Can't Stop Loving You' is not to be compared to the 1969 Las Vegas version. What is noteworthy is the superb drumming, guitar and brass work. In 'Hound Dog', and 'Blue Suede Shoes', Presley mumbles words for effect – not for their musical impact.

The Gilbert Becaud song 'What Now My Love?' was a big hit for Shirley Bassey in 1962. This is the only recording by Presley of this fine number. He sings the first verse with great strength, but does not begin the second verse so well. The performance has a committed quality, but there are rough edges which would have been ironed out in a studio, although it is unlikely the fine ending would have been captured so well.

If the last few songs show a falling away from the performances at the beginning of the show, 'Fever' is a superb performance. Although Presley had recorded it before, this is hypnotic, and there is an imaginative use of quadraphonic sound, as the tenor drums flick across the rear images behind the listener. 'Welcome To My World' is another one-time only recording. Presley continues in fine voice, and the sole drawback is the eruption from the audience when they eventually recognize the song. 'Suspicious Minds' shows Presley at full stretch. The sudden drop to half-speed, and the return to the *first* tempo is electrifying. 'I'll Remember You' continues this high standard. The gentle tempo (with a nice use of flutes in the orchestra) is beautifully phrased. The mixture of 'Long Tall Sally'/'Whole Lotta Shakin' Goin' On' has an infectious drive, and is better than the earlier 'reminiscence' of Presley's old rocking days. In 'American Trilogy' Presley is superb, and his final top A thoroughly deserves the ovation. In 'A Big Hunk O'Love' the driving rocker is a classic performance, with Glen Harding's thrilling pianism. After this 'Can't Help Falling In Love' is a disappointment: words are either incoherent or missed out, and Presley is breathless. By this time it did not matter, for he had achieved the most extraordinary live recording of his career, and convincingly showed that he was still the undisputed master of popular music.

21/25 July 1973. *Venue:* Stax Studios, Memphis.
*Titles recorded:* 'Find Out What's Happening', 'For Old Times' Sake', 'Girl Of Mine', 'If You Don't Come Back', 'I've Got A Thing About You Baby', 'Just A Little Bit', 'Raised On Rock', 'Take Good Care Of Her', 'Three Corn Patches'.

These were Presley's first studio recordings for sixteen months, and the first he had made at Stax. During the 1960s the Stax sound had been distinctive and influential, with a string of hits from such artists as William Bell, Judy Clay, and Booker T. and the M.G.s. Presley's last studio recording in Memphis was in February 1969, at the American Studios, but by 1973 they had closed their Memphis branch. 'Find Out What's Happening' is a good number, fast and bouncy and featuring a tight blend of female voices with Presley's fine vocal quality. Once again, we must mention James Burton's guitar as well as Bobby Emmons's excellent organ work. 'For Old Times' Sake' is a sentimental ballad, not out of the top drawer. Nor is Presley at his best.

Although the sessions were spread over five days, for the last two the personnel of the band was changed considerably, owing to previous commitments. This meant that Presley then had to work with unfamiliar musicians and it became clear on July 24 that the ensemble was not proving successful. Elvis left the studios to allow the musicians to lay down tracks for him to over-dub later. While this is by no means unusual in pop sessions, it was almost unheard-of for Presley. The only song completed in this way, 'Girl Of Mine', shows up this patchwork splicing. There is stiffness in the performance. 'If You Don't Come Back' is a superb 'dark' soul song by Lieber and Stoller. It has a wild choir in the right distance, and receives a splendid performance, full of thick undertones and smouldering power, although the guitar solo at the end lets it down. 'I've Got A Thing About You Baby' shows the influence of the Stax Studios. This unpretentious song gets a suitably gentle performance. At first, it appears ordinary, but soon the magic begins to work. 'Just A Little Bit' is a faster number. This is another superb performance by Presley, with tight drumming from both Jerry Carrigan and Ronnie Tutt. The Stax influence is also noticeable in 'Raised On Rock': the bass-line, brilliantly played by Tommy Cogbill, is worthy of special mention. The first three days recordings were superior to those done later, but the pianist Bobby Wood played throughout the five days. He begins 'Take Good Care Of Her', on which strings (or possibly synthesizer) were over-dubbed. Kathy Westmoreland sings a later verse well. Finally, 'Three Corn Patches' returns to rock'n'roll, but in a curious way this song sums up these sessions. Presley seems in two minds and several voices throughout this number — from the hesitant opening to the raunchy middle section. But whereas in the best songs he was able to mould this variety into one experience, here he fails. One must mention the dynamic chunky and boppy rock piano playing of Bobby Wood on this track.

This session is one of the most interesting Presley had undertaken for years, but the results are ultimately disappointing. First, the change in personnel was a serious mistake, but this did not affect the eight previously-recorded songs. The material is variable, but contains enough good songs to have been successful; and the musicians (of the first three days) could hardly be improved upon. However, this was the first time they had recorded in these studios. By the early 1970s, the importance of the sound engineer in rock music had grown enormously. Many rock musicians will testify that much of their success is due to the skill in balance and acoustic of those responsible for capturing the music on tape. In no way were the Stax Studios inferior — they had proved their merit by the important hits produced there. The problem for Presley was that they were the wrong type of studios. Used to producing the distinctive 'Stax' sound, the constricting effects of their methods of sound production have given these recordings a feeling that 'something' is missing. What was missing was the relaxed atmosphere which Presley needed to produce his best work.

24 September 1973. *Venue:* Elvis Presley's home, Palm Springs, Los Angeles.
*Titles recorded:* 'Are You Sincere?', 'I Miss You', 'Sweet Angeline'.

The intention at these sessions, the first at one of Presley's homes, was to salvage something from the abortive last two days at Stax the previous July. At his home in Palm Springs, 'Sweet Angeline' was resurrected for vocal over-dubbing. Presley and the other singers decided to record two other songs as well. 'Are You Sincere?' and 'I Miss You' are both slow ballads — but uninspired. They do not deserve commercial release, although they are well enough done. 'Sweet Angeline' is another slow ballad. It has parts of considerable interest and beauty, and given the circumstances can be counted a success. But the flaws noted in the original Stax sessions are still apparent, and the song fails to catch fire.

10/16 December 1973. *Venue:* Stax Studio, Memphis.
*Titles recorded:* 'Good Time Charlie's Got The Blues', 'Help Me', 'I Got A Feeling In My Body', 'If That Isn't Love', 'If You Talk In Your Sleep', 'It's Midnight', 'Love Song Of The Year', 'Loving Arms', 'Mr Song Man', 'My Boy', 'Promised Land', 'She Wears My Ring', 'Spanish Eyes', 'Talk About The Good Times', 'There's A Honky-Tonk Angel', 'Thinking About You', 'You Asked Me To', 'Your Love's Been A Long Time Coming'.

This was the second series of sessions recorded at Stax Studios in Memphis, and this time a smaller band played throughout the seven days. The varied material contains some remarkable performances. The problems with the Stax sound appear to have been overcome, perhaps by the use of a smaller band. In 'Good Time Charlie's Got The Blues' additional instruments were over-dubbed. This is an unusual song; it is a slow, blues-influenced number, without being a blues. Presley sings this very well, with a sensitive and restrained feel, and is helped by fine vocal backing work from J. D. Sumner and The Stamps. But the character of this number only reveals itself after several hearings. 'Help Me' is again enhanced by the male backing group, and this religious medium up-tempo song shows Presley's ability to blend with harmony singers.

'I Got A Feeling In My Body' has a distinctive Stax sound. Presley's voice is placed in the rear middle image. It has a strange quality, and the use of echo also detracts. In spite of all this, the performance is urgently infectious, and the result an unusual example of Presley being 'produced' to great effect. His repeated 'I-got-a, I-got-a, I-got-a' is sensational. 'If That Isn't Love' is a slow waltz, with a honky-tonk piano wandering in and out. There is more than a hint of Tom Jones in this performance, but Presley suffers from production drawbacks. 'If You Talk In Your Sleep', a song partly written by Red West, is a tremendous recording. It begins arrestingly, full of menace and flickering speed; and the orchestral arrangement is startingly good. Occasionally the interest passes from Presley to the orchestra. But there is no doubt who is in charge, and this little-known number has to be counted one of Presley's greatest recordings of this period. A fine orchestral arrangement also appears on 'It's Midnight', but this is very different. From the humid opening, with a gentle acoustic guitar, harmonica and a soft yet solid bass, the song builds dramatically. This is a serious song, and Presley's performance is full of foreboding and horror. This constitutes another remarkable performance which can plunge the listener into depression.

In 'Love Song Of The Year' solo violin and piano trace a delicate embroidery around Presley, but the overall effect is not of the best. The Stax sound is again in evidence in 'Loving Arms' which begins in slow moody fashion. Presley is relaxed in 'Mr Song Man' but the drawback is the song. 'My Boy' proved a major hit in Britain; it is a sentimental ballad, similar in message to Tammy Wynette's D.I.V.O.R.C.E. but more dramatic. Presley is well suited to this strong meat and surely his divorce two months before added poignancy to the lyrics. The Chuck Berry number 'Promised Land' blows away the gloom with its fast burning power. As in 'I Got A Feeling In My Body', 'Promised Land' Presley sounds constricted, but the effect is appropriate and the tight performance is good. In 'She Wears My Ring' Presley revives a Solomon King hit of six years before. This is a simple and effective song but demands a clear, unfettered sound, and the echo distorts Presley's natural voice.

In 1973 Capital Records re-issued the Al Martino song 'Spanish Eyes', which became a major hit. Presley revives it here, but although his performance is professional, and the recording good, the result hardly justifies the effort. Presley counts into 'Talk About The Good Times', a fun revival number with box-piano; the backing of Voice is a great asset.

In spite of the outrageous title and the church organ introduction, 'There's A Honky-Tonk Angel' is another astonishing performance from Presley. The song is surprisingly good. In slow-waltz tempo, the words have personal significance for Presley, who turns in a very moving performance. 'Thinking About You' is equally good, but is more obviously a pop song, a medium-tempo number with a fluent bass line. The arrangement is good, and it is clearly recorded. Presley is in excellent voice but the performance lacks the involvement which is a feature of the best of these sessions. 'You Asked Me To' begins like 'The Jimmy Brown Song': it is a simple arrangement, sung in straightforward style. The fine guitar work towards the end is possibly by Johnny

Christopher. The final song 'Your Love's Been A Long Time Coming' is best forgotten — a slow number without distinction.

20 March 1974. *Venue:* Midsouth Coliseum, Memphis.

*Titles recorded and released:* (in order on album) 'See See Rider', 'I Got A Woman', 'Love Me', 'Trying To Get To You', 'Long Tall Sally', 'Whole Lotta Shakin' Goin' On', 'Mama Don't Dance', 'Flip, Flop and Fly', 'Jailhouse Rock', 'Hound Dog', 'Why Me Lord', 'How Great Thou Art', 'American Trilogy', 'Let Me Be There', 'My Baby Left Me', 'Lawdy, Miss Clawdy', 'Can't Help Falling In Love'.

This album is the most superfluous of Presley's career. Every title had been recorded by him at least once before, in performances which are invariably better. Those here are often below Presley's best, the band is not 'tight', many words are slurred, with scant regard for sense or atmosphere, and the audience constantly interrupts. The performances say nothing new. As if this was not bad enough, the record is packaged with the most inept sleeve in a succession of generally mediocre packagings. The sales for this album, by all accounts, flopped badly, and caused — perhaps for the first time — some hard thinking concerning the wisdom of churning out similar 'live' albums by Presley.

# 11 The Final Years 1975-7

9/12 March 1975. *Venue:* RCA Studios, Hollywood.

*Titles recorded:* 'And I Love You So', 'Bringin' It Back', 'Fairytale', 'Green Green Grass Of Home', 'I Can Help', 'Pieces Of My Life', 'Shake A Hand', 'Susan When She Tried', 'T-R-O-U-B-L-E', 'Woman Without Love'.

This session was Presley's first studio visit for sixteen months. Following the failure of the 'Live in Memphis' album, new material, recorded under the best conditions, was becoming urgently needed. The result was good, but only after substantial overdubbing in Nashville. With one or two exceptions, Presley seemed content to record songs which had already been hits for other singers. While this may be interesting, musically it did nothing for his career.

'And I Love You So', the Don Maclean song, was a hit on RCA for Perry Como in 1973. Presley's performance is not outstanding. 'Bringin' It Back' is even less memorable. The same is true of 'Fairytale', a good example of Nashville in the 1970s — although much of it was done in Hollywood! With 'Green, Green Grass Of Home', Presley revived a smash hit for Tom Jones, released in 1966. Presley's performance is tremendous, but adds nothing to what Jones did with it. However, with Billy Swan's 'I Can Help', Presley seems out of touch. The song was a hit for Swan in 1974, but Presley's hectoring style is completely out of place. The electric piano and guitar are obtrusive. 'Pieces Of My Life' is a superlative performance: Presley is right in tune, and every word is clear and given its due. 'Shake A Hand' is very slow, in old rocker style, updated by modern recording. This is a fine performance, showing that Presley had no peer in songs of this type. The quality of the musicians is remarkable, but the song which they try to bring to life remains rooted to the spot.

'Susan When She Tried' is excellent; this toe-tapping number was a hit for the Statler Brothers in the U.S.A. It is enhanced here by fabulous guitar work, but driving the song, over Ronnie Tutt's solid drumming, is Presley's voice. 'T-R-O-U-B-L-E' is also outstanding. This is a fine rocker, with Presley urging it along with terrific verve. The piano (either Glen Hardin or David Briggs) is fabulous, and the only criticism is the restricted sound image — it should have been spread wider. Finally, 'Woman Without Love' is a good performance of a nondescript song.

2/8 February 1976. *Venue:* Graceland, Memphis.

*Titles recorded:* 'Bitter They Are, Harder They Fall', 'Blue Eyes Cry In The Rain', 'Danny Boy', 'For The Heart', 'Hurt', 'I'll Never Fall In Love Again', 'Love Comin' Down', 'Moody Blue', 'Never Again', 'She Thinks I Still Care', 'Solitaire', 'The Last Farewell'.

These sessions were the first to be held at Graceland. It is unclear why it was necessary to move engineers and equipment to Presley's home, but whatever the reason, these recordings (like most of his work at the time) were extensively over-dubbed, with variable results. The material lacks contrast, and it is impossible to avoid the feeling that this is a morbid collection, possibly affected by Presley's spells in hospital the previous year, and his father's heart attack a few months before.

The first song, 'Bitter They Are, Harder They Fall', is a slow, dramatic ballad, which receives a deeply-moving performance. This song will never become popular, but it could hardly be better performed. It is clear that Presley's divorce affected his singing. In 'Blue Eyes Cry In The Rain' Presley was possibly experimenting with different recording techniques. The song is no great stakes, being a slow ballad.

'Danny Boy' is quite different. This famous setting of the 'Londonderry Air' inspires Presley to one of his finest performances. He begins alone, to be joined by solo piano (Glen Hardin), and later by J. D. Sumner and The Stamps, to produce a sincere and restrained recording. 'For The Heart' is one of the few fast numbers in this session. In style it is typical of the mid-1970s, having a solid beat and a piano trying to update Floyd Cramer. This, plus the powerful instrumental backing and the optimistic nature of the song, makes a welcome change. Presley's singing was consistent at these sessions, and in 'Hurt' his voice is heard at its most startling. But the song is dated, and the accompaniment crude. This is not true of 'I'll Never Fall In Love Again', which was a major hit for Tom Jones. The influence of the Welsh singer is obvious. Occasionally Presley's voice falters as though overcome by emotion. This is great singing, and the effect is shattering. 'Love Comin' Down' is another slow ballad. But although Presley sings this well enough, the song lacks distinction.

In 'Moody Blue', we hear a fine arrangement of a mediocre song. It has an up-tempo beat, but Presley sounds less than totally-committed. The song does not suit his voice, but the arrangement almost compensates for the continuous sense of strain.

'Never Again' is another ballad with heavily over-dubbed strings, which make a sickly-sounding background. Presley sounds unusual and probably reveals his voice showing signs of wear and tear.

'She Thinks I Still Care' is good Nashville-influenced material, but Presley's voice lacks something. Perhaps he is set too far back. But the vocal quality fades and breaks as if he is suffering from breathing or throat troubles.

'Solitaire', a famous Neil Sedaka song, proved a great hit for Andy Williams. Again the words have personal significance for Presley, and his performance is outstanding, although he does not eclipse Williams. Presley chose the songs for these sessions and the material displays his discrimination. The final song, 'The Last Farewell', the international hit for Roger Whitaker (who wrote it), receives a very fine performance. The tempo is measured, and this fine song is given by Presley with due regard for the excellent lyrics.

29/31 October 1976. *Venue:* Graceland, Memphis.
*Titles recorded:* 'He'll Have To Go', 'It's Easy For You', 'Pledging My Love', 'There's A Fire Down Below' (unissued, probably not completed), 'Way Down'.

Once more, Presley's inability to achieve consistent studio work forced these sessions to be held at his home. Although these were spread over three days, only four songs were recorded (the fifth was apparently unfinished, without Presley recording the vocal track). The songs could only be released after much additional work, in some cases in January 1977 in Nashville. This cosmetic work is generally successful.

'He'll Have To Go', the first hit for Jim Reeves in the U.K. (1960), was a surprising choice. The song is well-known, and had long passed the peak of its popularity. Presley's performance is very slow and very long, at 4′.28″. Although he is in good voice, the quality is not as good as in the past, apart from a deep G on the word 'low'. 'It's Easy For You' is another slow ballad, by Tim Rice and Andrew Lloyd Webber. As recorded, Presley's voice is placed very far back, almost constricted at first. The performance seems good enough, but the backing musicians are so outstanding (especially Ronnie Tutt) that they tend to detract from Presley.

'Pledging My Love' is another curiosity: at least twenty years out of date, this slow, rocking ballad, with its heavy dragging triplets, is musically nothing.

The session is redeemed by 'Way Down'. This was Presley's last original hit, and shows him at the height of his powers. In spite of the troubles which beset the session, this magnificent rock number brought out the best in this great artist. The throbbing bass line at the beginning catches the spirit of its bluesy coarseness, echoed by the flaying piano line. 'Way Down' was one of the most unusual hits for Presley, because a large part of its appeal is in the backing vocals and instrumental colour. However, he was the only singer who could have handled the lead vocal line with such aplomb.

25 April 1977. *Venue:* Civic Center, Saginaw.
*Titles recorded:* 'If You Love Me', 'Little Darlin'', 'Unchained Melody'.

Three live numbers, which were subjected to considerable overdubbing and other cosmetic treatment in the studio to make them acceptable for album release. 'If You Love Me', a medium-sized hit for Mary Hopkin in the U.K. in 1976, is well performed by Presley. The arrangements and dubbings are added with skill, but the result is mediocre. 'Little Darlin' makes a change from the morbid material which Presley had concentrated on for some time. It is a good-humoured performance of a song with tongue-in-cheek reminiscences of late 1950s soft-rock. This 'red-blue-jeans-and-a-pony tail' atmosphere is a breath of clean air, and British listeners who recall the palmy days of the Vernon Girls will know what to expect. 'Unchained Melody' is remarkable. The live recording featured Presley accompanying himself on the piano. For an album release, the idea to overdub a better backing track was right. In the live performance, Presley was carried away and his singing takes on a freedom which had not been heard on disc for many years. The additions are in keeping with the spirit of his performance. This is an outstanding example of Presley in his last years, and thanks are due to those who brought about this realization of what at first might have seemed poor material.

19/21 June 1977. *Venue:* Omaha, Rapid City.
*Titles recorded:* 'Also Sprach Zarathustra', 'See See Rider', 'That's All Right', 'Are You Lonesome Tonight?', 'Teddy Bear'/'Don't Be Cruel', 'You Gave Me A Mountain', 'Jailhouse Rock', 'How Great Thou Art', 'I Really Don't Want to Know', 'Hurt', 'Hound Dog', 'My Way', 'Can't Help Falling In Love', 'I Got A Woman'/'Amen', 'Love Me', 'If You Love Me', 'O Sole Mio'/'It's Now or Never', 'Trying To Get To You', 'Hawaiian Wedding Song', 'Fairytale', 'Little Sister', 'Early Morning Rain', 'What'd I Say', 'Johnny B. Goode', 'And I Love You So'.

These were Presley's last recordings, taken live at concerts on the above dates. The concerts were filmed for a CBS television spectacular, and the recordings were issued after his death as a two-record set, *Elvis In Concert*. The strictures which applied to his earlier live recordings are not so relevant here, for the recording quality is easily the best of Presley's live recordings. Nevertheless the issue is largely a sentimental exercise. None of the material is new, and some songs — 'Love Me', for example — had been recorded as many as five times before.

Presley's comments between songs show him still a shy person; although he was a magisterial performer of charismatic quality, his half-apologetic comments, his slight stammering, the nervous laughs and sometimes garbled speech all reveal the shy boy from Tupelo, Mississippi. But Presley is in superb voice. Not for a long time had the ringing power and tenderness, the range of expression and the certainty of feeling been so clearly displayed. These performances needed no cosmetic surgery before release. In 'How Great Thou Art', for example, Presley's top A's are amazing: they would be a credit to any singer. Some performances are given with great care: 'My Way' especially, a better performance than on the *Aloha from Hawaii* double-album, suffers nothing from comparison with Frank Sinatra. The appearance of Sherrill Nielsen in the Italian verse of 'O Sole Mio' is a nice touch; it is a pity it was cut from the televison show. 'Are You Lonesome Tonight?' begins magnificently, but unfortunately Presley messes up the words in the middle section. Although he recovers well by making a joke of it, the sincerity of the opening verses show that he did not mean this to be a send-up. However, one cannot escape the suspicion that some of the earlier rockers are put in — in very abbreviated form — for old times' sake; the performances are little more than sketches, with hectic, garbled words.

Comments from some of Presley's fans add to the memorial nature of the album. Although they were recorded at the time, nobody could have realized how significant they would shortly become. The most poignant comment is by Presley's father, recorded after his son's death. But Vernon is incorrect when he says the recordings were of Presley's last appearance. Elvis Presley's *last* concert was in Indianapolis, five days later, on 26 June.

# PART III

# THE MUSICIAN

# Conclusion

As Elvis Presley passed into history, his premature end left a grieving family and dejected friends. Millions of people all over the world who never met him, but heard him sing, shared in a sense of loss. But he also left a recorded legacy of around seven hundred songs — his life's work as a singer — which we have examined in the course of this book. As we have seen, by no means all of these are worthy of detailed attention. But it must be clear, even to the most casual reader, that with his death a remarkable singer had passed from the face of the earth. During his lifetime, Elvis Presley appeared before millions of people, and sales of his records numbered many tens of millions. At this level, when nobody can say — or really cares — exactly how many records he sold, the sheer weight of numbers is itself the strongest reason for examining his legacy.

If some disaster were to wipe out our books, tapes, film and records of historical and contemporary events, and a future generation found only a few clues as to Elvis Presley's identity, what would they make of him? If they knew merely that he was born the only son of very poor parents, and that when he died, aged forty-two, millions mourned him all over the world, tens of thousands flocked to his home in a vain attempt to glimpse his body, and countless others attended memorial services in many countries, buying all manner of objects connected with him, they would surely wonder what sort of man could have made such an impact. A religious leader? A politician? A general? A king? None of these: he was a man who sang songs.

The reactions to Elvis Presley's death constitute the most extraordinary demonstration for decades of the power of music to reach the hearts and minds of millions of people. When Beethoven died, in March 1827, many thousands followed his coffin through the streets of Vienna — at a time when modern communications did not exist, and when the population of Vienna itself was not much greater than the number of mourners. The number of people moved to attend Elvis Presley's burial was similar to those who flocked to Beethoven's; but what sets Presley apart is that modern communications enable millions to watch an event without leaving their homes. If tens of thousands felt impelled to go to Presley's home and camp for days and nights, how many more all over the world watched the events on television?

Yet premature deaths of popular singers are not unknown. Other figures in popular music have died in much more violent and degrading circumstances than Presley. Buddy Holly and Eddie Cochran were killed while travelling, and the list of later rock stars who took their own lives — Janis Joplin, Jimi Hendrix, Paul Kossoff, Jim Morrison, Keith Moon, Sid Vicious, among many others — is regrettably, longer. None of these made such an impact as Elvis Presley. It could be argued that they died when their lives were not even half-finished so far as their music-making was concerned while at forty-two Presley's name was already of legendary proportions. In a sense this is true, but two things must be remembered. The first is that if Presley's career was unlikely to show much further development, the millions for whom and to whom Presley spoke through his performances regarded him as a vital force in popular music. Secondly Elvis Presley was not only the most important figure in world rock music — he was also the *first* rock performer of any consequence.

With some artists who have died prematurely, greater success occasionally comes after death. Buddy Holly is a case in point, and the country singer, Jim Reeves, is possibly the most remarkable example. This posthumous success is partly explained by the amount of unreleased material available at the time of the singer's death. But soon after Presley's death the single 'Way Down' became a massive international hit, and although it is possible that the emotion generated by his death contributed to the success, the record is such an outstanding example of pop music *and* one of Presley's best performances, that it would have been a hit at any time.

Presley's success as the most important figure in pop music from 1956 until his death has to be measured by its length and its international appeal. For more than twenty years Elvis Presley produced a string of major international hits which transcended language, culture and fashion. In Britain, for example, during these years Elvis Presley had an unprecedented total of ninety-four different singles enter the Top 50 charts. Wherever the music was heard, from the coffee bars of the 1950s to the discos of the late 1970s, the enjoyment, raw energy, good humour and sentimentality — in short, all of those things which go to make up the pleasure of being young and alive — are enshrined in hundreds of Presley's records. For several generations, the youth of many countries were set free by this man's music. Presley became synonomous with having a good time, and this string of hits, from 'Heartbreak Hotel' to 'Way Down', entered the subconsciousness of millions of people. To hear the song again brings back the memory, which itself meant so much. When people learned that Presley had died, then the sympathy and sadness of all those to whom he meant so much was released.

Another reason for the sympathy goes beyond music. Ten years after Presley burst upon the musical world, the Beatles breathed new life into popular music. At first they marked a return to a basic, raw quality, which Presley himself had revealed. The mid-1960s, however, were notable for other things: political protest, fed by the Vietnam war, the increase in drug-taking by young people all over the world, a rise in the numbers of young people, a sexual freedom made easy by more liberal laws and the pill. A collective culture-shock ran counter to the established standards of older generations. Many singers found themselves caught up in one or more of these movements. Other sections of the public were alienated, and rock music became exclusive, only for initiates who conformed in dress, behaviour, and mores.

Elvis Presley remained aloof from these changes. He preached no public sermons on politics, sex or drugs. He remained true to himself, and true to the one thing which for him really mattered — his music. This meant that when he died, no factions hated him. Acknowledged as the most important popular singer of his day, Presley remained above all an entertainer.

A large number of the mourners at the memorial services following Presley's death were teenagers. Where one might have expected such congregations to be made up of Presley's contemporaries, for whom he personified their hopes and aspirations, a large number were not even born when Presley had already established himself as the dominant force in rock music. Clearly Presley's greatest performances transcend those years and speak as vividly as when first released. Whereas most singers of his time have faded into obscurity, the compulsive quality of his best performances have lost none of their magic; indeed they have actually taken on a more significant character.

Why should this be so? Is it a purely musical phenomenon? In many ways it is; but success in popular music has also to be viewed in a sociological light.

By the early 1950s a new generation — the first post-war generation — had begun to arise. Each generation tends to react against its immediate predecessor, in an attempt to establish its own identity. If the popular music of the early 1950s was based on that of the dance-floor, dominated by dance styles, then it was clear that a different form of popular music was needed, to which the youth of the new generation could relate. The new generation had already begun to assert its individuality in dress and hair-style. In Britain, for example, the 'Teddy-Boy' fashion had begun to catch on; but the dance associated with it — the Creep, as opposed to the jive — was a lethargic stroll around the floor.

With Elvis Presley's 'Heartbreak Hotel', the dam was burst, and the floodgates opened. Here was a man who sang without any pretence at sophistication. The words — in so far as they could be understood at all — seemed to erupt from his body. The music was raw, basic, totally unsubtle. Stripped of all pretension, cut to the bone, lean, lithe, agile — this was the angry music of revolution.

As time went by, Presley became a more varied singer, instilling his own distinctive character into all he sang. He possessed a rare gift: the recognizable voice. A few words from any of his songs, and it could *only* be Elvis Presley singing. Why did it mean so much to young people when he died? In some ways, the conditions were similar to those which existed when Presley first appeared. The West experienced severe economic recession during the early 1970s. Many young people found themselves less well-off than in the intervening period. The pop music establishment failed to note this sociological change, and at first rejected the grass-roots reaction against the sophisticated music of a handful of jet-setting millionaire stars. But there was a return to basic, raw music, which Presley first personified and which led ten years later to the emerging careers of a new generation of rock stars. When Bob Dylan hitched down the freeways in the early 1960s to visit the ailing Woody Guthrie in hospital, and wrote 'Lonesome Traveller', the post-Beat generation could identify with the song. By the early 1970s, with Dylan travelling in his own jet, he was a lonesome traveller for very different reasons. Few of his original followers could identify with the millionaire and his trappings.

In addition, the 1960s saw the consolidation of soul music, a welcome black-based popular music, which by the early 1970s had become a dominant force. But what had not happened for a long time was a distinctive youth music — predominantly white — which marked a return to basic roots. As out-of-work teenagers have no money to spend, it was also clear that the conditions existed for music of a violent reaction. Presley's death coincided with this, and as music of the archetypal white working-class boy from a deprived background, the early Presley records took on a new lease of life. They spoke again to a young generation — and to an older one, too, for a general nostalgia for the 1950s — quickly capitalized upon by films — manifested itself.

Popular music, as understood today, is so often bound up with other things that it is difficult to remember that it *is* still music. Advertising, promotion, films, television, concerts, articles, and the hundred-and-one other things which a record company has to employ to bend the ear of the public towards a particular artist seem to take over. The details of Elvis Presley's early life appear to come from a bygone age: with six teachers in a high school of 1,700 pupils, what chance did he have of a good education? With a strict nonconformist upbringing and a mother who walked him to school until he was fifteen, what independence could he aspire to?

Presley's importance was achieved solely through music. He had nothing else to give, no sermon or political creed to preach. Nor, I suspect, did he seek the wealth which came his way. Obviously a truck driver would like extra money; but I do not believe that Elvis Presley actively set out to become a superstar. The child of two, barely able to talk, so fascinated by the sound of singing that he leaves his mother's arms to get nearer the choir — could there be more convincing proof that he was naturally musical? The boy who looked forward to going to church, because of the opportunity it gave him to sing? The shy, diffident youth, who confounded his friends by finding the courage to stand to sing in front of 1,500 fellow-pupils? The stammering truck-driver, who plucked up the courage to go into a recording studio, alone, 'just to hear what I sounded like'? The man who broke down in tears when he was told to quit singing and go back to driving a truck — just when he had finished an appalling performance at the country's leading country music venue — and then go on to confound his critics at an illustrious venue a few weeks later?

By all rational standards, Elvis Presley's career should never have got started at all. Sam Phillips of Sun Records was not at first impressed, and neither were Bill Black or Scotty Moore. But Presley's persistence, strangely at odds with his non-musical behaviour, was deep-seated.

Presley's was the most important formative and influential singing voice in popular music of the last quarter-century — possibly of all time. There could have been no more opportune place for him to have been born than in the deep South of the U.S.A. For it was there that the two main streams of popular music — black and white — met.

Although many years were to pass before the blacks in the South achieved a measure of equality, when Presley was about ten years old — at about the time of the end of World War II — the early signs of a change in society were beginning to appear. In some ways, the war had promoted a measure of integration, with black soldiers enlisted alongside white.

Memphis had been a capital of both blues and country music for some time. The economic recession of the 1930s had opened up a wider market for both types of music. RCA and CBS, for example, discovered in the 1930s that records by black blues artists sold well in the big cities of the north-eastern U.S.A. and the far west. Country music too was exportable, although it later came to be called country-and-western, as the western part included instruments from the western states — drums, electric guitars and fuller use of piano. The upshot was that blues and country music found a bigger audience. It is significant that one of the most prolific of the black blues singers — Tampa Red (Hudson Whittaker) — devoted most of his recording time between 1935 and 1936 to 'popular' songs, especially for the white market. The growth of radio in the 1930s as the popular entertainment medium meant that these recordings reached the ears of those who would previously not have heard such music.

In this way, the young Elvis Presley heard the black blues singers who greatly influenced him. He would not have been allowed to attend the black clubs where they performed. Tampa Red, Blind Willie McTell and artists such as James DeBerry and his Memphis Playboys as well as Sonny Boy Williamson the first are all traceable influences on Presley's rare blues recordings.

White and black singers met more frequently in the field of gospel music; and this was clearly another major influence on Presley's life. In this regard, Memphis — and the state of Mississippi — was in the heart of gospel country. The old hymns with their four-square harmony, which had such an effect on the young boy, are not so very different in harmonic structure from the blues. The gospel songs stemmed from the white settlers, who brought with them the Lutheran chorales of West European protestantism. But while the blues is secular music, gospel songs are sacred, and this means the the revival meetings, for all their fire-and-brimstone sermons, found the congregation rooted to the spot. In other words, it is not possible to dance to church music, for the congregation in pews is physically prevented from dancing. Musically the interest must fall not on the rhythm of the hymn, but on its harmony. As a result the harmonic interest of gospel music is much more important than in the blues music. You never hear a choir sing the blues.

The other important influence is the other main musical stream in the south — country music. Again it is curious how Presley seemed to have been born at just the right time.

If one man put country music on the map, it was the legendary Hank Williams. Williams died in 1953, at the age of 29. Few who heard him will ever forget him. In the post-War years, Hank Williams greatly broadened the appeal of what came to be called country-and-western, largely through his appearances in the immensely popular Louisiana Hayride shows.

But it was also due to the efforts of earlier singers that this branch of music had developed outside of the farmsteading communities of the rural southern states. People such as Jimmie Rodgers, the Carter Family, Red Foley (who composed 'Old Shep' and was the first country artist to have his own networked radio show — *Avalon Time* — in 1939), and Ernest Tubbs, were household names to many — including the Presleys.

By the late 1940s and early 1950s this branch of music was developing further offshoots. The growth of radio and television, rising living standards, and the greater sophistication brought about in recordings by the advent of tape all conspired to deal a mortal blow to the *ethnic* country-and-western music. Of course, it remained as a specialist field, but tended to become subordinated to a new phenomenon, 'Blue-Grass Music'. This was at first almost the single-handed invention of Bill Monroe, whose haunting high tenor voice, occasionally in duet with other, lower, male singers and accompanied by a small group in which the banjo predominated, seemed to personify the music of the Appalachian mountains. It became enormously successful, and was a clear early influence on Elvis Presley. In his very first recording session for Sun, in July 1954, Presley recorded Bill Monroe's 'Blue Moon of Kentucky', in a performance that reveals the Bluegrass roots.

Nor were these the only influences which saturated the young Presley. His stint as a cinema usher in Loew's Theater brought him into contact with the musical film, and the mainstream popular music of the day. The 1952 movie, *With A Song In My Heart,* has an extended sequence featuring 'Blue Moon', and this may have been where Presley learned it. Apart from this 'standard' repertoire, white singers as diverse as Johnnie Ray (whose 'Such A Night' must have been a seminal influence), Red Ingle and his Natural Seven, and more urban singers such as Frankie Laine (who betrays a strong country lineage) are in the Presley mix.

There is little pure folk-music in Presley's make-up. More significant is the close-harmony style of the barber-shop quartets (the Jordanaires, founded in 1948 in Springfield, Missouri, specialized in this music for a time), and the patriotic fervour of much popular music during the decade 1935-1945. This was not so much expressed in hit songs of the time, as in 'popular cantatas' such as Earl Robinson's 'Ballad For Americans' — which became a sensational vehicle for Paul Robeson during the War. More important is George Kleinsinger's 'I Hear America Singing', which was a similar vehicle for John Charles Thomas, whose politics were as far to the right as Robeson's were to the left. The patriotism of these highly successful works, with their solo baritones commandingly calling America to action, was infectious, and again left deep marks on the young Presley's musical mind, surfacing decades later in his great recordings of the 'American Trilogy'.

Against this background of curiously interlinked musical influences runs the deep river of jazz. Apart from the blues, there was nothing of traditional, or modern jazz in Presley's music-making, except for the technical features of his singing, which are quite jazz-like.

A classically-trained singer or instrumentalist will spend years perfecting a style in which purity of tone, consistency of timbre, clarity of expression and proper intonation all become second nature, to be used to interpret a wide variety of music, which must first adhere faithfully to the written instructions of the composer. In jazz, none of these things apply. There is no such thing as an inelegant jazz sound. No note is considered out of tune if it is sung or played flat. It is by no means necessary to pronounce every syllable correctly, as long as the character of the song is conveyed. All effects in jazz are acceptable, and may be used at the discretion of the performer — even though his realization of the number may be almost unrecognizable to the composer.

Popular singers of the mid-1950s — that is, those who were not rock singers — frequently adopted elements of classical style. It was considered important to sing in tune, to pronounce words, and to breathe properly. What Presley brought to popular music was the deliberate 'dirtiness' of jazz — *not* a style in which anything goes, but a style in which anything was acceptable, if it worked. This is not to be found in any other rock singer of his time — or before. Up to a point, Johnnie Ray had done the same, but this was against the background of a big-band sound.

Why was it then that Sam Phillips wanted a white man who sounded like a black singer? Was it because black singers had better voices? No — but because the black singer had two priceless attributes largely denied the white singer. First, an instinctive feel for the blues, and second, a highly-developed sense of rhythm. Nobody needs reminding that the negroes of the United States were carried to that country from Africa, and carried with them their own music. A characteristic free yet highly-complex syncopation was carried to America by the early slaves, and transformed into the expressive lines of jazz and blues music. But a chordal structure of European origin, was added to give an undercurrent of simple duple or triple beats. It was a small step from this to rock music, and in two of Presley's most famous numbers — 'Heartbreak Hotel' and 'Hound Dog' — these roots are revealed for all to hear.

If Presley's achievements in rock music are unassailable, then his ability as a blues singer is by no means so widely known. It is sad that he never recorded blues albums, for he was a natural blues singer, as Sam Phillips certainly knew. His reputation would have done much to make this branch of music more popular. His classic blues recordings, 'Reconsider Baby' and 'Merry Christmas Baby', dating from 1960 and 1971 respectively, are both outstanding performances.

Since Presley's achievements as a blues singer are so little known, let us look at 'Merry Christmas Baby' in some detail. It is a basic 12-bar blues in G minor; but what is astonishing is that, for perhaps the only time in his career, Presley reveals the full range of his voice and his natural feel for the blues. He uses his voice as an instrument as he endeavours to match the amazing guitar-work of James Burton (surely influenced by Johnny 'Guitar' Watson). Presley hums, moans and shouts. The piano is free and florid — the use of the high keyboard register is unusual and distinctive; but it is Presley's earthy, yet subtle and hypnotic singing in the opening verse that inspires the musicians. The gamut of his voice — from low, growly G's to a staggering, thrilling top B-flat — *sung*, not falsetto — is so surprising, and so unlike anything else Presley did, as to cause one to entirely rethink one's attitude to this singer. Even Presley's cries of 'Dig it, James, dig it!' become part of the musical fabric. Nothing is more remarkable than the complete understanding of these performers, and the way in which they slightly anticipate the beat. This is not only the essence of blues, but the essence of rock, and runs completely counter to European classical music. (This is clearly revealed in the several attempts during the last ten or fifteen years to get rock bands to play concerts with symphony orchestras.) On paper, the music looks the same; but the instinct of the rock musician is slightly to anticipate the beat, especially if it is not the first beat of a bar. This is precisely what is found in the work of the best blues performers. Hearing Presley's instinctive blues work on 'Merry Christmas Baby', it is easy to picture the young boy, sitting close to the radio, enthralled by the blues coming from the loudspeaker.

We should not forget, however, that Presley was first a country singer. His fame did much to reawaken interest in this distinctive musical style. Running through his career, one can find many examples of excellent country material. However the development of Nashville into one of the major popular recording centres of the world was not solely due to Presley: RCA must take much of the credit, as well as Chet Atkins and other major figures, such as Carl Perkins, Charlie Rich and Johnny Cash. But Elvis Presley never forgot his country roots. The album *Elvis Country* is an excellent example of how Nashville developed.

Presley's importance extends into other areas too. In gospel music and in modern popular songs by his younger contemporaries his achievement was considerable. But it was as a top rock singer that his effect was most widely felt. His influence on a wide range of singers was very marked. Naturally his influence was most potent at the time of his greatest early success, during 1956 and 1957. We have seen how singers such as Gene Vincent and Eddie Cochran were clearly influenced by him; but a whole host of other stars also acknowledge his dominance.

In many ways, the most interesting of these was Buddy Holly. Holly, who was killed in January 1959, was one of the few singers at the time who seemed able to challenge Presley's popularity.

Holly remains a fascinating figure, for he was a highly creative and individual rock star on his own. There is no doubt, however, that Presley influenced Holly to some degree; and it should be remembered that Holly's success came at a time (1958-59) when Presley was preoccupied by films, his army call-up, and his mother's death. But this was two-way traffic. Holly also influenced Presley; the change of emphasis into 'soft-rock' of 1959-1962 stems in part from Holly's more subtle and less bludgeoning approach.

But one other American singer, even more wide-ranging in scope than Presley, also had a mutual influence with him. This was Bobby Darin, a great singer and composer who, since his death at Christmas 1972, has been largely forgotten. Darin's own rock numbers, especially the classic song, 'Bullmoose', were eclipsed by his own versatility. Darin was one of Presley's favourite singers, and Elvis frequently attended Darin's performances.

However, Presley's achievement was so vast, and the scope of his singing so wide and long-lasting, that few singers in the last twenty-five years have remained untouched by one or other of his styles. Singers as different as Johnny Burnette, Chris Farlowe, Glen Campbell, Alice Cooper, Sam Cooke and Pat Boone along with countless others, have all at one time or another acknowledged their debt to him.

But above all Presley reached many millions of ordinary men and women, who were moved by the manner of his singing. Presley's importance transcends the influences which moulded him, and those which he had on other people. His importance also transcends the nature of his originality. It finally resides in the hearts and minds of millions of people who, whether for one brief moment or for a lifetime, found in his music-making the expression of their own hopes and aspirations.

# Appendix I — Filmography

## Feature Films

1956
LOVE ME TENDER CinemaScope
Release date: 16 November 1956. Studio: Twentieth-Century Fox.
Running time: 89 minutes.

Cast:
Clint Elvis Presley
Vance Richard Egan
Cathy Debra Paget
Siringo Robert Middleton
Brett Reno William Campbell
Mike Gavin Neville Brand
The Mother Mildred Dunnock
Major Kincaid Bruce Bennett
Ray Reno James Drury
Ed Galt Russ Conway
Kelso Ken Clark
Davis Barry Coe

Credits:
Producer David Weisbart
Director Robert D. Webb
Screenplay Robert Buckner
Story Maurice Geraghty
Photographer Leo Tover
Music Lionel Newman
Art Direction Lyle R. Wheeler/ Maurice Ransford
Special Effects Ray Kellogg
Technical Advisor Col Tom Parker

Songs: 'Love Me Tender', 'Let Me', 'Poor Boy', 'We're Gonna Move'.

1957
LOVING YOU VistaVision and Technicolor.
Release date: 9 July 1957. Studio: Paramount Pictures.
Running time: 101 minutes.

Cast:
Deke Rivers Elvis Presley
Glenda Lizabeth Scott
Tex Warner Wendell Corey
Susan Jessup Dolores Hart
Carl James Gleason
Tallman Ralph Dumke
Skeeter Paul Smith
Wayne Ken Becker
Daisy Jana Lund

Credits:
Producer Hal B. Wallis
Director Hal Kanter
Screenplay Herbert Baker/ Hal Kanter
Story Mary Agnes Thompson
Photographer Charles Lang, Jr.
Editor Howard Smith
Special Photographic Effects John P. Fulton
Art Director Hal Pereira/ Albert Nozaki
Assistant Director James Rosenberger
Technical Advisor Col Tom Parker

Songs: 'Teddy Bear', 'Got A Lot O' Livin' To Do', 'Loving You', 'Lonesome Cowboy', 'Hot Dog', 'Mean Woman Blues', 'Let's Have A Party'.

JAILHOUSE ROCK   CinemaScope
Release date: 21 October 1957. Studio: Metro-Goldwyn-Mayer.
Running time: 96 minutes.

Cast:
Vince Everett   Elvis Presley
Peggy van Alden   Judy Tyler
Hunk Houghton   Mickey Shaughnessy
Sherry Wilson   Jennifer Holden
Eddy Talbot   Dean Jones
Laury Jackson   Anne Neyland
Warden   Hugh Sanders

Credits:
Producer   Pandro S. Berman
Director   Richard Thorpe
Screenplay   Guy Trosper
Story   Ned Young
Photographer   Robert Bronner
Editor   Ralph E. Winters
Assistant Producer   Kathryn Hereford
Music Supervisor   Jeff Alexander
Art Directors   William A. Horning/Randell Duell
Special Effects   A. Arnold Gillespie
Assistant Director   Robert E. Reylen
Technical Advisor   Col Tom Parker

Songs: 'Jailhouse Rock', 'Treat Me Nice', 'Young And Beautiful', 'I Wanna Be Free', 'Don't Leave Me Now', 'Baby, I Don't Care', 'One More Day'.

1958
KING CREOLE
Release date: 4 June 1958. Studio: Paramount Pictures.
Running time: 115 minutes.

Cast:
Danny Fisher   Elvis Presley
Ronnie   Carolyn Jones
Nellie   Dolores Hart
Mr Fisher   Dean Jagger
'Forty' Nina   Liliane Montevecchi
Maxie Fields   Walter Matthau
Mimi   Jan Shepard
Charlie LeGrand   Paul Stewart
Shark   Vic Morrow

Credits:
Producer   Hal B. Wallis
Director   Michael Curtiz
Associate Producer   Paul Nathan
Screenplay   Herbert Baker/Mivhael Vincente Gazzo
Story Harold Robbins' *A Stone For Danny Fisher*
Photographer   Russell Harlan
Editor   Warren Low
Art Directors   Hal Pereira/Joseph MacMillan Johnson
Special Photographic Effects John P. Fulton
Assistant Director   D. Michael Moore
Technical Advisor   Col Tom Parker

Songs: 'King Creole', 'As Long As I Have You', 'Hard Headed Woman', 'Trouble', 'Dixieland Rock', 'Don't Ask Me Why', 'Lover Doll', 'Crawfish', 'Young Dreams', 'Steadfast, Loyal And True', 'New Orleans', 'Turtles, and Gumbo', 'Banana'.

1960

G.I. BLUES Technicolor

Release date: 20 October 1960. Studio: Paramount Pictures.

Running time: 104 minutes.

Cast:

Tulsa MacCauley Elvis Presley
Rick James Douglas
Cooky Robert Ivers
Lili Juliet Prowse
Tina Leticia Roman
Marla Sigrid Maier
Sgt McGraw Arch Johnson

Credits:

Producer Hal B. Wallis
Director Norman Taurog
Associate Producer Paul Nathan
Screenplay Edmund Beloin and Henry Garson
Photographer Loyal Griggs
Editor Warren Low
Music scored and conducted by Joseph L. Lilley
Music numbers staged by Charles O'Curran
Art Directors Hal Pereira and Walter Tyler
Technical Advisor Col Tom Parker

Songs: 'G.I. Blues', 'Tonight Is So Right For Love', 'Frankfurt Special', 'Wooden Heart', 'Pocketful Of Rainbows', 'Didya Ever', 'What's She Really Like?', 'Shoppin' Around', 'Big Boots', 'Doin' The Best I Can'.

FLAMING STAR CinemaScope, De Luxe Color

Release date: 20 December 1960. Studio: Twentieth-Century Fox.

Running time: 101 minutes.

Cast:

Pacer Burton Elvis Presley
Clint Burton Steve Forrest
Roslyn Pierce Barbara Eden
Neddy Burton Dolores Del Rio
Pa Burton John McIntyre
Buffalo Horn Rudolfo Acosta
Doc Phillips Ford Rainey
Dred Phillips Karl Swenson
Angus Pierce Richard Jaeckel
Dorothy Howard Anne Benton
Tom Howard L. O. Jones
Will Howard Douglas Dick
Jute Tom Reese

Credits:

Producer David Weisbart
Director Don Siegel
Screenplay Clair Huffaker and Nunnally Johnson
Photographer Charles G. Clarke
Editor Hugh S. Fowler
Art Directors Duncan Cramer and Walter M. Simonds
Music Cyril Mockridge
Musical Director Lionel Newman
Technical Advisor Col Tom Parker

Songs: 'Flaming Star', 'A Cane And A High-Starched Collar'.

1961

WILD IN THE COUNTRY CinemaScope, De Luxe Color
Release date: 15 June 1961. Studio: Twentieth-Century Fox.
Running time: 114 minutes.

Cast:
Glenn Tyler Elvis Presley
Irene Sperry Hope Lange
Noreen Tuesday Weld
Betty Lee Millie Perkins
Davis Rafer Johnson
Phil Macy John Ireland
Cliff Macy Gary Lockwood
Uncle Rolfe William Mims
Dr Underwood Raymond Greenleaf
Monica George Christina Crawford
Flossie Robin Raymond
Mrs Parsons Doreen Lang
Mr Parsons Charles Arnt

Credits:
Producer Jerry Wald
Director Philip Dunne
Screenplay Clifford Odets
Story J. R. Salamanca
Photographer William C. Mellor
Editor Dorothy Spencer
Associate Producer Peter Nelson
Music Kenyon Hopkins
Art Directors Jack Martin Smith and Preston Ames
Technical Advisor Col Tom Parker

Songs: 'Lonely Man', 'I Slipped, I Stumbled, I Fell', 'In My Way', 'Wild In The Country'.

BLUE HAWAII Panavision, Technicolor
Release date: 14 November 1961. Studio: Paramount Pictures.
Running time: 101 minutes.

Cast:
Chad Gates Elvis Presley
Maile Duval Joan Blackman
Abigail Prentace Nancy Walters
Fred Gates Roland Winters
Sarah Lee Gates Angela Lansbury
Jack Kelman John Archer
Mr Chapman Howard McNear
Mrs Manaka Flora Hayes
Mr Duval Gregory Gay
Mr Garvey Steve Brodie
Mrs Garvey Iris Adrian
Patsy Darlene Tomkins
Sandy Pamela Alkert
Beverly Christian Kay

Credits:
Producer Hal B. Wallis
Director Norman Taurog
Associate Producer Paul Nathan
Screenplay Hal Kanter
Story Allan Weiss
Photographer Charles Lang
Editors Warren Low and Terry Morse
Special Photographic Effects John P. Fulton
Music — scored and conducted by Joseph L. Lilley
Music — numbers staged by Charles O'Curran
Art Directors Hal Pereira and Walter Tyler
Technical Advisor Col Tom Parker

Songs: 'Blue Hawaii', 'Almost Always True', 'Aloha Oe', 'No More', 'Can't Help Falling in Love', 'Rock-a-Hula Baby', 'Moonlight Swim', 'Ku-u-i-po', 'Ito Eats', 'Slicin' Sand', 'Hawaiian Sunset', 'Beach Boy Blues', 'Island Of Love', 'Hawaiian Wedding Song', 'Stepping Out Of Line'.

1962

FOLLOW THAT DREAM Panavision, De Luxe Color
Release date: 29 March 1962. Studio: United Artists.
Running time: 110 minutes.

Cast:
Toby Kwimper Elvis Presley
Pop Kwimper Arthur O'Connell
Holly Jones Anne Helm
Alicia Claypole Joanna Moore
Carmine Jack Kruschen
Nick Simon Oakland
Eddy and Teddy Bascomb Gavin and Robert Koon
Adriane Pam Ogles

Credits:
Producer David Weisbart
Director Gordon Douglas
Screenplay Charles Lederer
Story: based on the play, *Pioneer, Go Home!* by Richard Powell
Photographer Leo Tover
Editor William B. Murphy
Music Hans J. Salter
Music Editor Robert Tracy
Technical Advisor Col Tom Parker

Songs: 'What a Wonderful Life', 'I'm Not the Marrying Kind', 'Sound Advice', 'Follow That Dream'.

KID GALAHAD Color by DeLuxe
Release date: 25 July 1962. Studio: United Artists.
Running time: 95 minutes.

Cast:
Walter Gulick Elvis Presley
Willy Grogan Gig Young
Dolly Fletcher Lola Albright
Rose Grogan Joan Blackman
Lew Nyack Charles Bronson
Lieberman Ned Glass
Maynard Robert Emhardt
Otto Danzig David Lewis
Joie Shakes Michael Dante
Zimmerman Judson Pratt
Sperling George Mitchell
Marvin Richard Devon

Credits:
Producer David Weisbart
Director Phil Karlson
Screenplay William Fay
Story Francis Wallace
Photographer Burnett Guffey
Editor Stuart Gilmore
Art Director Cary Odell
Music Jeff Alexander
Technical Advisor Col Tom Parker
Presentation The Mirisch Company

Songs: 'King Of The Whole Wide World', 'This Is Living', 'Riding The Rainbow', 'Home Is Where The Heart Is', 'I Got Lucky', 'A Whistling Tune'.

GIRLS! GIRLS! GIRLS! Panavision, Technicolor
Release date: 2 November 1962. Studio: Paramount Pictures.
Running time: 106 minutes.

Cast:
Ross Carpenter Elvis Presley
Robin Ganter Stella Stevens
Laurel Dodge Laurel Goodwin
Wesley Johnson Jeremy Slate
Chen Yung Guy Lee
Kin Yung Benson Fong
Madame Yung Beulah Quo
Sam Robert Strauss
Alexander Starvos Frank Puglia
Madama Starvos Lili Valenty
Leona and Linda Starvos Barbara and Betty Beal
Arthur Morgan Nestor Paiva
Mrs Morgan Ann McCrea
Mai and Lai Ting Ginny and Elizabeth Tiu

Credits:
Producer Hal B. Wallis
Director Norman Taurog
Associate Producer Paul Nathan
Screenplay Edward Anhalt and Allan Weiss
Story Allan Weiss
Photographer Loyal Griggs
Art Directors Hal Pereira and Walter Tyler
Music Joe Lilley
Music staged by Charles Curran
Assistant Director Mickey Moore
Technical Advisor Col Tom Parker

Songs: 'Girls! Girls! Girls!' 'I Don't Wanna Be Tied', 'Where Do You Come From?', 'I Don't Want To', 'We'll Be Together', 'A Boy Like Me, A Girl Like You', 'Earth Boy', 'Return To Sender', 'Thanks To The Rolling Sea', 'Song Of The Shrimp', 'The Walls Have Ears', 'We're Coming In Loaded'.

1963
IT HAPPENED AT THE WORLD'S FAIR Panavision, Metrocolor
Release date: 3 March 1963. Studio: Metro-Goldwyn-Mayer.
Running time: 105 minutes.

Cast:
Mike Edwards Elvis Presley
Diane Warren Joan O'Brien
Danny Burke Gary Lockwood
Sue-Lin Vicky Tu
Vince Bradley H. M. Wynant
Miss Steuben Edith Atwater
Barney Thatcher Guy Raymond
Miss Ettinger Dorothy Green
Walter Ling Kam Tong
Dorothy Johnson Yvonne Craig

Credits:
Director Norman Taurog
Screenplay Si Rose and Seaman Jacobs
Photographer Joseph Ruttenberg
Editor Frederic Steinkamp
Music Leith Stevens
Art Directors George W. Davis and Preston Ames
Music staged by Jack Baker
Assistant Director Al Jennings
Technical Advisor Col Tom Parker
A Ted Richmond Production

Songs: 'I'm Falling In Love Tonight', 'Relax', 'How Would You Like To Be', 'Beyond The Bend', 'One Broken Heart For Sale', 'Cotton Candy Land', 'A World Of Our Own', 'Take Me To The Fair', 'They Remind Me Too Much Of You', 'Happy Ending'.

FUN IN ACAPULCO Technicolor
Release date: 21 November 1963. Studio: Paramount Pictures.
Running time: 98 minutes.

Cast:
Mike Windgren Elvis Presley
Margarita Dauphine Ursula Andress
Dolores Gomez Elsa Cardenas
Maximillian Paul Lukas
Raoul Almeido Larry Domasin
Moreno Alejandro Rey
Jose Robert Carricart
Jamie Harkins Teri Hope

Credits:
Producer Hal B. Wallis
Director Richard Thorpe
Screenplay Allan Weiss
Photographer Daniel L. Fapp
Editor Warren Low
Art Directors Hal Pereira and Walter Tyler
Technical Advisor Col Tom Parker

Songs: 'Fun In Acapulco', 'Vino, Dinero Y Amor', 'Mexico', 'El Toro', 'Marguerita', 'The Bullfighter Was A Lady', 'There's No Room To Rhumba In A Sports Car', 'I Think I'm Gonna Like it Here', 'Bossa Nova Baby', 'You Can't Say No In Acapulco', 'Guadalajara'.

1964
KISSIN' COUSINS Panavision, Metrocolor
Release date: 6 March 1964. Studio: Metro-Goldwyn-Mayer.
Running time: 96 minutes.

Cast:
Josh Morgan Elvis Presley
Jodie Tatum Elvis Presley
Pappy Tatum Arthur O'Connell
Ma Tatum Glenda Farrell
Capt. Robert Salbo Jack Alvertson
Selena Tatum Pam Austin
Midge Cynthia Pepper
Azalea Tatum Yvonne Craig
General Donford Donald Woods
Sgt Bailey Tommy Farrell
Trudy Beverly Powers
Dixie Hortense Petra
General's Aide Robert Stone

Credits:
Producer Sam Katzman
Director Gene Nelson
Screenplay Gerald Drayson Adams and Gene Nelson
Story Gerald Drayson Adams
Photographer Ellis W. Carter
Editor Ben Lewis
Music Supervised and conducted by Fred Karger
Art Directors George W. Davis and Eddie Imazu
Assistant Director Eli Dunn
Technical Advisor Col Tom Parker

Songs: 'Kissin' Cousins' (Nos 1 and 2), 'One Boy, Two Little Girls', 'There's Gold In The Mountains', 'Catchin' On Fast', 'Barefoot Ballad', 'Once Is Enough', 'Smoky Mountain Boy', 'Tender Feeling'.

VIVA LAS VEGAS Panavision, Metrocolor
Release date: 20 April 1964. Studio: Metro-Goldwyn-Mayer.
Running time: 86 minutes.

Cast:
Lucky Jordan Elvis Presley
Rusty Martin Ann-Margret
Count Elmo Mancini Cesare Danova
Mr Martin William Demarest
Shorty Fransworth Nicky Blair

Credits:
Producer Jack Cummings and George Sidney
Director George Sidney
Screenplay Sally Benton
Photographer Joseph Biroc
Editor John McSweeney, Jr.
Music George Stoll
Assistant Director Milton Feldman
Technical Advisor Col Tom Parker

Songs: 'Viva Las Vegas', 'If You Think I Don't Need You', 'The Lady Loves Me', 'I Need Somebody To Lean On', 'C'mon Everybody', 'Today, Tomorrow And Forever', 'Santa Lucia'.

ROUSTABOUT Techniscope, Technicolor
Release date: 12 November 1964. Studio: Paramount Pictures.
Running time: 101 minutes.

Cast:
Charlie Rogers Elvis Presley
Maggie Morgan Barbara Stanwyck
Cathy Lean Joan Freeman
Joe Lean Leif Erickson
Madame Mijanou Sue Ann Langdon
Harry Carver Pat Buttram
Marge Joan Staley
Arthur Nielson Dabd Greer
Fred Steve Brodie
Sam Norman Grabowski
Lou Jack Albertson
Cody Marsh Joel Fluellen
Hazel Jane Dulo
Little Egypt Wilda Taylor

Credits:
Producer Hal B. Wallis
Associate Producer Paul Nathan
Director John Rich
Screenplay Anthony Lawrence and Allan Weiss
Story Allan Weiss
Photographer Lucien Ballard
Music Joseph L. Lilley
Art Directors Hal Pereira and Walter Tyler
Assistant Director D. Michael Moore
Technical Advisor Col Tom Parker

Songs: 'Roustabout', 'Poison Ivy League', 'Wheels On My Heels', 'It's A Wonderful World', 'It's Carnival Time', 'Carny Town', 'One Track Heart', 'Hard Knocks', 'Little Egypt', 'Big Love, Big Heartache', 'There's A Brand New Day On The Horizon'.

1965

GIRL HAPPY Panavision, Metrocolor
Release date: 22 January 1965. Studio: Metro-Goldwyn-Mayer.
Running time: 96 minutes.

Cast:
Rusty Wells Elvis Presley

Credits:
Producer Joe Pasternak

Cast: *continued*
Valerie Shelley Fabares
Big Frank Harold J. Stone
Andy Gary Crosby
Wilbur Jody Baker
Sunny Daze Nita Talbot
Deena Mary Ann Mobley
Romano Fabrizio Mioni
Doc Jimmy Hawkins
Sgt Benson Jackie Coogan
Brentwood von Durgenfeld Peter Brooks
Mr Penchill John Fiedler
Betsy Chris Noel
Laurie Lyn Edington
Nancy Gale Gilmore
Bobbie Pamela Curran
Linda Rusty Allen

Credits: *continued*
Director Boris Sagal
Screenplay Harvey Bullock and R. S. Allen
Photographer Philip H. Lathrop
Editor Rita Roland
Music George Stoll
Assistant Director Jack Aldworth
Technical Advisor Col Tom Parker

Songs: 'Girl Happy', 'Spring Fever', 'Fort Lauderdale Chamber Of Commerce', 'Startin' Tonight', 'Wolf Call', 'Do Not Disturb', 'Cross My Heart And Hope To Die', 'The Meanest Girl In Town', 'Do The Clam', 'Puppet On A String', 'I've Got To Find My Baby'.

TICKLE ME Panavision, DeLuxe Color
Release date: 15 June 1965. Studio: United Artists.
Running time: 90 minutes.

Cast:
Lonnie Beale Elvis Presley
Pam Merritt Jocelyn Lane
Vera Radford Julie Adams
Stanley Potter Jack Mullaney
Estelle Penfield Merry Anders
Hilda Connie Gilchrist
Brad Bentley Edward Faulkner
Deputy Sturdivent Bill Williams
Henry Louis Elias
Adolph John Dennis
Janet Laurie Burton
Clair Kinnamon Linda Rogers
Sibyl Ann Morel
Ronnie Lilyan Chauvin

Credits:
Producer Ben Schwalb
Director Norman Taurog
Story and Screenplay Elwood Ullman and Edward Bernds
Photographer Loyal Griggs
Editor Archie Marshek
Music Director Walter Scharf
Art Director Arthur Lonergan
Assistant Director Artie Jacobson
Technical Advisor Col Tom Parker

Songs: 'Tickle Me', 'I'm Yours', 'I Feel That I've Known You Forever', 'Dirty, Dirty Feeling', 'Put The Blame On Me', 'Easy Question', 'Slowly But Surely'.

HARUM SCARUM Metrocolor
Release date: 15 December 1965. Studio: Metro-Goldwyn-Mayer.
Running time: 95 minutes.

Cast:
Johnny Tyronne Elvis Presley
Princess Shalimar Mary Ann Mobley
Aishah Fran Jeffries
Prince Drana Michael Ansara
Zacha Jay Novello
King Toranshad Philip Reed
Sinan Theo Marcuse
Baba Billy Barty
Mohar Dirk Harvey
Juina Jack Castanzo
Captain Heret Larry Chance
Leilah Barbara Werle
Emerald Brenda Benet
Sapphire Gail Gilmore
Amethyst Wilda Taylor
Sari Vicki Malkin

Credits:
Producer Sam Katzman
Director Gene Nelson
Screenplay Gerald Drayson Adams
Photographer Fred H. Jackman
Editor Ben Levin
Music supervised and conducted by Fred Karger
Art Directors George W. Davis and H. McClure Capps
Technical Advisor Col Tom Parker

Songs: 'Harem Holiday', 'My Desert Serenade', 'Go East — Young Man', 'Mirage', 'Kismet', 'Shake That Tambourine', 'Hey Little Girl', 'Golden Coins', 'So Close Yet So Far'.

1966

FRANKIE AND JOHNNY Technicolor
Release date: 20 July 1966. Studio: United Artists.
Running time: 87 minutes.

Cast:
Johnny Elvis Presley
Frankie Donna Douglas
Nellie Bly Nancy Kovack
Mitzi Sue Ann Langdon
Braden Anthony Eisley
Cully Harry Morgan
Pog Audrey Christie
Blackie Robert Strauss
Wilbur Jerome Cowan
Earl Barton Dancers Wilda Taylor, Larri Thomas, Dee Jay Mattis, Judy Chapman

Credits:
Producer Edward Small
Director Fred de Cordova
Screenplay Alex Gottlieb
Story Nat Perrin
Photographer Jacques Marquette
Editor Grant Whytock
Music Director Fred Karger
Technical Advisor Col Tom Parker

Songs: 'Frankie and Johnny', 'Come Along', 'Petunia, The Gardener's Daughter', 'Chesay', 'What Every Woman Lives For', 'Look Out, Broadway', 'Beginner's Luck', 'Down By The Riverside', 'When The Saints Go Marching In', 'Shout It Out', 'Hard Luck', 'Please Don't Stop Loving Me', 'Everybody Come Aboard'.

PARADISE – HAWAIIAN STYLE Technicolor
Release date: 8 June 1966. Studio: Paramount Pictures.
Running time: 91 minutes.

Cast:
Rick Richards Elvis Presley
Judy Hudson Suzanne Leigh
Danny Kohana James Shigeta
Jan Kohana Donna Butterworth
Lani Marianna Hill
Pua Irene Tsu
Lehua Linda Wong
Joanna Julie Parrish
Betty Kohana Jan Shepard
Donald Belden John Doucette
Moki Philip Ahn
Mr Cubberson Grady Sutton
Andy Lowell Don Collier
Mrs Barrington Doris Packer
Mrs Belden Mary Treen
Peggy Holdren Gigi Verone

Credits:
Producer Hal B. Wallis
Associate Producer Paul Nathan
Director Michael Moore
Screenplay Allan Weiss and Anthony Lawrence
Story Allan Weiss
Photographer W. Wallace Kelley
Editor Warren Low
Music Joseph J. Lilley
Art Directors Hal Pereira and Walter Tyler
Technical Advisor Col Tom Parker

Songs: 'Paradise, Hawaiian Style', 'House of Sand', 'Queenie Wahine's Papaya', 'Scratch My Back', 'Drums Of The Islands', 'Dog's Life', 'Datin' ', 'Stop Where You Are', 'This Is My Heaven'.

SPINOUT Panavision, Metrocolor
Release date: 14 December 1966. Studio: Metro-Goldwyn-Mayer.
Running time: 95 minutes.

Cast:
Mike McCoy Elvis Presley
Cynthia Foxhugh Shelley Fabares
Diane St Clair Diane McBain
Les Deborah Walley
Susan Dodie Marshall
Curly Jack Mullaney
Lieut. Tracy Richards Will Hutchins
Philip Short Warren Berlinger
Larry Jimmy Hawkins
Howard Foxhugh Carl Betz
Bernard Ranley Cecil Kellaway
Violet Ranley Una Merkel
Blodgett Frederic Warlock
Harry Dave Barry

Credits:
Producer Joe Pasternak
Director Norman Taurog
Screenplay Theodore J. Flicker and George Kirgo
Photographer Daniel L. Fapp
Editor Rita Roland
Music George Stoll
Associate Producer Hank Moonjean
Technical Advisor Col Tom Parker

Songs: 'Spinout', 'I'll Be Back', 'All That I Am', 'Am I Ready', 'Stop, Look, Listen'.

1967

EASY COME, EASY GO Technicolor

Release date: 14 June 1967. Studio: Paramount Pictures.
Running time: 95 minutes.

Cast:
Ted Jackson Elvis Presley
Jo Symington Dodie Marshall
Dina Bishop Pat Priest
Judd Whitman Pat Harrington
Gil Carey Skip Ward
Schwartz Sandy Kenyon
Captain Jack Frank McHugh
Cooper Ed Griffith
Ship's Officers Reed Morgan, Mickey Elley
Vicki Elaine Beckett
Mary Shari Nims
Zoltan Diki Lawrence
Artist Robert Lawrence
Madame Neherina Elsa Lanchester

Credits:
Producer Hal B. Wallis
Associate Producer Paul Nathan
Director John Rich
Screenplay Allan Weiss and Anthony Lawrence
Photographer William Margulies
Editor Archie Marshek
Music Joseph J. Lilley
Art Directors Hal Pereira and Walter Tyler
Technical Advisor Col Tom Parker

Songs: 'Easy Come, Easy Go', 'The Love Machine', 'Yoga Is As Yoga Does', 'You Gotta Stop', 'Sing, You Children', 'I'll Take Love'.

DOUBLE TROUBLE Panavision, Metrocolor

Release date: 24 May 1967. Studio: Metro-Goldwyn-Mayer.
Running time: 90 minutes.

Cast:
Guy Lambert Elvis Presley
Jill Conway Annette Day
Gerald Waverly John Williams
Claire Dunham Yvonne Romain
The Wiere Brothers Themselves
Archie Brown Chips Rafferty
Arthur Babcock Norman Rossington
Georgie Monty Landis
Morley Michael Murphy
Inspector DeGrotte Leon Askin
Iceman John Alderson
Captain Roach Stanley Adams
The G Men Themselves

Credits:
Producers Judd Bernard and Irwin Winkler
Director Norman Taurog
Screenplay Jo Heims
Story Marc Brandel
Photographer Daniel L. Fapp
Editor John McSweeney
Music Jeff Alexander
Art Directors George W. Davis and Merrill Pye
Assistant Director Claude Binyon, Jr.
Technical Advisor Col Tom Parker

Songs: 'Double Trouble', 'Baby, If You'll Give Me All Your Love', 'Could I Fall In Love', 'Long-Legged Girls With Short Dresses On', 'City Of Night', 'Old MacDonald', 'I Love Only One Girl', 'There's So Much World To See', 'It Won't Be Long'.

CLAMBAKE Techniscope, Technicolor
Release date: 4 December 1967. Studio: United Artists.
Running time: 99 minutes.

Cast:
Scott Heywood Elvis Presley
Dianne Carter Shelly Fabares
Tom Wilson Will Hutchins
James Jamison III Bill Bixby
Sam Burton Gary Merrill
Duster Heywood James Gregory
Ellie Amanda Harley
Sally Suzy Kaye
Gloria Angelique Pettyjohn

Credits:
Producers J. Levy, A. Gardner, A. Laven
Director Arthur Nadel
Screenplay Arthur Brown, Jr
Story Arthur Brown, Jr
Photographer William Margulies
Editor Tom Rolf
Music Jeff Alexander
Technical Advisor Col Tom Parker

Songs: 'Clambake', 'Who Needs Money', 'A House That Has Everything', 'Confidence', 'Hey, Hey, Hey', 'You Don't Know Me', 'The Girl I Never Loved'.

1968
STAY AWAY, JOE Panavision, Metrocolor
Release date: 14 March 1968. Studio: Metro-Goldwyn-Mayer.
Running time: 98 minutes.

Cast:
Joe Lightcloud Elvis Presley
Charlie Lightcloud Burgess Meredith
Glenda Callahan Joan Blondell
Annie Lightcloud Katy Jurado
Grandpa Thomas Gomez
Hy Slager Henry Jones
Bronc Hoverty L. Q. Jones
Mamie Callahan Quentin Dean
Mrs Hawkins Anne Seymour
Congressman Morrissey Douglas Henderson
Lorne Hawkins Angus Duncan
Frank Hawk Michael Lane
Mary Lightcloud Susan Trustman
Hike Bowers Warren Vanders
Bull Shortgun Buck Kartalian
Marlene Standing Rattle Caitlin Wyles

Credits:
Producer Douglas Laurence
Director Peter Tewksbury
Screenplay Michael A. Hoey
Story Dan Cushman
Photographer Fred Koenekamp
Editor George W. Brooks
Music Score Jack Marshall
Assistant Director Dale Hutchinson
Technical Advisor Colonel Tom Parker

Songs: 'Stay Away', 'All I Needed Was The Rain', 'Stay Away, Joe', 'Dominic'. 'Dominic'.
(NB: Presley also sings a few bars of a song, 'Lovely Mamie', in the course of the film.)

SPEEDWAY Panavision, Metrocolor
Release date: 13 June 1968. Studio: Metro-Goldwyn-Mayer.
Running time: 90 minutes.

Cast:
Steve Grayson Elvis Presley
Susan Jacks Nancy Sinatra
Kenny Donford Billie Bixby
R. W. Hepworth Gale Gordon
Abel Esterlake William Schallert
Ellie Esterlake Victoria Meyerink
Paul Dado Ross Hagen
Birdie Kebner Carl Ballantine
Juan Medala Ponice Ponce
The Cook Harry Hickox
Billie Jo Christopher West
Mary Ann Miss Beverly Hills
Ted Simmons Harper Carter
Lloyd Meadows Bob Harris
Carrie Courtney Brown
Billie Dana Brown

Credits:
Producer Douglas Laurence
Director Norman Taurog
Screenplay Phillip Shuken
Photographer Joseph Ruttenberg
Editor Russell Farrell
Music Jeff Alexander
Art Directors George W. Davis and Leroy Coleman
Assistant Director Dale Hutchinson
Technical Advisor Col Tom Parker

Songs: 'Speedway', 'Let Yourself Go', 'Your Time Hasn't Come Yet, Baby', 'He's Your Uncle, Not Your Dad', 'Your Groovy Self', 'There Ain't Nothing Like A Song'.

LIVE, A LITTLE, LOVE A LITTLE Panavision, Metrocolor
Release date: 9 October 1968. Studio: Metro-Goldwyn-Mayer.
Running time: 89 minutes.

Cast:
Greg Elvis Presley
Bernice Michele Carey
Mike Landsdown Don Porter
Penlow Rudy Vallee
Harry Dick Sargent
Milkman Sterling Holloway
Ellen Celeste Yarnall
Delivery Boy Eddie Hodges
Robbie's Mother Joan Shawlee
Miss Selfridge Mary Grover
Receptionist Emily Banks

Credits:
Producer Douglas Laurence
Director Norman Taurog
Screenplay Michael A. Hoey and Dan Greenburg
Story Dan Greenburg
Photographer Fred Koenekamp
Editor John McSweeney
Music Billy Strange
Art Directors George Davis and Preston Ames
Assistant Director Al Shenberg
Technical Advisor Col Tom Parker

Songs: 'Almost In Love', 'A Little Less Conversation', 'Edge of Reality', 'Wonderful World'.

1969

CHARRO Panavision, Metrocolor
Release date: 3 September 1969. Studio: National General Pictures.
Running time: 98 minutes.

Cast:
Jesse Wade Elvis Presley
Tracey Ina Balin
Vince Victor French
Sara Barbara Werle
Billy Roy Solomon Sturges
Marcie Lynn Kellogg
Gunner James Sikking
Opie Keetch Paul Brinegar
Heff Harry Landers
Lt Rivera Tony Young
Sheriff Ramsey James Almanzar
Mody Charles H. Gray
Jerome Selby John Pickard
Martin Tilford Garry Walberg
Gabe Duana Grey
Lige Rodd Redwing
Henry Carter J. Edward McKinley

Credits:
Executive Producer
Harry A. Caplan
Producer/Director
Charles Marquis Warren
Screenplay Charles Marquis Warren
Story Frederic Louis Fox
Photographer Ellsworth Fredericks
Editor Al Clark
Art Director James Sullivan
Music Hugo Montenegro
Music Editor John Mick
Assistant Director Dink Templeton
Technical Advisor Col Tom Parker

Song: 'Charro'.

THE TROUBLE WITH GIRLS Panavision, Metrocolor
Release date: 10 December 1969. Studio: Metro-Goldwyn-Mayer.
Running time: 99 minutes.

Cast:
Walter Hale Elvis Presley
Charlene Marlyn Mason
Betty Nicole Jaffe
Nita Nix Sheree North
Johnny Edward Andrews
Mr Drewcolt John Carradine
Caril Anissa Jones
Mr Morality Vincent Price
Maude Joyce Van Polten
Willy Pepe Brown
Harrison Wilby Dabney Coleman
Mayor Gilchrist Bill Zuchert
Mr Perper Pitt Herbet
Clarence Anthony Teague
Constable Med Flory

Credits:
Producer Lester Welch
Director Peter Tewksbury
Screenplay Arnold and
Lois Peyser
Story Day Keene/Dwight Babcock
Photographer Jacques Marquette
Editor George W. Brooks
Music Billy Strange
Art Directors George W. Davis
and Edward Carfagno
Technical Advisor Col Tom Parker

Songs: 'Almost', 'Clean Up Your Own Backyard'.

1970

CHANGE OF HABIT Technicolor

Release date: 21 January 1970. Studio: NBC—Universal.
Running time: 93 minutes.

Cast:
Dr John Carpenter Elvis Presley
Sister Michelle Mary Tyler Moore
Sister Irene Barbara MacNair
Sister Barbara Jane Elliot
Mother Joseph Leorna Dana
Lieut. Moretti Edward Asner
The Banker Robert Emhart
Father Gibbons Regis Toomey
Rose Doro Merande
Lily Ruth McDevitt
Bishop Finley Richard Carlson
Julio Hernandez Nefti Millet
Desiree Laura Figuerosa
Amanda Lorena Rich

Credits:
Producer Joe Connelly
Director William Graham
Associate Producer Irving Paley
Screenplay James Lee, S. S. Schweitzer, Eric Bercovici
Story John Joseph and Richard Morris
Photographer Russell Metty
Editor Douglas Stewart
Music William Goldenberg
Technical Advisor Col Tom Parker

Songs: 'Change of Habit', 'Rubberneckin'', 'Let Us Pray', 'Have a Happy'

## Documentary Films

1970

ELVIS – 'THAT'S THE WAY IT IS' Panavision, Metrocolor

Release date: 15 December 1970. Studio: Metro-Goldwyn-Mayer.
Running time: 107 minutes.

Credits:
Director Denis Sanders
Photographer Lucien Ballard
Editors Henry Berman and George Folsey
Assistant Director John Wilson
Technical Advisor Colonel Tom Parker

Songs: Extracts, rehearsal sequences and live performances of over 27 songs.

1973

ELVIS ON TOUR Metrocolor

Release date: 6 June 1973. Studio: Metro-Goldwyn-Mayer.
Running time: 93 minutes.

Credits:
Producer/Director Pierre Adidge and Robert Abel
Associate Producer Sidney Levin
Photographer Robert Thomas
Technical Advisor Colonel Tom Parker

Songs: Extracts and live performances of 24 songs.

# Appendix II

## Select Bibliography

Although there have been many books published on Elvis Presley, the following are especially recommended, and have been invaluable in providing information. Those interested in pursuing aspects of Presley's career are directed to them.

*The A-Z of Elvis Presley,* edited by Todd Slaughter, Albert Hand Publications, 1976.
*Elvis Presley,* Todd Slaughter, Mandabrook, 1977.
*Elvis Recording Sessions,* Ernst Jørgensen, Erik Rasmussen and Johnny Mikkelsen, JEE-production, Baneringen, Denmark, 1977.
*Elvis: What Happened?*, Red West, Sonny West and Dave Hebler, Ballantine/William Collins, 1977.
*My Life With Elvis,* Becky Yancey and Cliff Lindecker, Granada. W. H. Allen, 1977.
*The Films and Career of Elvis Presley,* Steven Zimijesky and Boris Zmijewsky, Citadel Press, Secaucus, New Jersey 1976.
*Elvis*, Jerry Hopkins, Abacus, 1974.
*African Rhythm*, A. M. Jones, International African Institute, London, republished 1972.

# Appendix III

## Select Discography

With the considerable number of recoupling, reissues and the custom packaging of many of the Presley recordings, it is not possible to provide a fully detailed discography. Those who wish to pursue this subject are referred initially to *Elvis Recording Sessions.* This selected discography lists only long-playing records; singles, EPs and other records not included. Broadly speaking, the albums are listed in order of release, not of recording; but the album of almost all of the Sun recordings, for example, is listed not in the year in which it appeared (1976) but at the head of the list. I have not hesitated to adopt a different order where it proved more sensible to do so.

With regard to record numbers, I have restricted this to the original U.S. number, and the U.K. number as adopted by RCA (at the beginning of Elvis Presley's career with RCA, these recordings were issued in the U.K. by EMI on the HMV label; these have not been listed since all the songs are available in other forms on different albums).

Finally there is a rough guide to the worth of each album: a record is awarded a number of stars (a maximum of three) according to its importance. Detailed comment can be found, of course, in the description of the sessions involved. When a record is listed without stars, it is generally unsatisfactory, although it may have the odd good track. Unlisted single albums are considered unworthy.

This listing does not include the two four-record sets, each containing Presley's top 50 hits, nor the various compilation albums (often double-albums) for Pickwick, television campaigns or the like, as all the material is available on the single albums listed.

1. 1954/55
THE SUN SESSIONS That's All Right/Blue Moon of Kentucky/I Don't Care if the Sun Don't Shine/Good Rockin' Tonight/Milkcow Blues Boogie/You're a Heartbreaker/I'm Left You're Right She's Gone/Baby Let's Play House/Mystery Train/I Forgot To Remember To Forget/I'll Never Let You Go/I Love You Because/Trying To Get To You/Blue Moon/Just Because. APM1-1675 HY 1001 ***

2. 1956
ROCK 'N' ROLL Blue Suede Shoes/I'm Counting On You/I Got A Woman/One-Sided Love Affair/I Love You Because/Just Because/Tutti Frutti/Trying To Get To You/I'm Gonna Sit Right Down and Cry/I'll Never Let You Go/Blue Moon/Money Honey. LPM 1254 SF 8233 ***

3. 1956
ROCK 'N' ROLL No 2 (U.S. title ELVIS) Rip It Up/Love Me/When My Blue Moon Turns To Gold Again/Long Tall Sally/First in Line/Paralyzed/So Glad You're Mine/Old Shep/Ready Teddy/Anyplace is Paradise/How's The World Treating You/How Do You Think I Feel. LPM 1283 SF 7528 ***

4. 1957
LOVING YOU Mean Woman Blues/Teddy Bear/Loving You/Got A Lot O' Livin' To Do/Lonesome Cowboy/Hot Dog/Party/Blueberry Hill/True Love/Don't Leave Me Now/Have I Told You Lately That I Love You/I Need You So. LPM 1515 PL 42358**

5. 1957
ELVIS' CHRISTMAS ALBUM Santa Claus is Back in Town/White Christmas/Here Comes Santa Claus/I'll Be Home For Christmas/Blue Christmas/Santa Bring My Baby Back To Me/O Little Town Of Bethlehem/Silent Night/Peace in the Valley/I Believe/Take My Hand, Precious Lord/It Is No Secret. LOC 1035 RD 27052 ***

6. 1958
ELVIS' GOLDEN RECORDS (vol. I) Hound Dog/Loving You/All Shook Up/Heartbreak Hotel/Jailhouse Rock/Love Me/Too Much/Don't Be Cruel/That's When Your Heartaches Begin/Teddy Bear/Love Me Tender/Treat Me Nice/Any Way You Want Me/I Want You, I Need You, I Love You. LPM 1707 RB 16069 ***

7. 1958
KING CREOLE King Creole/As Long As I Have You/Hard Headed Woman/Dixieland Rock/Don't Ask Me Why/Lover Doll/Young Dreams/Crawfish/Steadfast, Loyal And True/New Orleans. LPM 1884 RD 27088**

8. 1959
FOR LP FANS ONLY/ELVIS That's All Right/Lawdy Miss Clawdy/Mystery Train/Playing For Keeps/Poor Boy/My Baby Left Me/I Was The One/Shake, Rattle And Roll/I'm Left, You're Right, She's Gone/You're A Heartbreaker. LPM 1990 RD 27120 ***

9. 1959
A DATE WITH ELVIS Blue Moon Of Kentucky/Young And Beautiful/Baby I Don't Care/Milkcow Blues Boogie/Baby, Let's Play House/Good Rockin' Tonight/Is It So Strange/We're Gonna Move/I Want To Be Free/I Forgot To Remember To Forget. LPM 2011 RD 27128 **

10. 1959
ELVIS' GOLDEN RECORDS (vol II) 50,000,000 ELVIS FANS CAN'T BE WRONG I Need Your Love Tonight/Don't/Wear My Ring Around Your Neck/My Wish Came True/I Got Stung/One Night/A Big Hunk O' Love/I Beg Of You/A Fool Such As I/Doncha' Think It's Time. LPM 2075 RD 27159 ***

11. 1960
ELVIS IS BACK Make Me Know It/The Girl Of My Best Friend/I Will Be Home Again/Dirty Dirty Feeling/The Thrill Of Your Love/Soldier Boy/Such A Night/It Feels So Right/The Girl Next Door/Like A Baby/Reconsider Baby. LSP 2231 SF 5060 ***

12. 1960
G.I. BLUES Tonight Is So Right For Love/What's She Really Like/Frankfurt Special/Wooden Heart/GI Blues/Pocketful Of Rainbows/Shoppin' Around/Big Boots/Didja Ever/Blue Suede Shoes/Doin' The Best I Can. LSP 2256 SF 5078 **

13. 1961
HIS HAND IN MINE His Hand in Mine/I'm Gonna Walk Dem Golden Stairs/In My Father's House/Milky White Way/Known Only to Him/I Believe in the Man in the Sky/Joshua Fit the Battle/He Knows Just What I Need/Swing Down Sweet Chariot/Mansion Over the Hilltop/If We Never Meet Again/Working On The Building. LSP 2328 SF 5094 ***

14. 1961
SOMETHING FOR EVERYBODY There's Always Me/Give Me The Right/It's A Sin/Sentimental Me/Starting Today/Gently/I'm Comin' Home/In Your Arms/Put The Blame On Me/Judy/I Want You With Me/I Slipped, I Stumbled, I Fell. LSP 2370 SF 5106 **

15. 1961
BLUE HAWAII Blue Hawaii/Slicin' Sand/Almost Always True/Aloha Oe/Can't Help Fallin' In Love/Rock-A-Hula-Baby/Moonlight Swim/Ku-U-I-Po/Ito Eats/Hawaiian Sunset/Beach Boy Blues/Island Of Love/Hawaiian Wedding Song. LSP 2426 SF 8145

16. 1962
POT LUCK Kiss Me Quick/Just For Old Time's Sake/Gonna Get Back Home Somehow/Easy Question/Steppin' Out Of Line/I'm Yours/Something Blue/Suspicion/I Feel That I've Known You Forever/Night Rider/Fountain Of Love/That's Someone You Never Forget. LSP 2523 SF 5135 **

17. 1962
GIRLS! GIRLS! GIRLS! Girls! Girls! Girls!/I Don't Wanna Be Tied/Where Do You Come From/I Don't Want To/We'll Be Together/A Boy Like Me, A Girl Like You/Return To Sender/Because Of Love/Thanks To The Rolling Sea/Song Of The Shrimp/The Walls Have Ears/We're Coming In Loaded. LSP 2621 SF 7534

18. 1963
IT HAPPENED AT THE WORLD'S FAIR Beyond the Bend/Relax/Take Me To The Fair/They Remind Me Too Much of You/One Broken Heart For Sale/I'm Falling In Love Tonight/Cotton Candy Land/A World Of Our Own/How Would You Like To Be/Happy Ending. LSP 2697 SF 7565

19. 1963
ELVIS' GOLDEN RECORDS (vol. III) It's Now Or Never/Stuck On You/Fame and Fortune/I Gotta Know/Surrender/I Feel So Bad/Are You Lonesome Tonight?/His Latest Flame/Little Sister/Good Luck Charm/Anything That's Part of You/She's Not You. LSP 2765 SF 7630 ***

20. 1963
FUN IN ACAPULCO Fun in Acapulco/Vino Dinero Y Amor/Mexico/El Toro/Marguerita/The Bullfighter Was A Lady/No Room To Rhumba In A Sports Car/I Think I'm Gonna Like It Here/Bossa Nova Baby/You Can't Say No in Acapulco/Guadalajara/Love Me Tonight/Slowly But Surely. LSP 2756 PL 42357

21. 1964
KISSIN' COUSINS Kissin' Cousins No 2/Smokey Mountain Boy/There's Gold In The Mountains/One Boy, Two Little Girls/Catchin' On Fast/Tender Feeling/Anyone/Barefoot Ballad/Once is Enough/Kissin' Cousins/Echoes of Love/Long Lonely Highway. LSP 2894 PL 42355

22. 1964
ROUSTABOUT Roustabout/Little Egypt/Poison Ivy League/Hard Knocks/It's A Wonderful World/Big Love, Big Heartache/One Track Heart/It's Carnival Time/Carny Town/There's A Brand New Day on the Horizon/Wheels On My Heels. LSP 2999 PL 42356

23. 1965
GIRL HAPPY Girl Happy/Spring Fever/Fort Lauderdale Chamber of Commerce/Startin' Tonight/Wolf Call/Do Not Disturb/Cross My Heart And Hope To Die/The Meanest Girl In Town/Do The Clam/Puppet On A String/I've Got To Find My Baby/You'll Be Gone. LSP 3338 SF 7714

24. 1965
ELVIS FOR EVERYONE Your Cheatin'Heart/Summer Kisses Winter Tears/Finders Keepers Losers Weepers/In My Way/Tomorrow Night/Memphis Tennessee/For The Millionth and Last Time/Forget Me Never/Sound Advice/Santa Lucia/I Met Her Today/When It Rains It Really Pours. LSP 3450 SF 7752

25. 1965
HARUM SCARUM/HAREM HOLIDAY Harem Holiday/My Desert Serenade/Go East Young Man/Mirage/Kismet/Shake That Tambourine/Hey Little Girl/Golden Coins/So Close Yet So Far/Animal Instinct/Wisdom Of The Ages. LSP 3468 SF 7767

26. 1966
FRANKIE AND JOHNNY Frankie And Johnny/Come Along/Petunia The Gardener's Daughter/Chesay/What Every Woman Lives For/Look Out Broadway/Beginner's Luck/Down By The Riverside/When The Saints Go Marching In/Shout It Out/Hard Luck/Please Don't Stop Loving Me/Everybody Come Aboard. LSP 3553 SF 7793

27. 1966
PARADISE HAWAIIAN STYLE Paradise Hawaiian Style/Queenie Wahine's Papaya/Scratch My Back/Drums of the Island/Datin'/A Dog's Life/House of Sand/Stop Where You Are/This Is My Heaven/Sand Castles. LSP 3643 SF 7810

28. 1966
SPINOUT (U.K. title CALIFORNIA HOLIDAY) Stop Look And Listen/Adam And Evil/All That I Am/Never Say Yes/Am I Ready/Beach Shack/Spinout/Smorgasbord/I'll Be Back/Down In The Alley/Tomorrow Is A Long Time. LSP 3702 SF 7820

29. 1967
HOW GREAT THOU ART How Great Thou Art/In The Garden/Somebody Bigger Tham You And I/Farther Along/Stand By Me/Without Him/So High/Where Could I Go But To The Lord/By And By/If The Lord Wasn't Walking By My Side/Run On/Where No-One Stands Alone/Crying in the Chapel. LSP 3758 SF 8206 ***

30. 1967
DOUBLE TROUBLE Double Trouble/Baby If You'll Give Me All Your Love/Could I Fall In Love/Long Legged Girl/City By Night/Old MacDonald/I Love Only One Girl/There's So Much World To See/It Won't Be Long/Never Ending/Blue River/What Now, Where Next, Where To? LSP 3787 SF 7892

31. 1967
CLAMBAKE Guitar Man/Clambake/Who Needs Money/A House That Has Everything/Confidence/Hey Hey Hey/You Don't Know Me/The Girl I Never Loved/How Can You Lose What You Never Had/Big Boss Man/Singing Tree/Just Call Me Lonesome. LSP 3893 SF 7917

32. 1968
ELVIS GOLD RECORDS (vol. IV) Love Letters/Witchcraft/It Hurts Me/What'd I Say/Please Don't Drag That String Around/Indescribably Blue/Devil in Disguise/Lonely Man/A Mess Of Blues/Ask Me/Ain't That Loving You Baby/Just Tell Her Jim Said Hello. LSP 3921 SF 7924 **

33. 1968
SPEEDWAY Speedway/There Ain't Nothing Like A Song/Your Time Hasn't Come Yet Baby/Who Are You/He's Your Uncle, Not Your Dad/Let Yourself Go/Your Groovy Self (*sung by Nancy Sinatra*)/Five Sleepy Heads/Western Union/Mine/Goin' Home/Suppose. LSP 3989 SF 7957

34. 1968
ELVIS SINGS FLAMING STAR Flaming Star/Wonderful World/Night Life/All I Needed Was The Rain/Too Much Monkey Business/Yellow Rose Of Texas/The Eyes Of Texas/She's A Machine/Do The Vega/Tiger Man. CAS 2304 INTS 1021 *

35. 1968
ELVIS NBC-TV SPECIAL Trouble/Guitar Man/Lawdy Miss Clawdy/Baby What You Want Me To Do/Heartbreak Hotel/Hound Dog/All Shook Up/Can't Help Falling In Love/Jailhouse Rock/Love Me Tender/Where Could I Go But To The Lord/Up Above My Head/Saved/Blue Christmas/One Night/Memories/Nothingville/Big Boss Man/Guitar Man/Little Egypt/Trouble/I Can Dream. LPM 4088 RD 8011

36. 1969
FROM ELVIS IN MEMPHIS Wearing That Loved On Look/Only The Strong Survive/I'll Hold You in My Heart/Long Black Limousine/It Keeps Right On A-Hurtin'/I'm Moving On/Power Of My Love/Gentle On My Mind/After Loving You/True Love Travels On A Gravel Road/Any Day Now/In The Ghetto. LSP 4155 SF 8029 ***

37. 1969
FROM MEMPHIS TO VEGAS – FROM VEGAS TO MEMPHIS: *Rec. 1* Blue Suede Shoes/Johnny B. Goode/All Shook Up/Are You Lonesome Tonight/Hound Dog/I Can't Stop Loving You/My Babe/Mystery Train/Tiger Man/Words/In The Ghetto/Suspicious Minds/Can't Help Falling In Love; *Rec. 2* Inherit The Wind/This Is The Story/Stranger In My Own Home Town/A Little Bit Of Green/And The Grass Won't Pay No Mind/Do You Know Who I Am/From A Jack To A King/The Fair's Moving On/You'll Think Of Me/Without Love. LSP 6020 SF 8080/1 **

38. 1970
LET'S BE FRIENDS Stay Away Joe/If I'm A Fool/Let's Be Friends/Let's Forget About The Stars/Mama/I'll Be There/Almost/Change Of Habit/Have A Happy. CAS 2408 INTS 1103 *

39. 1970
ON STAGE See See Rider/Release Me/Sweet Caroline/Runaway/The Wonder of You/Polk Salad Annie/Yesterday/Proud Mary/Walk a Mile in My Shoes/Let It Be Me. LSP 4362 SF 8128 *

40. 1970
ALMOST IN LOVE Almost In Love/Long Legged Girl/Edge Of Reality/My Little Friend/A Little Less Conversation/Rubberneckin'/Clean Up Your Own Backyard/U.S. Male/Charro/Stay Away Joe. CAS 2440 INTS 1206 *

41. 1970
ELVIS Blue Christmas/Silent Night/White Christmas/Santa Claus is Back In Town/I'll Be Home For Christmas/If Every Day Was Like Christmas/Here Comes Santa Claus/O Little Town of Bethlehem/Santa Bring My Baby Back/Mama Liked the Roses. CAL 2428 INTS 1126 **

42. 1970
THAT'S THE WAY IT IS I Just Can't Help Believin'/Twenty Days and Twenty Nights/How The Web Was Woven/Patch It Up/Mary In The Morning/You Don't Have To Say You Love Me/You've Lost That Loving

Feeling/I've Lost You/Just Pretend/Stranger In The Crowd/The Next Step Is Love/Bridge Over Troubled Water. LSP 4445 SF 8162 *

43. 1971
ELVIS COUNTRY Snowbird/Tomorrow Never Comes/Little Cabin On The Hill/Whole Lotta Shakin' Goin' On/Funny How Time Slips Away/I Really Don't Want To Know/There Goes My Everything/It's Your Baby, You Rock It/The Fool/Faded Love/I Washed My Hands In Muddy Water/Make The World Go Away. LSP 4460 SF 8172 **

44. 1971
YOU'LL NEVER WALK ALONE You'll Never Walk Alone/Who Am I/Let Us Pray/Peace in the Valley/We Call On Him/I Believe/It Is No Secret/Sing You Children/Take My Hand Precious Lord. CAL 2472 INTS 1286 *

45. 1971
C'MON EVERYBODY C'mon Everybody/Angel/Easy Come Easy Go/A Whistling Tune/Follow That Dream/King of the Whole Wide World/I'll Take Love/I'm Not the Marrying Kind/This is Living/Today, Tomorrow and Forever. CAL 2518 INTS 1286 *

46. 1971
ELVIS SINGS THE WONDERFUL WORLD OF CHRISTMAS O Come All Ye Faithful/The First Noel/On A Snowy Christmas Night/Winter Wonderland/The Wonderful World of Christmas/It Won't Seem Like Christmas/I'll Be Home on Christmas Day/If I Get Home on Christmas Day/Holly Leaves and Christmas Trees/Merry Christmas Baby/Silver Bells. LSP 4579 SF 8221 **

47. 1972
ELVIS NOW Help Me Make It Through The Night/Miracle Of The Rosary/Hey Jude/Put Your Hand In The Hand/Until It's Time For You To Go/We Can Make The Morning/Early Morning Rain/Sylvia/Fools Rush In/I Was Born About 10,000 Years Ago. LSP 4671 SF 8266 **

48. 1972
HE TOUCHED ME He Touched Me/I've Got Confidence/Amazing Grace/Seeing Is Believing/He Is My Everything/Bosom Of Abraham/An Evening Prayer/Lead Me, Guide Me/There is No God But God/A Thing Called Love/I John/Reach Out To Jesus. LSP 4690 SF 8275 **

49. 1972
ELVIS AS RECORDED AT MADISON SQUARE GARDEN Also Sprach Zarathustra/That's All Right/Proud Mary/Never Been To Spain/You Don't Have To Say You Love Me/You've Lost That Loving Feeling/Polk Salad Annie/Love Me/All Shook Up/Heartbreak Hotel/Teddy Bear/Don't Be Cruel/Love Me Tender/The Impossible Dream/Hound Dog/Suspicious Minds/For the Good Times/American Trilogy/Funny How Time Slips Away/I Can't Stop Loving You/Can't Help Falling In Love. LSP 4776 SF 8296 *

50. 1972
BURNING LOVE AND HITS FROM HIS MOVIES Burning Love/Tender Feeling/Am I Ready/Tonight is So Right For Love/Guadalajara/It's A Matter of Time/No More/Santa Lucia/We'll Be Together/I Love Only One Girl. CAS 2595 INTS 1414 *

51. 1973
ALOHA FROM HAWAII VIA SATELLITE Also Sprach Zarathustra/See See Rider/Burning Love/Something/You Gave Me A Mountain/Steamroller Blues/My Way/Love Me/Johnny B. Goode/It's Over/Blue Suede Shoes/I'm So Lonesome I Could Cry/I Can't Stop Loving You/Hound Dog/What Now My Love/Fever/Welcome To My World/SuspiciousMinds/I'll RememberYou/Long Tall Sally/Whole Lotta Shakin' Goin' On/American Trilogy/A Big Hunk O' Love/Can't Help Falling In Love. VPSX 6089 DPS 2040 *

52. 1973
ELVIS
ELVIS Fool/Where Do I Go From Here/Love Me Love/The Life I Lead/It's Still Here/It's Impossible/For Lovin' Me/Padre/I'll Take You Home Again, Kathleen/I Will Be True/Don't Think Twice, It's Alright. APL1 0283 SF 8378 *

53. 1973
RAISED ON ROCK Raised on Rock/Are You Sincere?/Find Out What's Happening/I Miss You/Girl Of Mine/For Ol' Times Sake/If You Don't Come Back/Just A Little Bit/Sweet Angeline/Three Corn Patches. APL1 0388 APL1 0388 **

54. 1974
ELVIS A LEGENDARY PERFORMER *Vol. I* That's All Right/I Love You Because/Heartbreak Hotel/Love Me/Trying to Get To You/Love Me Tender/Peace In The Valley/A Fool Such As I/Tonight's All Right For Love/Are You Lonesome Tonight/Can't Help Falling In Love. CPL1 0341 CPL1 0341 **

55. 1974
GOOD TIMES Take Good Care of Her/Loving Arms/I Got A Feeling in My Body/If That Isn't Love/She Wears My Ring/I've Got A Thing About You Baby/My Boy/Spanish Eyes/Talk About The Good Times/Good Time Charlie's Got The Blues. CPL1 0475 APL1 0475 *

56. 1974
ELVIS AS RECORDED LIVE ON STAGE IN MEMPHIS See See Rider/I Got A Woman/Love Me/Trying to Get To You/Long Tall Sally/Whole Lotta Shakin' Goin' on/Mama Don't Dance/Flip Flop and Fly/Jailhouse Rock/Hound Dog/Why Me Lord/How Great Thou Art/Blueberry Hill/I Can't Stop Loving You/Help Me/American Trilogy/Let Me Be There/My Baby Left Me/Lawdy Miss Clawdy/Can't Help Falling In Love. APL1 0606 APL1 0606

58. 1975
TODAY T-R-O-U-B-L-E/And I Love You So/Susan When She Tried/Woman Without Love/Shake a Hand/Pieces of My Life/Fairytale/I Can Help/Bringin' it Back/Green Green Grass of Home. APL1 1039 APL1 1039 **

59. 1976
ELVIS A LEGENDARY PERFORMER Vol. 2 Harbor Lights/I Want You, I Need You, I Love You/Blue Suede Shoes/Blue Christmas/Jailhouse Rock/It's Now Or Never/A Cane And A High Starched Collar/Blue Hawaii/Such A Night/Baby What You Want Me To Do/How Great Thou Art/If I Can Dream. CPL1 1349 CPL1 1349 ***

60. 1976
FROM ELVIS PRESLEY BOULEVARD, MEMPHIS, TENNESSEE Hurt/Never Again/Blue Eyes Crying in the Rain/Danny Boy/The Last Farewell/For the Heart/Bitter They Are/Harder They Fall/Solitaire/Love Coming Down/I'll Never Fall in Love Again. APL1 1506 APL1 1506 **

61. 1977
WELCOME TO MY WORLD Welcome to My World/Help Me Make It Through the Night/Release Me/I Really Don't Want To Know/For The Good Times/Make The World Go Away/Gentle on My Mind/I'm So Lonesome I Could cry/Your Cheatin' Heart/I Can't Stop Loving You. APL1 2274 PL 12274 *

62. 1977
ELVIS IN DEMAND Suspicion/Hi Heel Sneakers/Got A Lot O' Livin' To Do/Have I Told You Lately That I Love You?/Please Don't Drag That String Around/It's Only Love/The Sound Of Your Cry/Viva Las Vegas/Do Not Disturb/Tomorrow is a Long Time/It's A Long Lonely Highway/Puppet on a String/The First Time Ever I Saw Your Face/Summer Kisses, Winter Tears/It Hurts Me *(without Jordanaires)*/Let It Be Me. PL 42003 ***

63. 1977
ELVIS IN CONCERT Also Sprach Zarathustra/See See Rider/That's All Right/Are You Lonesome Tonight?/Teddy Bear/Don't Be Cruel/You Gave Me A Mountain/Jailhouse Rock/How Great Thou Art/I Really Don't Want To Know/Hurt/Hound Dog/My Way/Can't Help Falling In Love/I Got A Woman/Amen/Love Me/If You Love Me/O Sole Mio (*sung by Sherill Nielsen*)/It's Now Or Never/Trying To Get To You/Hawaiian Wedding Song/Fairytale/Little Sister/Early Morning Rain/What'd I Say/Johnny B. Goode/And I Love You So. APL2 2587 PL 02587 (23) **

64. 1978
ELVIS A LEGENDARY PERFORMER Vol. 3 Hound Dog/Danny/Fame and Fortune/Frankfurt Special/Britches/Crying In The Chapel/Surrender/Guadalajara/It Hurts Me/Let Yourself Go/In The Ghetto/Let It Be Me. CPL1 3082 PL 13082 **

65. 1979
OUR MEMORIES OF ELVIS Are You Sincere/It's Midnight/My Boy/Girl Of Mine/Take Good Care Of Her/I'll Never Fall In Love Again/Your Love's Been A Long Time Coming/Spanish Eyes/Never Again/She Thinks I Still Care/Solitaire. (N.B. *These performances are without later overdubbings by backing vocalists.*) AQL1 3279 PL 13279 **

# Index I – List of Songs Recorded and Released, with page references


A Big Hunk O'Love 43, 95, 97, 137
A Boy Like Me, A Girl Like You 58, 124, 138
A Cane And A High Starched Collar 51, 121
Adam And Evil 67, 140
A Fool Such As I 46, 137
After Loving You 80, 141
A House That Has Everything 71, 131, 140
Ain't That Loving You Baby 46, 140
A Little Bit Of Green 78, 141
A Little Less Conversation 74, 132, 141
All I Needed Was The Rain 73, 131, 140
All Shook Up 40, 75, 76, 84, 94, 137, 141, 142
All That I Am 67, 129, 140
Almost 78, 133, 141
Almost Always True 54, 122, 138
Almost In Love 74, 132, 141
Aloha-Oe 54, 122, 138
Also Sprach Zarathustra 94, 95, 105, 142
Always On My Mind 93
Amazing Grace 89, 142
Amen 105
American Trilogy 93, 94, 95, 97, 101, 142
A Mess Of Blues 48, 140
Am I Ready? 67, 129, 140
And I Love You So 102, 105
And The Grass Won't Pay No Mind 80, 81, 141
An Evening Prayer 90, 91, 142
Angel 56, 142
Animal Instinct 64, 139
Any Day Now 80, 81, 141
Anyone 62, 139
Any Place is Paradise 38, 39, 137
Anything That's Part Of You 56, 139
Any Way You Want Me 37, 137
Are You Lonesome Tonight? 48, 49, 75, 77, 84, 105, 106, 139, 141
Are You Sincere 99, 143
Ask Me 63, 140
As Long As I Have You 44, 45, 120, 137
A Thing Called Love 90, 91, 142
Aurora Lee 78
A Whistling Tune 56, 57, 123, 142
A World Of Our Own 59, 124, 138
Baby I Don't Care 42, 43, 120, 137
Baby, If You'll Give Me All Your Love 70, 130, 140
Baby, Let's Play House 34, 136, 137
Baby What You Want Me To Do 75, 76, 77, 141
Barefoot Ballad 62, 125, 139
Beach Boy Blues 54, 122, 138
Beach Shack 67, 140
Because Of Love 58, 138
Beginner's Luck 65, 128, 139
Beyond The Bend 59, 124, 138
Big Boots 50, 121, 138
Big Boss Man 22, 72, 75, 77, 140, 141
Big Love, Big Heartache 63, 126, 139
Bitter They Are, Harder They Fall 103
Blueberry Hill 41, 80, 137
Blue Christmas 43, 75, 76, 137, 141
Blue Eyes Cry In The Rain 103
Blue Hawaii 54, 55, 66, 95, 122, 138
Blue Moon 31, 115, 136
Blue Moon Of Kentucky 31, 33, 115, 136, 137
Blue River 60, 140
Blue Suede Shoes 36, 50, 55, 75, 77, 84, 95, 96, 136, 138, 141
Bosom Of Abraham 93, 142
Bossa Nova Baby 59, 60, 125, 139
Bridge Over Troubled Water 86, 88, 142
Bringing It Back 102
Britches 51
Burning Love 93, 95, 96
By And By 68, 140

Can't Help Falling In Love 54, 55, 75, 76, 84, 94, 95, 97, 101, 105, 122, 138, 141, 142
Carny Town 63, 126, 139
Casual Love 8
Catchin' On Fast 62, 125, 139
Change Of Habit 23, 82, 134, 141
Charro 23, 77, 133, 141
Chesay 65, 128, 139
Cindy, Cindy 86
City By Night 70, 130, 140
Clambake 22, 71, 73, 131
Clean Up Your Own Backyard 78, 133, 141
C'Mon Everybody 61, 126, 142
Come Along 65, 128, 139
Come Out 78
Come What May 68
Confidence 71, 131, 140
Cotton Candy Land 59, 124, 138
Could I Fall In Love 70, 130, 140
Crawfish 44, 45, 120, 137
Cross My Heart And Hope To Die 64, 127, 139
Crying In The Chapel 52, 140

Danny 44, 45
Danny Boy 103
Datin' 40, 66, 129
Devil In Disguise 60, 61, 140
Didja Ever 50, 121, 138
Dirty, Dirty Feeling 48, 49, 127, 138
Dixieland Rock 44, 45, 120, 137
Dog's Life, 66, 129

Doin' The Best I Can 50, 121, 138
Dominic 73, 131
Don'cha Think It's Time 46, 137
Do Not Disturb 64, 127, 139
Don't 43, 44
Don't Ask Me Why 44, 45, 120, 137
Don't Be Cruel 37, 38, 75, 94, 95, 105, 137, 142
Don't Cry Daddy 78
Don't Leave Me Now 41, 42, 43, 120, 137
Don't Think Twice It's All Right 90, 91
Do The Clam 64, 127, 139
Do The Vega 61, 140
Double Trouble 70, 130, 140
Down By The Riverside 65, 128, 139
Down In The Valley 68, 140
Do You Know Who I Am? 80, 81, 141
Drums Of The Island 66, 129, 140

Early Morning Rain 89, 90, 95, 105, 142
Earth Boy 58, 124
Easy Come, Easy Go 71, 130, 142
Easy Question 57, 127, 138
Echoes Of Love 60, 61, 139
Edge Of Reality 74, 132, 141
El Toro 59, 60, 125, 139
Everybody Come Aboard 65, 128, 139

Faded Love 86, 142
Fairytale 102, 105
Fame And Fortune 48, 139
Farther Along 68, 140
Fever 48, 49, 95, 97
Finders Keepers, Losers Weepers 60, 61, 139
Find Out What's Happening 97
First In Line 38, 39, 137
Five Sleepy Heads 72, 140
Flaming Star 20, 23, 51, 52, 121, 140
Flip Flop And Fly 101
Follow That Dream 56, 123, 142
Fool 93, 94
Fools Fall In Love 68
Fools Rush In 90, 91, 142
Forget Me Never 52, 139
For Loving Me 89, 90
For Old Times Sake 97
For The Good Times 94, 95, 142
For The Heart 103
For The Millionth And The Last Time 56, 139
Fort Lauderdale Chamber Of Commerce 64, 127, 139
Fountain Of Love 57, 138
Frankfort Special 50, 51, 121, 138
Frankie And Johnny 65, 128, 139
From A Jack To A King 78, 79, 141
Fun In Acapulco 59, 60, 125, 139
Funny How Time Slips Away 86, 94, 95, 142

Gentle On My Mind 78, 79, 141
Gently 53, 138
G.I. Blues 18, 19, 20, 50, 51, 61, 121, 138
Girl Happy 64, 127, 139
Girl Next Door (Went A'Walking) 48, 49, 138
Girl Of Mine 97, 98, 143
Girls! Girls! Girls! 58, 124, 138
Give Me The Right 53, 54, 138
Go East - Young Man 64, 65, 128, 139
Going Home 73, 140
Golden Coins 64, 65, 128, 139
Gonna Get Back Home Somehow 57, 138
Good Luck Charm 56, 139
Good Rockin' Tonight 10, 32, 136, 137
Good Time Charlie's Got The Blues 99
Got A Lot O'Livin' To Do 40, 42, 119, 137
Got My Mojo Working 86
Green, Green Grass Of Home 102
Guadalajara 59, 60, 125, 139
Guitar Man 22, 72, 73, 75, 76, 77, 140, 141

Happy Ending 59, 124, 138
Harbour Lights 10, 33
Hard Headed Woman 44, 45, 46, 120, 137
Hard Knocks 63, 126, 139
Hard Luck 65, 128, 139
Harem Holiday 64, 65, 128, 139
Have A Happy 82, 134, 141
Have I Told You Lately That I Love You 41, 137
Hawaiian Sunset 54, 55, 122, 138
Hawaiian Wedding Song 54, 55, 95, 105, 122, 138
Heartbreak Hotel (V), 12, 35, 38, 46, 75, 76, 94, 110, 111, 116, 137, 141, 142
Heart Of Rome 86, 87
He Is My Everything 93, 142
He Knows Just What I Need 138
He'll Have To Go 104
Help Me 99
Help Me Make It Through The Night 90, 91, 142
Here Comes Santa Claus 43, 44, 137, 141
He's Your Uncle, Not Your Dad 72, 132, 140
He Touched Me 90, 91, 142
Hey, Hey, Hey 71, 131, 140
Hey Jude 78, 79, 85, 142
Hey Little Girl 64, 65, 128, 139
High Heel Sneakers 72, 73
His Hand In Mine 52, 53, 138
His Latest Flame 55, 139
Holly Leaves And Christmas Trees 90, 91, 142
Home Is Where The Heart Is 56, 57, 123
Hot Dog 42, 119, 137

Hound Dog 13, 37, 38, 75, 76, 84, 94, 95, 96, 101, 105, 116, 137, 141, 142
House Of Sand 66, 129, 140
How Can You Lose What You Never Had 71, 140
How Do You Think I Feel 38, 39, 137
How Great Thou Art 68, 101, 105, 106, 140
How's The World Treating You 38, 39, 137
How The Web Was Woven 86, 87, 141
How Would You Like To Be 59, 124, 138
Hurt 103, 105

I Beg Of You 40, 41, 137
I Believe 40, 137, 142
I Believe In The Man In The Sky 52, 53, 138
I Can Dream 141
I Can Help 102
I Can't Stop Loving You 84, 94, 95, 96, 141, 142
I Don't Care If The Sun Don't Shine 10, 32, 33, 136
I Don't Wanna Be Tied 58, 124, 138
I Don't Want To 58, 124, 138
I Feel So Bad 53, 54, 139
I Feel That I've Known You Forever 57, 127, 138
If Every Day Was Like Christmas 69, 70, 141
If I Can Dream 75, 77
If I Get Home On Christmas Day 90, 91, 142
If I'm Fool 80, 81, 141
If I Were You 86, 87
I Forgot To Remember 34, 136, 137
If The Lord Wasn't Walking By My Side 68, 140
If We Never Meet Again 52, 53, 138
If You Don't Come Back 97, 98
If You Love Me 105
If You Talk In Your Sleep 99, 100
If You Think I Don't Need You 61, 126
I Got A Feeling In My Body 99, 100
I Got A Woman 101, 105, 136
I Got Lucky 57, 123
I Got Stung 46, 47, 137
I Gotta Know 48, 49, 139
I, John 93, 142
I Just Can't Help Believing 88, 141
I'll Be Back 67, 129, 140
I'll Be Home For Christmas 43, 44, 137, 141
I'll Be Home On Christmas Day 90, 91, 93, 142
I'll Be There 78, 79, 141
I'll Hold You In My Heart 78, 79, 141
I'll Never Fall In Love Again 103, 143
I'll Never Know 86, 87
I'll Never Let You Go 10, 34, 136
I'll Never Stand In Your Way 8
I'll Remember You 69, 70, 95, 97
I'll Take Love 71, 130, 142
I'll Take You Home Again Kathleen 90, 91
I Love Only One Girl 70, 130, 140
I Love You Because 8, 31, 136
I'm Comin' Home 53, 54, 138
I'm Counting On You 35, 36, 136
I Met Her Today 56, 139
I'm Falling In Love Tonight 59, 138
I'm Gonna Sit Right Down and Cry 36, 136
I'm Gonna Walk Dem Golden Stairs 52, 53, 138
I Miss You 99
I'm Leaving 90,91
I'm Left, You're Right, She's Gone 10, 33, 136, 137
I'm Moving On 78, 79, 141
I'm Not The Marrying Kind 56, 123, 142
I'm So Lonesome I Could Cry 95, 96
I'm Yours 55, 127, 138
Indescribably Blue 69, 70, 140
I Need Somebody To Lean On 61, 126
I Need Your Love Tonight 46, 47, 137
I Need You So 41, 42
Inherit The Wind 78, 79, 141
In My Father's House 52, 53, 138
In My Way 52, 122, 139
In The Garden 68, 69, 140
In The Ghetto 23, 78, 79, 84, 141
In Your Arms 53, 54, 138
I Really Don't Want To Know 86, 87, 105, 142
I Slipped, I Stumbled, I Fell 52, 121, 138
Is It So Strange 41, 137
Island Of Love 54, 122, 138
It Ain't No Big Thing 86, 87
It Feels So Right 48, 138
I Think I'm Gonna Like It Here 59, 60, 125, 139
It Hurts Me 63, 75, 140
It Keeps Right On A-Hurtin' 80, 81, 141
Ito Eats 54, 55, 122
It Is No Secret 41, 137, 142
It's A Matter Of Time 93
It's A Sin 53, 138
It's A Wonderful World 63, 126, 139
It's Carnival Time 63, 126, 139
It's Easy For You 104
It's Impossible 93
It's Midnight 99, 100, 143
It's Now Or Never 19, 48, 49, 53, 105, 139
It's Only Love 90, 91
It's Over 95, 96
It's Still Here 90, 91
It's Your Baby, You Rock It 86, 87, 142
It Won't Be Long 70, 130, 140
It Won't Seem Like Christmas 90, 92, 142
I've Got A Thing About You Baby 97, 98
I've Got Confidence 90, 92, 142

I've Got To Find My Baby 64, 127, 139
I've Lost You 86, 87, 88, 142
I Want To Be Free 42, 43, 120, 137
I Want You, I Need You, I Love You 37, 137
I Want You With Me 53, 54, 138
I Was Born About Ten Thousand Years Ago 86, 87, 142
I Washed My Hands In Muddy Waters 86, 87, 142
I Was The One 35, 36, 137
I Will Be Home Again 48, 49, 138
I Will Be True 90, 92

Jailhouse Rock 15, 19, 43, 44, 75, 76, 101, 105, 120, 137, 141
Jesus Knows Just What I Need 52, 53
Johnny B. Goode 84, 95, 96, 105, 141
Joshua Fit The Battle 52, 53, 138
Judy 53, 54, 138
Just A Little Bit 97, 98
Just Because 10, 32, 33, 136
Just Call Me Lonesome 72, 73, 140
Just For Old Time's Sake 57, 138
Just Pretend 86, 87, 142
Just Tell Her Jim Said Hello 57, 140

Keep Your Hands Off (Her) 86
Kentucky Rain 80, 81
King Creole 16, 19, 44, 46, 76, 120, 137
King Of The Whole Wide World 57, 123, 142
Kismet 64, 65, 128, 139
Kissin' Cousins 62, 125, 139
Kissin' Cousins (No. 2) 62, 125, 139
Kiss Me Quick 55, 138
Known Only To Him 52, 53, 138
Ku-U-I-Po 54, 55, 95, 122, 138

Lawdy Miss Clawdy 36, 37, 75, 76, 101, 137, 141
Lead Me, Guide Me 90, 92, 142
Let It Be Me 85, 141
Let Me 38, 119
Let Me Be There 101
Let's Be Friends 82, 141
Let's Forget About The Stars 82, 141
Let Us Pray 82, 134, 142
Let Yourself Go 72, 75, 132, 140
Life 86, 87
Like A Baby 48, 49, 138
Little Cabin On The Hill 86, 87, 142
Little Darling 105
Little Egypt 63, 75, 77, 126, 139, 141
Little Sister 55, 105, 139
Lonely Man 52, 122, 140
Lonesome Cowboy 42, 119, 137
Long Black Limousine 78, 79, 141
Long Legged Girl(s. With Short Dresses On) 70, 130, 140, 141
Long Lonely Highway 60, 61, 139
Long Tall Sally 38, 39, 95, 97, 101, 137
Look Out, Broadway 65, 128, 139
Love Coming Down 103
Love Letters 68, 69, 86, 87, 140
Lovely Mamie (not yet released) 131
Love Me 38, 39, 75, 77, 94, 95, 96, 101, 105, 137, 142
Love Me Love The Life I Lead 90, 92
Love Me Tender 14, 38, 75, 76, 94, 95, 119, 137, 141, 142
Love Me Tonight 60, 61, 139
Lover Doll 44, 120, 137
Love Song Of The Year 99, 100
Loving Arms 99, 100
Loving You 40, 41, 42, 119, 137

Make Me Know It 48, 138
Make The World Go Away 86, 87, 142
Mama 141
Mama Don't Dance 101
Mama Liked The Roses 78, 79, 141
Mansion Over The Hilltop 52, 53, 138
Marguerita 59, 60, 125, 139
Mary In The Morning 86, 87, 141
Mean Woman Blues 40, 42, 119, 137
Memories 75, 77, 141
Memory Revival 80
Memphis, Tennessee 63, 139
Merry Christmas, Baby 24, 90, 91, 92, 116, 117, 142
Mexico 59, 60, 125, 139
Milkcow Blues Boogie 10, 33, 136, 137
Milky White Way 52, 53, 138
Mine 72, 73, 140
Miracle Of The Rosary 90, 92, 142
Mirage 64, 65, 128, 139
Money Honey 35, 36, 136
Moody Blue 103
Moonlight Swim 54, 55, 122, 138
Mr Song Man 99, 100
My Babe 84, 141
My Baby Left Me 36, 37, 101, 137
My Boy 99, 100, 143
My Desert Serenade 64, 65, 128, 139
My Happiness 7
My Little Friend 78, 80, 141
Mystery Train 34, 84, 136, 137, 141
My Way 95, 96, 105, 106
My Wish Came True 43, 44, 46, 137

Never Again 103, 143
Never Been To Spain 94, 142
Never Ending 60, 61, 140

Never Say Yes 67, 140
New Orleans 44, 120, 137
Night Life 61, 140
Night Rider 56, 57, 138
No More 54, 55, 95, 122
Nothingsville 75, 77, 141

O Come All Ye Faithful 90, 92, 142
O Little Town Of Bethlehem 43, 44, 137, 141
Old MacDonald 70, 130 140
Old Shep 3, 6, 38, 39, 137
On A Snowy Christmas Night 90, 92, 142
Once Is Enough 62, 125, 139
One Boy, Two Little Girls 62, 125, 139
One Broken Heart For Sale 59, 124, 138
One Night 41, 42, 75, 76, 141
One Sided Love Affair 36, 37, 136
One Track Heart 63, 126, 139
Only Believe 86, 87
Only The Strong Survive 80, 81, 141
O Sole Mio 105

Padre 90, 92
Paradise Hawaiian Style 66, 129, 140
Paralyzed 38, 39, 137
Party 42, 137
Patch It Up 86, 87, 88, 89, 141
Peace In The Valley 40, 41, 137, 142
Petunia, The Gardener's Daughter 65, 66, 128, 139
Pieces Of My Life 102
Playing For Keeps 38, 39, 137
Please Don't Drag That String Around 60, 61, 140
Please Don't Stop Loving Me 65, 66, 128, 139
Pledging Of Love 104
Pocketful Of Rainbows 50, 121, 138
Poison Ivy League 63, 126, 139
Polk Salad Annie 85, 94, 141, 142
Poor Boy 38, 137
Poor Man's Gold 78
Power Of My Love 80, 81, 141
Promised Land 99, 100
Proud Mary 85, 94, 141, 142
Puppet On A String 64, 127, 139
Put The Blame On Me 53, 54, 127, 138
Put Your Hand In The Hand 93, 142

Queenie Wahine's Papaya 66, 129, 140

Rag Mop 8
Rags To Riches 89
Raised On Rock 97, 98
Reach Out To Jesus 93, 142
Ready Teddy 38, 39, 137
Reconsider Baby 48, 49, 116, 138
Relax 59, 124, 138
Release Me 85, 141
Return To Sender 58, 59, 61, 124, 138
Riding The Rainbow 57, 123
Rip It Up 39, 137
Rock-A-Hula Baby 54, 55, 122, 138
Roustabout 63, 126, 139
Rubberneckin' 78, 80, 134, 141
Runaway 84, 141
Run On 68, 69, 140

Sand Castles 66, 140
Santa Bring My Baby Back To Me 43, 44, 137, 141
Santa Claus Is Back In Town 43, 44, 75, 137, 141
Santa Lucia 61, 62, 126, 139
Saved 75, 76, 141
Scratch My Back 66, 129, 140
Seeing Is Believing 90, 92, 142
See See Rider 85, 95, 101, 105, 141
Sentimental Me 53, 54, 138
Separate Ways 93, 94
Shake A Hand 102
Shake, Rattle And Roll 36, 37, 137
Shake That Tambourine 64, 65, 128, 139
She's A Machine 71, 140
She's Not You 139
She Thinks I Still Care 103, 143
She Wears My Ring 99, 100
Shoppin' Around 50, 51, 121, 138
Shout It Out 65, 66, 128, 139
Sign Of Zodiac 78
Silent Night 43, 44, 49, 137, 141
Silver Bells 90, 92, 142
Singing Tree 72, 73, 140
Sing You Children 71, 130, 142
Slicin' Sand 54, 55, 122, 138
Slowly But Surely 60, 61, 127, 139
Smokey Mountain Boy 62, 139
Smorgasbord 67, 140
Snowbird 89, 142
So Close, Yet So Far 64, 65, 128, 139
So Glad You're Mine 36, 37, 137
So High 68, 69, 140
Soldier Boy 48, 138
Solitaire 103, 104, 143
Somebody Bigger Than You And I 68, 69, 140
Something 95, 96
Something Blue 57, 138
Song Of The Shrimp 58, 124, 138
Sound Advice 56, 123, 139
Sound Of Your Cry 86, 88
Spanish Eyes 99, 100, 143
Speedway 72, 132, 140
Spinout 67, 69, 140
Spring Fever 64, 127, 139
Stand By Me 68, 69, 140
Starting Today 53, 54, 138
Starting Tonight 64, 127, 139
Stay Away 73, 131
Stay Away Joe 73, 74, 131, 141
Steadfast, Loyal And True 44, 120, 137

Steamroller Blues 95, 96
Steppin' Out Of Line 122, 138
Stop Look And Listen 67, 129, 140
Stop Where You Are 66, 129, 140
Stranger In My Own Home Town 80, 81, 141
Stranger In The Crowd 86, 88, 142
Stuck On You 48, 139
Such A Night 48, 49, 138
Summer Kisses, Winter Tears 51, 52, 139
Suppose 72, 140
Surrender 52, 53, 139
Susan When She Tried 102
Suspicion 57, 138
Suspicious Minds 78, 80, 84, 85, 94, 95, 96, 141, 142
Sweet Angeline 99
Sweet Caroline 85, 141
Swing Down Sweet Chariot 52, 53, 78, 138
Sylvia 86, 88, 142

Take Good Care Of Her 97, 98, 143
Take Me To The Fair 59, 124, 138
Take My Hand Precious Lord 40, 41, 137, 142
Talk About The Good Times 99, 100
Teddy Bear 42, 94, 95, 105, 111, 119, 137, 142
Tell Me Why 40, 41
Tender Feeling 62, 125, 139
Thanks To The Rolling Sea 58, 124, 138
That's All Right 8, 9, 31, 32, 75, 94, 105, 136, 137, 142
That's Someone You Never Forget 55, 138
That's When Your Heartaches Begin 7, 40, 41, 137
The Bullfighter Was A Lady 59, 60, 125, 139
The Eyes Of Texas 61, 62, 140
The Fair's Moving On 80, 81, 141
The First Noel 90, 92, 142
The First Time Ever I Saw Your Face 89, 90
The Fool 86, 88, 142
The Girl I Never Loved 71, 131, 140
The Girl Of My Best Friend 48, 50, 138
The Impossible Dream 94, 95, 142
The Lady Loves Me 126
The Last Farewell 103
The Love Machine 71, 130
The Meanest Girl In Town 64, 127, 139
The Next Step Is Love 86, 88, 142
There Ain't Nothing Like A Song 72, 132, 140
There Goes My Everything 86, 88, 142
There Is No God But God 93, 142
There's A Brand New Day On The Horizon 63, 126, 139
There's A Honky Tonk Angel 99, 100
There's Always Me 53, 54, 138
There's A Fire Down Below 104
There's Gold In The Mountain 62, 63, 125, 139
There's So Much World To See 70, 130, 140
There's No Room To Rhumba (In A Sports Car) 59, 60, 125, 139
The Thrill Of Your Love 48, 138
The Walls Have Ears 58, 124, 138
The Wonderful World Of Christmas 90, 92, 142
The Wonder Of You 85, 141
They Remind Me Too Much Of You 59, 124, 138
Thinking About You 99, 100
This Is Living 56, 123, 142
This Is My Heaven 66, 129, 140
This Is Our Dance 86, 88
This Is The Story 78, 80, 141
Three Corn Patches 97, 98
Tickle Me 127
Tiger Man 75, 77, 84, 140, 141
Today, Tomorrow And Forever 61, 62, 126
Tomorrow Is A Long Time 68, 69, 140
Tomorrow Never Comes 86, 88, 142
Tomorrow Night 34, 139
Tonight Is So Right For Love 50, 51, 121, 138
Tonight's All Right For Love 50, 51
Too Much 39, 40, 137
Too Much Monkey Business 74, 140
Treat Me Nice 43, 44, 120, 137
Trouble 44, 75, 76, 77, 120, 141
T-R-O-U-B-L-E 102
True Love 41, 42, 44, 137
True Love Travels On A Gravel Road 80, 81, 141
Tryin' To Get To You 34, 75, 77, 101, 105, 136
Tutti Frutti 36, 37, 136
Twenty Days And Twenty Nights 86, 88, 141

Unchanged Melody 105
Until It's Time For You To Go 90,92, 93, 142
Up Above My Head 75, 76, 141
U.S. Male 74, 141

Vino, Dinero Y Amor 59, 60, 125, 139
Viva Las Vegas 61, 126

Walk A Mile In My Shoes 85, 86, 141
Way Down 104, 110
Wearing That Loved On Look 78, 80, 141
Wear My Ring Around Your Neck 46, 137
We Call On Him 72, 73, 142
We Can Make The Morning 90, 92, 142
Welcome To My World 95, 97
We'll Be Together 58, 124, 138

We're Coming In Loaded 58, 124, 138
We're Gonna Move 38, 119, 137
Western Union 60, 61, 140
What A Wonderful Life 56, 123
What'd I Say 61, 62, 105, 140
What Every Woman Lives For 65, 66, 128, 139
What Now My Love 95, 96
What Now, What Next, Where To 60, 61, 140
What's She Really Like 50, 51, 121, 138
Wheels On My Heels 63, 126, 139
When I'm Over You 86, 88
When It Rains, It Really Pours 41, 42, 139
When My Blue Moon Turns To Gold 39, 40, 75, 137
When The Saints Go Marching In 65, 128, 139
Where Could I Go But To The Lord 68, 69, 75, 76, 140, 141
Where Did They Go Lord? 89
Where Do I Go From Here 93, 94
Where Do You Come From 124, 138
Where No One Stands Alone 68, 69, 140
White Christmas 43, 44, 137, 141
Who Am I? 80, 81, 142
Who Are You? 72, 140
Whole Lotta Shakin' Goin' On 89, 95, 97, 101, 142
Who Needs Money 71, 131, 140
Why Me Lord 101
Wild In The Country 52, 122
Winter Wonderland 90, 92, 142
Wisdom Of The Ages 64, 65, 139
Witchcraft 60, 61, 140
Without Him 68, 69, 140
Without Love 78, 80, 141
Without You 8
Wolf Call 64, 127
Woman Without Love 102
Wonderful World 74, 132, 140
Wooden Heart 121, 138
Words 84, 85, 141
Working On The Building 52, 53, 138

Yellow Rose Of Texas 61, 62, 140
Yesterday 84, 85, 141
Yoga Is As Yoga Does 71, 130
You Asked Me To 99, 100
You Can't Say No In Acapulco 125, 139
You Don't Have To Say You Love Me 86, 88, 94, 141, 142
You Don't Know Me 71, 72, 73, 131, 140
You Gave Me A Mountain 95, 96, 105
You Gotta Stop 71, 130
You'll Be Gone 57, 58, 139
You'll Never Walk Alone 72, 73, 142
You'll Think Of Me 78, 80, 141
Young And Beautiful 43, 120, 137
Young Dreams 45, 46, 120, 137
Your Cheatin' Heart 46, 139
You're A Heartbreaker 10, 33, 136, 137
You're Right, Im Left, She's Gone 10, 33
Your Groovy Self (Nancy Sinatra) 132, 140
Your Love's Been A Long Time Coming 99, 101, 143
Your Time Hasn't Come Yet Baby 72, 132, 140
You've Lost That Loving Feeling 88, 89, 94, 141, 142

## Index of persons mentioned in text (not including appendices)

Alden, Ginger 26
Acuff, Roy 3
Allen, Steve 13, 14
Arnold, Eddy 10, 11, 87
Atkins, Chet 34, 35, 36, 117

Bacharach, Burt 81
Baiter, Tammy 26
Bassey, Shirley 96
Beatles (see also Harrison, George; Lennon, John; McCartney, Paul) 14, 21, 32, 79, 83, 111
Beaulieu, Joseph P. 18
Becaud, Gilbert 85, 96
Bee-Gees 85
Beethoven, Ludwig van 109
Belafonte, Harry 45, 55, 67
Bell, William 97
Berlin, Irving 44
Berry, Chuck 63, 74, 100
Berry, Dave 63
Binder, Steve 22, 23
Black, Bill 8, 9, 31, 32, 38, 40, 113
Black, Cilla 89
Blue Caps 36
Booker T. and the MGs 97
Boone, Pat 118
Brahms, Johannes 72
Briggs, David 102
Brooks, Dudley 39, 40, 41, 42, 43, 44
Brown, James 85
Burnette, Johnny 118
Burton, James 84, 85, 90, 91, 95, 97, 116

Campbell, Glen 118
Carrigan, Jerry 98
Carter Family 114
Carter, President Jimmy 27
Caruso, Enrico 62
Cash, Johnny 7, 15, 21, 117
Charles, Ray 73
Christopher, Johnny 100
Clay, Judy 97
Clement, Governor 10
Cochran, Eddie 61, 110, 117
Cogbill, Tommy 98

Cole, Don 31
Collins, Judy 89, 90
Como, Perry 12, 88, 93, 102
Cooke, Sam 118
Cooper, Alice 118
Cramer, Floyd 35, 36, 49, 53, 54, 55, 56, 61, 63, 64, 72, 73, 103
Creedence Clearwater Revival 85
Crosby, Bing 44
Curtiz, Michael 16

Daffan, Ted 3
Darby, Ken 38
Darin, Bobby 49, 54, 58, 67, 118
Davis, Jimmy 3
Dean, James 14, 15
DeBerry and His Memphis Playboys, James 114
Demetrius, Claude 40
Diamond, Neil 81, 85
Domino, Fats 41
Dorsey, Jimmy 12
Dorsey, Tommy 12
Douglas, Donna 66
Dylan, Bob 69, 91, 112

Eastwood, Clint 77
Emmons, Bobby 97
Ertegun, Ahmet 11
Esposito, Joe 26

Farlowe, Chris 118
Fike, Lamar 16, 17
Flack, Roberta 90
Foley, Red 3, 114
Fontana, D. J. 10, 33, 35, 40, 44
Fucik 63

Gamble, Kenny 81
Garfunkel, Art 86
Garland, Hank 47
Gershwin, George 45
Graham, Dr Billy 19
Grimes, Mrs 3
Groom, Arthur 5
Guthrie, Woody 112

Haley, Bill 39
Harding, Glen 88, 96, 97, 102, 103
Harris, Mrs Faye 4
Harris, Woody 62
Harrison, George 65, 96
Hawkins, Hoyt 38
Hendrix, Jimi 110
Hepburn, Katherine 13
Hodge, Charlie 49, 70
Holder, Dave 26
Holly, Buddy 110, 117
Holmes, Marty 62
Hopkin, Mary 105
Hovartan, Marie Alice 26
Howlin' Wolf 7
Huff, Leon 81
Humperdinck, Engelbert 85, 88
Hutchins, Willie 71

Ifield, Frank 70
Ingle and His Natural Seven, Red 115

Jagger, Dean 16
Jarrett, Hugh 38, 46
Johnson, Juanita Joan 26
Jones, Carolyn 16
Jones, Tom 80, 87, 92, 99, 102, 103
Joplin, Janis 110
Jordanaires 38, 39, 40, 42, 43, 44, 45, 46, 50, 52, 53, 54, 62, 115
Justice, Jimmy 64

Keisker, Marion 7, 8, 9, 18
Kelly, Grace 42
Kitt, Eartha 81
King, B. B. 7
King, Dr Martin Luther 22
King, Solomon 100
Kirkham, Millie 53, 54, 56, 70
Kleinsinger, George 115
Kossoff, Paul 110
Kristofferson, Kris 91
Kubrick, Stanley 95

Laine, Frankie 40
Lancaster, Burt 13
Lennon, John 85
Lester, Ketty 69, 87
Lewis, Jerry Lee 7, 15, 21, 40, 41, 62
Lieber, Jerry 43, 76, 98
Lieberson, Goddard 11
Lightfoot, Gordon 90
Liszt, Franz 62
Logan, Horace 10
Long, Shorty 36
Marsden, Gerry 73
Martin, Dean 79
Martino, Al 100
Mathews, Neal 38
Matthau, Walter 16
Mayfield, Curtis 81
McCartney, Paul 85
McCoy, Charlie 73, 87, 88, 89, 90
Mclean, Don 102
McTell, Blind Willie 114
Mercer, Johnny 91
Miller, Ned 79
Montenegro, Hugo 77
Monroe, Bill 115
Moon, Keith 110
Moore, Bob 61
Moore, Scotty 8, 9, 32, 35, 36, 39, 40, 42, 45, 113
Moore, Dr Thomas 15
Morrison, Jim 110
Mozart, Wolfgang Amadeus 69
Muhoberac, Larry 85

Neal, Bob 10
Nicholoulos, Dr 26
Nietzche, Friedrich 95
Nielsen, Sherrill 106
Nixon, President Richard M. 24, 26

Offenbach, Jacques 51
Orbison, Roy 7, 96

Parker, Junior 7
Parker, Colonel Tom 10, 11, 12, 13, 14, 20, 21, 23, 87
Perkins, Carl 15, 21, 117
Phillips, Dewey 9
Phillips, Sam 7, 8, 9, 10, 11, 15, 18, 31, 32, 33, 89, 113, 116
Platters, The 33
Pomus, Doc 50, 55, 61
Porter, Cole 42
Presley, Dee (Davada) (Mrs Stanley), step-mother 17, 18, 20, 25, 26
Presley, Gladys (*née* Smith), mother 1, 2, 3, 4, 5, 7, 9, 11, 16, 17, 117
Presley, Jesse Garon, twin brother 2
Presley, Lisa Marie, daughter 22

Presley, Luther, grandfather 1
Presley, Minnie, grandmother 17
Presley, Priscilla (*née* Beaulieu), wife 18, 20, 22, 24, 25
Presley, Vernon, father 1, 2, 3, 4, 5, 9, 10, 11, 16, 17, 20, 25, 26, 106
Presley, Vester, uncle 3
Preston, Johnny 52

Randi, Don 76
Randolph, Boots 49, 54, 58, 61
Ray, Johnnie 49, 115, 116
Reed, Jerry 73
Reeves, Jim 104, 110
Rice, Tim 104
Rich, Charlie 7, 117
Richard, Little 39
Righteous Brothers, The 89
Robbins, Harold 16
Robeson, Paul 115
Robinson, Earl 115
Rodgers, Jimmie 3, 114
Royal Scots Dragoon Guards 90

Sanders, Denis 24
Scrivener, Mildred 5, 6
Sedaka, Neil 104
Sex Pistols, The 32
Shannon, Del 84
Sholes, Steve 11
Shuman, Mort 50, 55, 61
Simon, Paul 86
Sinatra, Frank 18, 19, 96, 106
Sinatra, Nancy 72
Slaughter, Henry 70
Snow, Hank 11
Spector, Phil 68
Speer, Ben and Brock 35
Springfield, Dusty 88, 94
Stafford, Terry 57
Stanley, Bill 17, 18
Statler Brothers, The 102
Stoker, Gordon 35, 38
Stoller, Mike 43, 76, 98
Stone, Mike 25
Strauss, Johann II, 51
Strauss, Richard 95
Sullivan, Ed 14, 40
Sumner, J. D. and the Stamps 99, 103
Swan, Billy 102

Tampa, Red (Hudson Whittaker) 113, 114
Thomas, John Charles 115
Thompson, Linda 25
Thorpe, Sister Rosetta 3
Tillotson, Johnny 81
Toof, Grace 15
Tubbs, Ernest 3, 114
Tucker, Tommy 73
Tutt, Ronnie 89, 93, 94, 96, 98, 102, 104

Vernon Girls 105
Vicious, Sid 110
Vincent, Gene 34, 36, 117
Voice 100

Walker, Ray 46, 49, 53
Wallis, Hal 13
Watson, Johnny 'Guitar' 116
Webber, Andrew Lloyd 104
Weisbart, David 14
West, Red 4, 5, 6, 17, 18, 26, 70, 100
West, Sonny 26
Westmoreland, Kathy 98
Wheeler, Treatise 26
Whittaker, Roger 104
Williams, Andy 104
Williams, Hank 46, 114
Williamson, Sonny Boy 114
Wills, Bob 3
Wood, Bobby 98
Wynette, Tammy 100

Yancey, Becky 26

Zenoff, Judge David 22.